GORDONSTOUN

AN ENDURING VISION

GORDONSTOUN
AN ENDURING VISION

EDITED BY **JILL HOLLIS**

THIRD MILLENNIUM
PUBLISHING, LONDON

© Third Millennium Publishing Limited

First published in 2011 by
Third Millennium Publishing Limited, a subsidiary
of Third Millennium Information Limited

2–5 Benjamin Street
London
United Kingdom
EC1M 5QL
www.tmiltd.com

ISBN 978 1 906507 29 9

British Library Cataloguing in Publication Data
A CIP catalogue record for this book is available from the British Library.

Editor: Jill Hollis
Designer: Helen Swansbourne
Production: Bonnie Murray
Repro by Studio Fasoli, Italy
Printed by Scotprint, Scotland

Front jacket image: South elevation of Gordonstoun House with part of the
Round Square in the foreground.

Back jacket image: Students walking to their next class though the arch
leading into the Round Square, and, in the background, one of the school
cutters leaving Hopeman harbour in the late 1940s.

Frontispiece: The south-east end of Gordonstoun House, seen from the
Round Square.

PICTURE ACKNOWLEDGEMENTS

The majority of the pictures reproduced in this book are owned by
Gordonstoun School. The identity of many of the photographers is
unknown; thanks are certainly due, however, to Sheila Lambie, David Selby,
Andy Thomas of Calcots Photography and Peter Thomas for their
contributions. Photographs on the following pages are reproduced by kind
permission of: David Bell 132, 133 (both); John Breckenridge 69, 70
(below), 71 (above), 72 (below left and right), 73; Howard Lester 55 (above
left and right, below right), 61 (below), 86 (right); Bill Mohr 173 (right);
Michael Newton 66 (below right), 71 (below), 72 (top), 159 (both), 177
(left), 187 (all); Charles K. Nissen 30–31, 60 (below left), 170 (all black and
white images); John Pownall 155 (below right); Helen Swansbourne 41, 43
(left), 64 (top), 67, 87, 99 (below), 198–199.

EDITOR'S ACKNOWLEDGEMENTS

A book of this kind is impossible to produce without the assistance of many, many people.
I would like to thank everyone who responded to the invitation to submit reminiscences.
Whether these contributions have appeared verbatim in the text or not, they have all
helped to inform the picture that has been drawn of life at Gordonstoun over the decades.
Invaluable accounts of many aspects of the school have been provided by members of staff,
both current and retired. The school's archivist, Louise Avery, has been endlessly helpful and
accommodating in tracking down pictures and helping me to tease out facts from fiction in
the sometimes very complicated history of the school; Steve Brown has been stalwart in his
administrative support; Mark Pyper has been an informative source as well as being
gracious and forbearing when the book took longer than expected to complete; and Mary
and David Byatt provided important historical background. Angus Miller, however, deserves
a special thank-you for his scrupulous attention to detail, his determination to get things
right and his wholehearted commitment to the book from the outset.

THE GORDONSTOUN ASSOCIATION

It is hoped that this book will, among other things, help to encourage Old Gordonstounians
(OGs) to keep in touch with one another and maintain contact with the school through the
Gordonstoun Association (GA). Originally formed in 1947, the GA is now run by a committee
of nine, supported by a GA Coordinator, an Assistant Coordinator and a full-time Secretary
all based at the school. It organises an extensive range of events, from a GA weekend at
Gordonstoun each spring to gatherings held around the UK (and occasionally overseas),
including annual carol services in both Edinburgh and London. Should you wish to get in
touch, please contact the Association either by e-mail at ga@gordonstoun.org.uk or by
telephone on +44 (0)1343 837922.

CONTENTS

PREFACE

KURT HAHN HAD already established his reputation as an enlightened educator by the time he opened the school at Gordonstoun. In the 1930s he had established a new type of boarding school, which, he believed, Germany needed after the traumas of the First World War. Salem is an enormous Cistercian monastery, which was owned by his previous chief, Prince Max of Baden. In essence, Hahn believed in a form of education that included both what might be described as normal curricular subjects and experience in extra-curricular subjects designed to add an extra dimension to the lives of his pupils.

An old family home looking out on the Moray Firth in the north of Scotland may not have seemed like an ideal spot for a new boarding school, but it turned out to be just the place for what Hahn had in mind. To the north were the sheltered waters of the Moray Firth, to the south lay the Scottish mountains. Hahn saw these as invaluable additional classrooms. He was not about re-inventing the wheel; academic education remained the main purpose of the school. The sea and the mountains were there to broaden experience, to develop skills and enterprise, to open the eyes of young people to the wider world beyond school and home.

Hahn was undoubtedly a visionary, and it was not always easy for traditional educators to grasp just how he wanted to achieve his vision. To many he was an eccentric, and it often took some time for them to appreciate what he was getting at. Many got the point; others, with less imagination, thought it best to humour him, and there were always those who would doubt anyone who dared to tinker with the hallowed English Public School System.

This very impressive publication tells the story of the unfolding of Hahn's great dream. Even so, it is only a part of his remarkable legacy, which also includes Outward Bound, the short-stay schools that introduce young people from the cities to his 'classrooms' on the sea and in the mountains; the United World Colleges that bring young people together; and the Duke of Edinburgh's Award, which aims to introduce young people to all those 'extra-curricular' challenges and activities that are so essential for a rewarding and fulfilling life. Hahn's enduring vision was that education needs to go far beyond the classroom.

Opposite: The south side of Gordonstoun House, seen from the lake.

HRH The Duke of Edinburgh

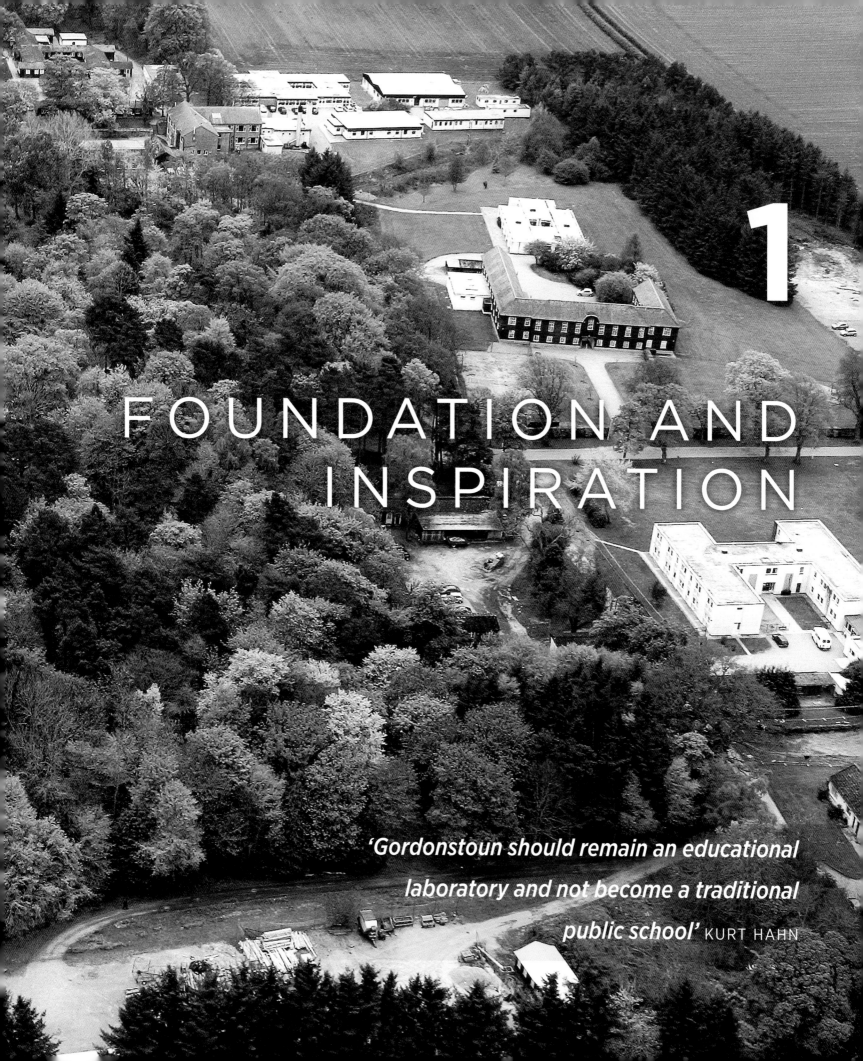

FOUNDATION AND INSPIRATION

1

'Gordonstoun should remain an educational laboratory and not become a traditional public school' KURT HAHN

THE ORIGINS OF Gordonstoun School, and its philosophy, are inextricably bound up with the visionary educational ambitions of its founder, Kurt Hahn. Some knowledge of the man and the context in which his very strong opinions were formed are essential to an understanding of Gordonstoun, both past and present. Salem, the school of which Hahn was Headmaster in Germany (1920–33), clearly established the template from which all his subsequent educational endeavours sprang.

Kurt Hahn, born in June 1886, was the second of four sons of a wealthy German Jewish industrialist. His father ran the Hahnsche-Werke steelworks, which had been started by his grandfather. The family enjoyed the privileged life of the Berlin bourgeoisie, and, for a while, Hahn was taught at home by an 'English tutor', in fact a Scot called Charlie Macpherson who hailed from Newtonmore. 'Perhaps,' wrote Evan Barron, who met the 22-year-old Hahn when he was on holiday in Scotland, 'Hahn's passionate love for the north of Scotland and its people began unconsciously from the first time he met his

Mountain Rescue group on the Five Sisters of Kintail looking down towards Shiel Bridge, west coast of Scotland, photographed by Jim Rawlings who led many such expeditions, 1960s.

Above: Kurt Hahn in the 1930s.

Opposite: Autumn on the Gordonstoun estate.

Highland tutor, who, to the end of his life, remained one of Hahn's firmest friends.'

As an older child, Hahn attended the Wilhelms Gymnasium, one of the leading humanistic schools in Prussia, and it was here that he was first introduced to the philosophy of Plato: *The Republic* was later to become the bedrock of his own educational theory. In 1902, as a sixteen-year-old, while on a hiking holiday in the Austrian Alps, he met three senior pupils from Abbotsholme School who spoke enthusiastically of their pioneering English school and of their responsibilities there as prefects. Abbotsholme, founded in 1887 by Cecil Reddie, was one of the very few schools to have broken away from the rigid system of education practised in most English private schools, a system likened by some critics to a cross between an orphanage and prison. Reddie also believed in expanding the focus of education from tedious learning by rote to a gentler, more humanistic and meaningful education of the whole person. He shared what became Hahn's hope that a school should be a community or an extended family rather than the harsher environment emerging from the 'make a man out of them' philosophy which so often prevailed in educational institutions of the time. Kurt Hahn was impressed and subsequently got hold of the writings of Cecil Reddie. Perhaps the seeds of the idea to found his own school were planted in Hahn's mind at this point. The other probable influence on his thinking at this time was Hermann Lietz (1868–1919), a German educational reformer who had taught at Abbotsholme in 1898 and, much impressed by its system, returned to Germany to found his own country boarding schools – three by 1904, another five before his death.

Kurt Hahn went to university in Berlin and also attended the universities of Heidelberg, Göttingen and Oxford. He first enrolled at Christ Church, Oxford, in 1904, but illness forced him to withdraw in 1906. He returned in 1910 and spent four happy years there reading Classics until war broke out in 1914. He is said to have found the contrast between the authoritarianism of Berlin University and the liberal intellectual freedom of Oxford very marked and much to his taste.

During World War I, Hahn worked in the English Section of the German Foreign Ministry, where one of his work colleagues was a long-standing family friend, Frau Professor Lina Richter. Here he learned to work with the press, and to read and interpret English newspapers. ('For the rest of his life', remarked Jocelin Winthrop Young, one of his pupils both at Salem and at Gordonstoun, 'he was to influence the powerful to advance what he considered to be right.') Also

working at the Ministry at the time was Prince Max von Baden, who owned the magnificent Schloss Salem close to Lake Constance in southern Germany. At the end of the war he briefly became the last Imperial Chancellor of Germany, and in 1919 Hahn moved to the Chancellery and became Prince Max's private secretary. According to her grandson, Andrew Ritchie, Frau Richter (who was friendly with Prince Max) and Hahn together persuaded him to make over a part of the Schloss for a school. Hahn's memory of the words spoken by Prince Max when he was told of the idea of starting a school at Salem are clearly echoed later in his stated ambition that schools should be 'islands of health' for the areas in which they were established: 'Please remember that you are on sacred ground. The Cistercians owned this castle and this countryside from 1134 to 1803; they were the roadbuilders, the farmers, the foresters, the doctors, the consolers and the teachers of this district . . . your school is only justified if it too gives health to the surrounding district.' Prince Max was once asked what he was particularly proud of in the school. He replied: 'I am proud of the fact that there is nothing original here. Our ideas come from Dr Arnold of Rugby, from Abbotsholme, from Eton, from everywhere', to which, on another occasion, he added Goethe, Plato and the Boy Scouts.

Hahn was headmaster, Frau Richter was administrator, and Salem School opened in April 1920 with two pupils: Frau Richter's son, Leo, and Berthold, son of Prince Max. Leo's sister Alice was the first girl to attend the school, and his brother Roland (who was to become a much-loved and long-standing teacher, 'Bex' Richter, at Gordonstoun) followed later.

Ekke von Kuenssberg, who arrived at Salem in 1925 aged twelve, relates that it was highly unusual to go to a boarding school in Germany at this time, but in his case, 'the most pressing reason was presumably the fact that I made

The great-granddaughter of Frau Richter, Phoebe Ritchie, in a performance of *Les Misérables*, 2009.

heavy weather and little progress in the local gymnasium, where my younger sister in the class below me was about to overtake me'. A family disaster had made his mother 'easily nervous when I seemed to be a somewhat quiet and lonely, secretive chap.' He continued, 'Salem's educational principle was simple enough. If you were occupied in sufficiently diverse and pre-arranged ways, you really had no time to get into mischief. Thus we had classes, interspersed with athletics, or were sent as apprentices to the local joiner or blacksmith. We sang as our musical activity, we organised plays and other theatricals, we played team games, and did our respective chores helping the school to run smoothly. No doubt this responsibility for the school community was the most valuable part of our education, though it was only in retrospect that this has been fully appreciated . . . As you progressed in the school, increasing responsibilities were placed on you, whether it was getting together the teams for hockey, or the music timetable, or library duties, or the tidiness of the various dormitories. If you did not make a hash of whatever was your task, you might be elected to become a Colour Bearer. The Colour Bearers collectively met as a kind of parliament, and elected additional Colour Bearers; there were various checks and balances so that there was no apparent misuse of the system. The most senior of the Colour Bearers had a ministerial department such as sport, juniors, etc., with the Head Boy as their leader.'

A British consular official who wrote to the British Ambassador in Berlin in 1933 in connection with Hahn's arrest by the Nazis remarked that 'Prince Max's conception seems to have been to bring up a new generation of Germans somewhat on the lines of an English public school. Discipline is maintained largely by the pupils themselves and more attention is devoted to the formation of character than to scholarship. Some of the principles of the Dalton system have been adopted and 20 boys were this autumn exchanged with Bryanston school in Dorset which is run on the Dalton system [an educational programme first trialled in the 1920s in Dalton, Massachusetts, which aimed to achieve a balance between each child's talents and the needs of the community]. The school fees at Salem range from R.M.2000 to R.M.6000 odd and it is left to the parents to assess themselves at the figure they can afford to pay. The school is a great success and is considered to be the best in Southern if not in the whole of Germany. Several branch schools had to be opened to cope with the number of applicants; these are all situated in the vicinity of Salem.' Geoffrey Winthrop Young, in a letter to *The Times* in August 1945 on the subject of German resistance to the Nazis, referred to the fact that,

Colour Bearer meetings: above, in the Guardian's Room in 1942 at Plas Dinam, when the school had been evacuated to Wales; and, left, with Mark Pyper at Gordonstoun, May 2004.

during World War I, Prince Max had opposed aggression and conquest and that Salem had succeeded 'in replacing Prussian regimentation by character training'. Winthrop Young was an accomplished mountaineer, poet and pacifist, who had served during World War I in the Ambulance Corps in Italy where he lost a leg (a disability which did not prevent him from resuming his climbing). He was a convinced supporter of the Salem educational experiment, sending his son Jocelin there, and when Hahn was being encouraged to found a British Salem School in Scotland, he provided Jocelin as one of the first pupils.

It was apparently while he was reading Classics at Oxford that Hahn, continually troubled by illness and spending long spells of convalescence in the solitude of a darkened room, reflected on the opening chapters of Plato's

Republic and resolved to found a school. A radio talk given by him in 1934 provides the clearest exposition of what he drew from this background: 'I will call the three views of education the Ionian view, the Spartan view and the Platonic view. In the fifth century B.C. the Ionians had the reputation for softness and self-indulgence. They believe that the individual ought to be nurtured and humoured regardless of the interests of the community. This is the Ionian view. According to the second, the individual may and should be neglected for the benefit of the State. This is the Spartan view. The third, the Platonic view, believes that any nation is a slovenly guardian of its own interests if it does not do all it can to make the individual citizen discover his own powers and serve the community.' In other words, the Ionian panders to the individual, ignoring the community; the Spartan view worships the scholar and the athlete in exams and games, but undervalues the others; the Platonic school aims to produce the all-rounder with a balance of body, mind and character. Hahn's stroke of genius was to extract from Plato's *Republic*, regarded by many as a blueprint for fascism and totalitarian regimes, a unique principle that marked off Salem and subsequently Gordonstoun not only from all other state and public schools but also from most major institutions in society.

As an educated, imaginative German of liberal persuasion, Hahn could not fail to be appalled by the disasters that had befallen his country when those who were equipped to challenge the wrongheadedness of their governments failed to do so. He sometimes quoted Yeats to underline his point: 'The best lack all conviction, while the worst/Are full of passionate intensity.' He had long been disillusioned by the German state education system that was highly centralised and bureaucratic. Much of his philosophy of education can be traced back to a desire to make rounded, responsible adults of the young people in his charge, capable of standing up for principle rather than unquestioningly accepting authority: 'The world is not ruined by the wickedness of the wicked but by the weakness of the good.' Hahn had been impressed that during the 1914–18 war young men (eighteen-year-olds, some of them), were given positions of great responsibility. The lives of other men and women could well depend upon the decisions made by inexperienced youths. Whilst he abhorred the carnage and destruction, he observed, nevertheless, that it had given young men and women opportunities to produce their 'best' and to discover unexpected reserves of resourcefulness, bravery, leadership and responsibility. 'But it is unthinkable', he said, 'to arrange a war in every generation to awaken these virtues in the

young.' It became part of his mission therefore to find 'a substitute for war'. Through this type of experience he hoped to make 'the tough compassionate and the timid enterprising'. The stimulating of a sense of responsibility is central to many of his ideas: 'I find among our bigger boys, English and German, that sense of passionate responsibility which we were able to introduce into Salem – fired by the example of your public schools. Our leading boys have responsibilities entrusted to them big enough to wreck the state if negligently performed.'

As early as the autumn of 1908, Kurt Hahn had started visiting Moray, invited there initially by William Calder, a friend made at Oxford whose family had farmed at Dunphail for generations (and who later married Renata, sister of Lola Hahn, Hahn's sister-in-law). Calder, needing the time to complete a thesis, introduced him to Evan Barron (subsequently editor and proprietor of the *Inverness Courier* and an energetic supporter of Gordonstoun): 'It was a glorious autumn day of the kind we frequently get in October in the Highlands, with the sun shining from a clear blue sky,' recalled Barron, 'and I accordingly suggested that we climb a neighbouring hill called The Cnoc [The Knock of Braemoray], from which there was a magnificent view, but he demurred, and on my asking why, he replied hesitantly, "Well, you see, I got sunstroke, two years ago".' At this Barron suggested that they explore the valleys of the Divie and the Findhorn instead, 'and that was how his passion for these rivers began'. The following summer, Barron received a telegram from Hahn asking to meet him at the Station Hotel at Inverness. 'When I got there, I found him

The Combined Services Parade outside Gordonstoun House, 1950s.

Kurt Hahn and Geoffrey Winthrop Young photographed on the banks of the Findhorn, one of Hahn's favourite spots in Moray.

duct that allows fluid to flow between the spinal cord and the brain). In 1913 Hahn was operated on by Sir Victor Horsley, the first brain surgeon in Britain, who (apparently) removed a section of vein from Hahn's ankle and grafted it to the duct at the back of his head. Hahn must have been warned to avoid the sun because of the risk that the graft might 'dry up' and cause further blockage. As a result, he was scrupulous, when outside, about covering his head with a variety of sometimes very broad-brimmed hats.

In the Upper Silesian town of Potempa, in the summer of 1932, five SA men, after a drinking bout, dragged a communist worker out of bed and literally trampled him to death in front of his horrified mother. The murderers were duly arrested, tried and condemned to death. On hearing the news, Hitler sent a congratulatory telegram to the indicted thugs and, together with various National Socialist leaders and other conservative groups, petitioned the Reichspräsident for clemency. The outcry alarmed the government, and Franz von Papen, the Chancellor, rushed through a pardon, commuting the sentence to life imprisonment. Kurt Hahn, outraged both by the brutality of the attack and by this scandalous undermining of justice sent a circular to all old Salem pupils – 'Our Christian civilisation, our military honour and our good name are at stake. I ask of you to break with Hitler or to break with Salem.' Hahn was fully aware of the likely impact of his action: 'I know that I have risked the survival of the school in this struggle, but the issue is worthy of it.' A few months later, when Hitler came to power, the murderers were set free, and it was not long before Kurt Hahn was arrested by the Nazis (on 11 March 1933). At this point, a kindness done by Hahn almost twenty years before was returned. Nevile Butler, now foreign policy adviser to the British Prime Minister Ramsay MacDonald, described how he had known Kurt Hahn 'since he befriended me, a stranded undergraduate, in Potsdam in August 1914. He eventually helped to get me exchanged without my requiring to undertake not to join H.M. Forces. I was not the only British subject that he befriended in the Internment Camp.' Butler proceeded to intercede on Hahn's behalf via the British Embassy in Berlin. A P.S. to a letter addressed to Basil Newton, Counsellor at the British Embassy in Berlin, reveals: 'I am told, but the P.M. does not know this, that the Nazis are trying to prosecute H. for high treason because Max of Baden accepted the Wilson fourteen points.' (Woodrow Wilson's Fourteen Points, first outlined in a speech he made to the American Congress in January 1918, became the basis for a peace programme on the back of which Germany and her allies agreed to an armistice in November 1918.)

accompanied by his younger brother, Franz, and Hahn told me that his sunstroke had got worse and his doctors had told him that he must not spend the summer in Germany but go to a cooler climate . . . Hahn wanted a place which, if possible, had some angling and shooting for the entertainment of his friends.' Barron found Glenernie, a house on the banks of the Dorback, a tributary of the Divie, and from then until shortly before World War I, Hahn spent his summers there. After the war he was able to resume the habit. His brother Rudolf was a keen sportsman, and the two rented Glenernie once again – a visit there from the painter Oskar Kokoschka is recorded in August 1929.

The 'sunstroke' that Hahn referred to was in fact nothing of the kind. Perhaps he did not wish to sow alarm by describing a more serious condition, perhaps he was simply being discreet, but Hahn allowed, even encouraged, the sunstroke myth to gain currency to such an extent that it is still sometimes referred to as the reason why he had to avoid sun falling directly on his head or the nape of his neck. After the investigation of serious recurrent headaches, he was diagnosed with a narrowing of the Sylvian Canal (a

At the same time, Frau Richter was seeking international help to have him released. After two days he was, in the words of a British consular official in Frankfurt, 'ordered or allowed to proceed to Berlin where he is now living. The only restriction imposed on him is that he is not allowed to return to Baden. The son of Prince Max has taken charge of the school.' As a result of a telegram sent by Jim Butler, brother of Nevile, at the behest of Geoffrey Winthrop Young, Ramsay MacDonald (another denizen of Moray) had written to the German Foreign Minister, Baron von Neurath, asking for Hahn's release. Though the letter almost certainly arrived just after his release, Hahn himself believed that it was MacDonald's intervention that had saved him.

By 13 April a member of the Embassy staff was writing, in a letter to Nevile Butler, '[Hahn is] in excellent health and by no means anxious about himself. He is apparently resigned to his dismissal from Salem. On the other hand he maintains that anti-Jewish atrocities are still being perpetrated, although they are now kept out of the press. He is determined to do his utmost to stop this state of affairs and if he is indiscreet in his efforts to prevent or expose these alleged atrocities, I can only fear that he may personally get into trouble once more.' But more than Hahn's personal survival was at stake. Now the issue was also the survival of the school. The Margrave Berthold, who had done all in his power to save Hahn and had taken over personal responsibility for the school, wrote to Geoffrey Winthrop Young in June 1933, 'I think it is time for your friend Kurt to understand that his waiting will not help. It has become absolutely necessary to convince him that he must leave his home country for a while.'

Clearly action was needed, and it now fell to Hahn's friends, especially the British contingent, to persuade him that for his own safety he must leave Germany. Hahn was 47. The educational experiment he had pursued at Salem had proved extraordinarily successful, and he was a man whose life was entirely devoted to his work. There remained one more thing he could do for the school, and that was to release all his former pupils from the commitment he had placed upon them in the famous telegram. This he did in a message to the school association enjoining its members now to concentrate all their loyalty on their old school; his attitude, summed up by a Salem old boy who visited him at the time was: 'You must love your own country even if it does not love you. Indeed that is the essence of patriotism.' It must have been hard, at first, to be enthusiastic about the idea of starting again, of establishing a 'British Salem'. But after some weeks, Hahn reluctantly agreed to the notion of finding a base for a school in Britain. As in much of the early

history of Hahn and Gordonstoun, various accounts of Hahn's 'escape' from Germany have circulated, one from Diana Pares (whose brother Norman Pares had taught at Salem and subsequently at Gordonstoun), who alleged that Hahn escaped to Holland on the arm of 'Aunt May' on the pretext of playing in a tennis tournament, and another account from Jack LeQuesne who claimed that during an attempt to arrest Hahn at Salem, May Cumming distracted the soldiers whilst Norman Pares drove Hahn down to the lake, enabling him to escape in a school boat to Switzerland. But the truth appears to be that in July 1933 he simply left Berlin by train.

DELIGHTFULLY SITUATED ON THE SEA COAST, SECLUDED AND WELL SHELTERED.

THE MANSION.   THE ROUND SQUARE.
TO BE LET FURNISHED OR UNFURNISHED FOR A TERM OF YEARS.
THE WELL-KNOWN HISTORICAL COUNTRY SEAT KNOWN AS
GORDONSTOUN, ELGIN.
Accommodation includes :—Three reception rooms, 20 bed rooms, nurseries, billiard room, six bath rooms, excellent servant's offices, laundry, three cottages, garage and stabling, &c. Beautiful grounds and gardens, including rose and rock gardens, tennis court, ornamental lake, kitchen garden, &c. PRIVATE AVENUE DOWN TO THE SEA. Electric light, telephone, central heating, &c.
For full particulars and appointment to view apply O. E. INGMAN, Land Agent, Park Estate Office, Pontypool.

View of the Gordonstoun estate in the 1950s. The Moray Firth can be seen in the distance as well as Ross and Sutherland beyond.

Inset: An advertisement for the lease of Gordonstoun, 1934.

Such was Hahn's attachment to Moray in 1933, fostered by now over 25 years, that his determination to look there for a home for a new school should not have been surprising. Hahn loved these lines of Plato: 'We would not have our children grow up amid images of moral deformity, as in some noxious pasture, and there browse and feed upon many a baneful herb and flower day by day, little by little, until they silently gather a festering mass of corruption in their own soul; our youth should dwell in the land of health, amid fair sights and sounds; and beauty, the effluence of fair works, will meet the sense like a breeze, and insensibly draw the soul even in childhood into harmony with the beauty of reason.' A school prospectus dating from 1935 describes the appeal of its location: 'Gordonstoun has been selected for the school because of the combination of advantages which it offers: a mild yet bracing climate, the driest in the British Isles; the beauty of the coastline and of the mountains within sight and reach; the expanse of open country immediately surrounding its sheltered position; the sailing and bathing for which the sea – a mile distant – gives opportunity; the character of the neighbouring population, and its own historic associations [. . .] It is a good pasture up there. I know there are many beautiful spots in England, as there are in Germany, and nearer the centre of things, but often they are distinguished by a sweet and honourable somnolence, fitting them better to frame the evening of life than the morning of life [. . .] Gordonstoun is situated in a peaceful and fertile land, but there is a challenge on the horizon; to the north the challenge of the sea, and to the south the challenge of high hills.'

'The system of education is the same as that which produced the physical and spiritual development noticeable in the pupils of the Salem Schools,' continued Hahn. 'By preserving their vitality and developing their strength, tenacity and sense of responsibility, the boys are trained to take an active part in the life of the community and fitted to face poverty or hardship, difficult decisions and changing social relationships.'

Reflecting on what was wrong with current attitudes, Hahn identified the following 'causes for the decline of modern youth: (1) The decline of initiative and self-discipline. (2) The decline of fitness. (3) The decline of care and skill. (4) The decline of compassion.' Jim Graham, a visiting member of staff at Gordonstoun in the 1960s, provides useful paraphrases of these concerns: 'a waning of personal motivation and initiative, the decline of physical fitness, a lack of concern for excellence in care and skill, and finally, a fear that individuals in society were increasingly indifferent to the plight of those less fortunate around them.' Hahn frequently gave lectures on his educational theories, and the numbers of 'declines' or 'decays' waxed and waned in these, probably according to the perceived sensibilities of his audiences or the points he particularly wished to emphasise at the time. By 1965, in the Essex Hall Lecture, he enumerated six declines 'which surround and influence us all, young and old. There is a decline in physical fitness due to the modern methods of locomotion . . . a decline of skill and care due to the weakened tradition of craftsmanship . . . of initiative due to the widespread disease of spectatoritis . . . of self discipline due to the ever present availability of tranquillizers and stimulants . . . of memory and imagination due to the confused restlessness of modern life, and the decline – the worst – of compassion, which William Temple calls "spiritual death".'

Hahn's solution to this complex set of problems and risks was intricate and far-reaching. Taking as his starting point the Platonic view of a healthy state deriving from the relationship between it and the individual, Hahn was convinced that the two major responsibilities of schools were to provide the means and opportunities by which students could discover themselves in order to develop as fully as possible and to equip their charges both morally and physically to serve the community. While he borrowed openly from the British public-school system, which he admired, there were aspects of it that he regarded as unhelpful or even pernicious.

Echoing Prince Max's belief that a healthy school contains a mixture of children of differing ability from a variety of social backgrounds, Hahn felt that the existing public schools were damagingly elitist; their fees meant that only students from well-off families could attend, and the

THE OBSTACLE COURSE

The obstacle course and the mystique surrounding it helped perpetuate the myth of the 'toughness' of Gordonstoun, especially when spoken of in the same breath as morning runs and cold showers. In fact, the obstacle course provided a training facility that was challenging, competitive, great fun and safe. There has been much debate as to which came first, the army version or the Gordonstoun course. Given the Founder's connections in Whitehall and his firmly held belief in training through challenge and physical endeavour, many Gordonstoun enthusiasts have no doubt as to the truth of the matter. Whatever the case, it provided a test of stamina, confidence and skill as well as team-building training without equal in a compact format. It was a popular component of the Gordonstoun International Summer School (GISS) programme from the late 1970s, and the annual inter-Services obstacle-course race was competed for enthusiastically. In spite of its blemish-free record (no serious injury had ever been sustained by its users), health and safety issues were in the end the reason for its demise in 2000.

The obstacle course in the 1950s: top, crossing the lake on the single rope; above, scaling the high wall.

Jenny Needham, director of the Summer School, was determined that it should once again have the use of an obstacle course. After discussion with the school's Outdoor Education Coordinator, a specialist company was commissioned to build a low-level course in the Windmill strip wood. James Thomas, former director of the Summer School, remarks that although the new course is fun and challenging, it doesn't come close to providing the sense of achievement felt by students after they had scaled the big wall or crossed the lake at the end of the original course.

entrance examination guaranteed that all students would be of superior academic ability. Hahn determined that his school would consist of a cross-section of society, from both an economic and an intellectual point of view, and he replaced entrance examinations with a thorough interview. He instituted an elaborate system of fees which required parents to assess their capacity to pay above or below the standard fee. Those who paid above were, in effect, subsidising those who could not afford the standard fee, and it was by this means that he avoided filling his school with an economic elite. 'It is quite impossible to conquer the enervating sense of privilege, and to engender the spirit of joyous exertion, unless a considerable minority of our boys come from homes where life is not only simple but hard.' A mixture of students of different nationalities was also an imperative: 'The boy growing in brotherhood with foreigners cannot help but learn to care about the rights and happiness of at least one other nation. Patriotism does not become diluted; on the contrary, it grows up stronger and nobler by including the love of humanity.' Mark Pyper, Headmaster 1990–2011, has remarked that the Founder would have been gratified by the extent to which this principle of internationalism has been followed: in these days of international mobility, there are now (2011) 44 nationalities represented within the school, and the trick of promoting the positive appreciation of difference by educating everyone together in a boarding community is as effective now as it ever was.

Hahn had distinct opinions about the perils of adolescence. He believed that, while having truly great potential, adolescents are in grave moral danger if they are not properly directed. He was convinced of the importance of channelling the emotional and moral development of children as they grow older. Part of his report on Gordonstoun 1934–35 clearly expresses his hopes and fears about the stage in a child's life that we would now refer to as teenage: 'Is Gordonstoun able, as Salem was, to maintain the child's spiritual strength undiluted and unbroken through adolescence? . . . I believe our boys do not fade, as they do so often in public school. When they leave, their love, their curiosity, their pugnacity are intact as they were when their mothers brought them to school. The nineteen-year-old responsible Helper still radiates the freshness of childhood . . . Again and again I have been weighed down in the last years by the fatalistic acquiescence of parents in the deforming influences of "puberty" that must destroy all promise of the nursery.' Paul Meyer, who attended Gordonstoun 1938–39 between finishing his Abitur in Germany and going to St Andrew's University, and

KURT HAHN BY ERICH MEISSNER

Erich Meissner was a historian, philosopher, educator and painter. For a time, in the 1920s, he worked with Hermann Lietz, who, after viewing the progressive educational methods at Cecil Reddie's school at Abbotsholme in the Lake District, set up a small number of schools in Germany along similar lines. After the Nazis forced Kurt Hahn to leave his post as headmaster of Salem, first the Margrave Berthold and then Meissner filled the position. It was not long, however, before Meissner, too, came into conflict with the Nazis, and soon he followed Hahn into exile in Britain, arriving at Gordonstoun to become Warden of the school and a Housemaster.

Meissner was a prolific painter. This painting, which now hangs in the Library, is one of his best known. The central panel shows Hahn on the southern shore of the Moray Firth, having arrived there in a small rowing boat. An exile from his native Germany, he has nothing with him but his ideas (clasped to his bosom in a Gladstone bag) and his hockey sticks (a reference to Hahn's favourite game).

To the left of the painting are images from the troubled past that led to Hahn's departure from his country of birth: at the top the horrors of World War I (which had led Hahn and Prince Max von Baden to establish the school at Salem) are evoked, and beneath, the Potempa murder. With tragic prescience, Prince Max von Baden had remarked as early as 1923:

'Germany no longer respects her own history. The morals of the Balkans have affected our towns, also our politics, so that in the end the younger generation, victims of deception, have come to believe that you can be a murderer in Germany without being discredited.' On hearing news of the trial of the storm troopers who had murdered the young communist, Hitler sent congratulations to them. Hahn, well aware that old boys from Salem were joining the Hitler Youth movement, reacted instantly, sending a telegram to all old boys telling them that they must break either with the Nazi party or with Salem – 'you cannot belong to both'.

To the right of the painting are, from top to bottom, the school yacht *Henrietta* sailing in the Moray Firth, a reference to Hahn's belief in the crucial educational importance of adventure outdoors; the Parthenon, representing the central significance to him of Plato's view of education; and, at the bottom, Gordonstoun House in the soft evening light of a northern summer, with the artist's large white poodle, Ponto, waiting patiently for his master in the foreground. The only other people awake are the Guardian, whose light burns in one of the dormer windows at the top of the house, and the boy on overnight telephone duty lest there be a call for the Fire Service or Coastguard Watchers.

described Hahn as 'coming from exactly the same stock as my own family – upper-middle class Berlin Jewish bourgeoisie', is blunt in his criticism of his 'sanctimoniousness, above all in matters sexual', finding that Hahn had 'an unwillingness to come to grips with the obvious problems facing normal adolescent males that even sports and cold showers will not completely exorcise.'

As far as we know, Hahn himself never had an intimate relationship. He had a fierce and unflinching concern for the well-being of the adolescents in his charge, as well as an extraordinarily accurate intuitive sense of their characters. Perhaps some of the emotional energy that many people invest in a relationship with a partner was instead directed towards the care of his pupils. Jocelin Winthrop Young remarks, 'Reading his reports and letters to parents, it is amazing to see how brilliantly he analysed and understood us, how carefully he thought out necessary help or correction to our development of character and how concerned he was that we should produce only the very best in carrying out our responsibilities. Above all he put his finger on any fundamental weakness and tried to get the individual to recognise this himself.' When Hahn talks of the dangers from which he seeks to protect older children, his language seems quaint, off-putting, even ridiculous, yet the sense that there is still something relevant in his thoughts on this subject persists. Many parents and teachers will recognise, for example, Hahn's characterisation of infuriatingly non-productive youthful attitudes: 'the law-abiding listless and the cantankerous listless' – no generation, it seems, is immune. How to harness the energies concealed by apparent listlessness was an abiding theme in many of Hahn's initiatives. Once children have reached 'the awkward age', he claimed, 'they often lose their freshness and their charm, sometimes forever . . . The Salem system tries to preserve a child's strength intact through the difficult loutish years, and to hand it to the man as a lifelong source of strength.'

'It is possible in modern surroundings, English or German, to kindle on the threshold of puberty non-poisonous passions which act as Guardian angels during the dangerous years', asserted Hahn. 'I go further – boys herded together are in greater need of this protection. Where the Guardian angels are absent or not firmly established the temptations of puberty either become irresistible or are resisted at a price, the price of youth. Faded voluptuaries may be more repulsive, but the spectacle of victorious puritans, low spirited and prematurely aged, is also sad to someone who knows that children can triumphantly and joyously emerge from puberty, unmolested and without repressions. They can do so on one condition, that healthy passions capable of fulfilment absorb their emotional energies.'

The adolescent, he believed, needed to feel a sense of victory. Often this was achieved through sport, but the problem with sport was that for every 'victor' there was, of necessity, a 'vanquished'. Too great an emphasis on winning could be counter-productive – the criticism of the heroic treatment of sporting prowess in many public schools at the time is clear. Hahn was a keen sportsman himself – an enthusiastic tennis and hockey player – and he believed strongly in physical activity and fitness. He nevertheless reacted against a system in which first-team colours had become the most coveted honour a school community had

to offer. A system of athletic standards was introduced to encourage every boy to compete against himself. In the annual athletics Chart Competition between houses, each boy would record his own achievement for the javelin, the long jump or the track and award himself a Gold, a Silver or a Bronze. The aim was for a pupil to improve his own personal record.

The idea of young people testing themselves against the elements was central to Hahn's philosophy, and he made sure that opportunities were provided wherever possible either up mountains or at sea. Seamanship and sailing provided an invaluable way of testing skill, endurance and ability to work in a team. Expeditions, mountaineering and associated activities such as rock climbing and abseiling provided similar opportunities. 'No boy', he said, 'should be compelled into opinions but it is criminal negligence not to impel him into experience.'

Hahn was passionate in his conviction that young people should be encouraged always to do their personal best, and in particular that they should be pushed to overcome whatever obstacles prevented them from succeeding physically – be it fear, physical disability or simply a disinclination to exert themselves. Jim Orr, who moved from Harrow to Gordonstoun in 1934, recalled two examples of Hahn's sure touch when it came to encouraging boys who faced physical difficulty: 'His greatest gift was to practise what he preached when it came to compassion. There was a boy at Gordonstoun who had had a foot amputated. "I'm afraid I can't play games", moaned the boy. "That is nonsense", said Hahn, "You will play hockey and you will play in goal. As you'll be wearing pads no-one will know of your handicap". The boy in question proved a courageous and competent goalkeeper and laughed about his infirmity. He used to put his artificial foot under motor cars and then tell the driver, "You've just run over my foot", much to the consternation of the poor person responsible . . . Another boy spent his time at Gordonstoun on a stretcher. Hahn placed him under a big tree near the West Door where every

Below left: A Gordonstoun entrant in the Scottish Schools Athletics Championships, 1938; below: Jocelin Winthrop Young in mid-jump, 1934. The high jump was an activity held in great regard by Hahn.

Above: Pre-war expedition.

Centre and right: Expedition to Norway on *Henrietta*, 1937.

member of the school passed at least twice a day. Sandy grew to love everyone as much as we loved him. Hahn promoted him to an important rank. He grew in confidence. His morale was sky high. He didn't live long but if ever a boy left his mark on us all, it was Sandy, a living symbol of courage facing the inevitable with his delicate features, all smiles, in the environment which Hahn had created.'

Hahn was determined to counter what he saw as a tendency in public schools towards introspection and separation from the communities in or near which they were located, regarding boarding schools as facing particular problems in this respect: 'I consider one of the chief dangers in an isolated school is the turning of the eye inward, domestic events are exaggerated, gossip fills every empty moment', he remarked in 1939. He believed that boys or girls must be educated in such a way that they were enabled to confront their own characters and then, equipped with greater self-knowledge, become responsible citizens in the communities in which they lived. 'You cannot overestimate the power of self-deception' was a favourite remark.

Central to Hahn's idea of developing a sense of social responsibility was the idea that an awareness of current social problems should be fostered, and active opportunities provided for students to be involved in solutions to them. 'A boarding school can contribute something essential to the health of the community immediately beyond it, and the community contributes something essential to the school.' He also believed in the transforming effect of rescue on the rescuer. Looking back on the achievements of Gordonstoun, he reflected on how the Services had begun in Moray: 'Before Gordonstoun started I had some leisure to look back on what was right and what was wrong with Salem. There was no doubt we had failed in the Cistercian purpose; dramatic opportunities had been seized by the school to be of use to the district, but there never was that epic continuity of service which the Cistercians had practised and preached. We made the discovery of Samaritan service accidentally in 1935, and I consider it the most important contribution, so far, that Gordonstoun has made to the training of the young. I should like to say something about this discovery. The Morayshire coast is dangerous and the strip on which Gordonstoun is situated is, for miles, hidden from the lookouts, both in Lossiemouth and Burghead. I had learnt that in the eighth century a monk, Gernadius, came over from Ireland to live in one of the Covesea caves, within our grounds. On stormy nights he used to walk about through all the hours of darkness, waving a lantern to warn the fishermen of rocks and shoals.' At a school meeting attended by officials from HM Coastguard, it was agreed that the Board of Trade would provide equipment if boys from the school would build and then man a coastguard station. And this was precisely what happened (see page 138).

The birth of the Coastguard Watchers was followed by a series of life-saving rescue services, the Fire Service, Mountain Rescue, Beach Rescue, to which Community Service was added later. The Bloodhound Service (with the hounds first kennelled in Duffus stables) may well have been inspired by the St Bernard dogs trained by the monks to aid travellers through the passes of the Alps. St Bernard of Clairvaux took part in the foundation of Salem in 1138.

'It was Hahn's ambition', notes Ian Lawson, 'that every pupil would find his *grande passion* which would absorb and stimulate even the unlikeliest student to strive for excellence. There were many startling successes creating an energy and satisfaction in some who found it hard to achieve conventional success.' Hahn believed that once a student had tasted success and a sense of achievement in his area of special interest he would begin to achieve in other areas as well, that the benefits for a discouraged and perhaps hitherto undervalued child who became passionately interested by an activity or pursuit would spill over into other areas of endeavour, unlocking potential that would otherwise go untapped. Jim Orr gives a touching instance of Hahn's lateral thinking in this regard: 'I have often repeated the story of the rather backward, awkward boy whom we all laughed at or ignored. Hahn got to hear that this boy loved maps and timetables. On one occasion an important businessman had overstayed his visit to the school and was worried about the urgent meeting awaiting his presence abroad. "I have just the man for you", said Hahn, using one of his favourite expressions, and promptly sent for X to seek his advice. X was like a dog with two tails, went off all smiles to his timetables and maps and produced the much-appreciated solution. For years that boy never missed an old boys' dinner at which we were all so pleased to see him.'

Time was set aside on one afternoon each week for Projects which, within reason, would open up interests of every kind. The range was unlimited: local biological and geographical surveys, science Projects, historical studies and art and craft of all kinds. Some of the most popular Projects involved cars and radios. Not all were successful: one boy, found sleeping during Projects time, was awoken and asked by his tutor what he was thinking of: 'I'm doing my Project, sir.' 'Which is?' 'Interpreting dreams, sir.'

Youthful enthusiasms allowed to blossom with little supervision sometimes produced results which went rather further than might have been expected. Pat Whitworth remembers that at Broneirion while the school was in Wales during the war there was a radio club in a cellar: 'To avoid too many inquisitive visitors, they arranged a series of

charged wires (2v and 200v) dangling from a beam over the entrance. Their first visitor was Dr Meissner [a member of staff]! The wires were removed but the staples that held them remain in the beam to this day.' Pat Whitworth recalls a fellow enthusiast for model-making and cars called Timothy Grey 'who had been caught at dead of night returning one of the school vehicles to its garage, after taking it on a tour round the district . . . Perhaps we were both into engines really and model-making legitimised

Michael Shea with bloodhounds Wizard and Hamlet, 1956.

Below: Building the first Watchers' Hut in 1935; below left, its replacement, made out of two ships' wheelhouses in 1946.

Opposite: The new Coastguard Watchtower, opened in 1955 and still in use today.

having model engines. I had a 3 cc diesel engine and he had a similar petrol one. He also had a portable radio, which items were not so common in those days. He must have had a vague knowledge of electronics, because, with the aid of this radio and other bits and pieces he contrived to bug the masters' common room which was not far away below the Round Square hobby room, on the ground floor. When the weekly, perhaps fortnightly Masters' Meeting took place, Timothy and others crouched over their radio to hear what the masters would say.'

'The members of the Engineering Guild', remembers another old boy, 'seemed to live in a world of their own. Their place of business was (invariably) in a Nissen hut just up a slope to the west of the Round Square and opposite the laundry – close to the san – and they spent every possible moment there. They also had a language of their own. Two of the leading lights were Pat Whitworth and Simon Rathbone. They built a three-wheeled wooden chassis, two wheels at the front, one at the back, and they fitted a motor-cycle engine into the chassis to drive the rear wheel along with a motor car steering system for the front wheels. This extraordinarily ugly contraption worked and they were familiar figures perched on a seat and endlessly

puttering along the east and west drives. Everyone knew they were coming due to the noise, since the motor-cycle engine did not seem to have a silencer.'

When Pat's brother Peter arrived at Aberlour House, Pat had an excuse to take the day off, and while looking round the outbuildings of this considerable country house, he spotted a 1911 Renault sitting in one of the garages: 'The school Governors were not going to give it away. Their final price meant that the only way to purchase it was to form a syndicate; shared between four of us, £7 10s was just about manageable. It was, of course, delivered free to Gordonstoun, on the school lorry. From then on, work began. All other school activities were minimised, including prep, of course. It was in better condition than we had feared, so before long, we were ready to give it a try. Cranking appeared to be non-productive, so the next option was pushing. At this point I must remind the reader that our Headmaster had some very strict safety rules. Anyway, we

The Pocock Workshops, in one of the Nissen huts installed on the estate during the war by the army, where many Projects were worked upon. Ralph Pocock, an artist, and his wife had been greatly impressed by the educational ambitions of the school and the conversion and fitting out were carried out after Pocock's death in his memory.

Below: The 1911 Renault bought by a syndicate of boys at the school.

Projects Exhibition in Duffus village hall, c. 1961, an event held from 1953 until the early 1970s.

cheering, engine noise or just chance, we will never know, but Headmaster Kurt Hahn was looking out of his study window. Shortly after this historic event I was duly summoned. Was I aware that I had broken seven safety rules? I was reminded that riding on the running board of a moving vehicle was forbidden. It is the driver's responsibility to make sure this does not happen. "Bend over".'

Once a year there would be a Projects Exhibition in Duffus village hall, judged by an outside panel of experts. Projects from a number of local schools were included, and the Gordonstoun embargo on prizes would be waived. The top prize was the Saltire Prize, followed by Special Commendations and Gold, Silver and Bronze Awards.

Hahn took a huge interest in the health of the children in his care. His was a world in which remedial health care was still very limited: there were no antibiotics, and illnesses of many kinds could be both life-threatening and chronically weakening. In 1928, while he was at Salem, for instance, there was an outbreak of polio for which there was no known treatment except quarantine. Hahn and Marina Ewald (daughter of an eminent Berlin doctor and a graduate of St Andrew's who had worked with Hahn at Salem since 1923) simply evacuated the whole school to a village in Switzerland, where, remarks a boy who was there at the time, 'sun and frost and altitude soon coped with the problem – at least there was no further case of polio [. . .] Of the initial two boys affected, one recovered completely, the other had a permanently weakened right arm and leg, all the more disastrous as he was the captain of tennis.' True to form, Hahn made sure the boy returned to the game 'and two years later he was able to give one a pretty good game in spite of the handicap.'

started pushing the Renault away from its workshop, the commandeered Fire Station. By the time we got to the drive a number of other boys had observed and joined in the push. Faster and faster. Halfway down the hill towards the main school some thumping and clonking noises. Yes! We had ignition, traction and acceleration! Whether it was the

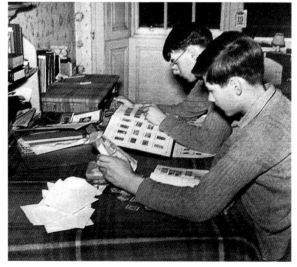

Projects: rug making, stamp collecting and, below, the result of a Project that involved converting a motorbike into a car with three wheels, 1950s.

Hahn attributed the health record of Gordonstoun boys (better, he observed, than in Salem) to the climate and 'the mode of living'. The food that was served has much in common with what is advocated now as a healthy diet: 'For lunch our boys have meat four times a week and fish once a week and they get plenty of fresh vegetables, and fruit all year round. They never have meat or fish in the evening.'

He regarded fitness as crucial (a healthy mind in a healthy body). 'When Plato demands that his future Guardians should be alert in starting, swift in pursuit and full of fight in the finish. I think we can say that we at least equip our young with willing bodies . . . There is an alertness in their bearing just as there was in Salem. I attribute it to our physical activities occurring not only once a day but at different intervals during the day; skipping and the run before breakfast; jumping, running and throwing four times a week during the morning break; games and seamanship twice a week, after lunch and after the rest period; practical work twice a week. We find that one can teach almost every English boy as one can teach almost every German boy, to run, to jump and to throw' (note that Hahn cleaved to the athletics favoured by the ancient Greeks: 'jumping develops decision; throwing, strength; running, the power to tap one's hidden reserves'). 'I am often asked,' reflected Hahn, ' "Do they like it?" and I answer, "I do not ask children whether they enjoy brushing their teeth or taking medicine, and I regard the Salem training as a medicine meant not only to help to ward off illness, but to turn health into fitness." In the end everybody enjoys fitness and thinks kindly of labours that have helped them to build it up.' Hahn's interest in health matters pervaded many aspects of daily life: the morning run, the salt gargle, the cold shower, no eating between meals, no drinking at meals, no aspirin whatever (considered a poison), no cycling uphill.

Mindful both of the model for promoting active citizenship laid out in Plato's *Republic* and of the plentiful evidence in Germany that a passive citizenry harbours great risk to the healthy functioning of a nation, Hahn laid great emphasis on 'character training'. This he set out to achieve with a 'Training Plan', which in its turn was dependent on a 'Trust System'.

Both at Salem and at Gordonstoun, trust was given to the pupils in return for their honesty to others and to themselves. 'There are two methods of governing the young' declared Hahn. 'You can tether them by distrust or bind them by trust. I would back a spirited boy to defeat the first method. I believe in the second method, which was Thomas Arnold's, but only on the condition you fortify it by a daily incentive to self supervision.' Jocelin Winthrop Young has pointed out that this daily incentive was only a

Below left: The first pupils at Gordonstoun.

Below: Athletic training on Covesea Beach, 1930s.

Opposite: Senior boys inter-house cross-country race, 2005.

means of aiding self-discipline, not an end in itself, meaning that the aim should be to work without it.

The Trust System was perhaps one of Gordonstoun's most remarkable characteristics. 'It was an anxious time for us to see how English public school boys would react to trust', recounted Hahn shortly after the opening of the school. 'I was confident of an honourable response even though, contrary to the standards in Dr Arnold's times, the public school boy's code in England at this moment permits of judicious cribbing and lying within limits in dealing with certain masters. I found that even with public school boys of 16 and 17 years of age, the veracity of the English nursery can be restored under a system which gives trust ungrudgingly and punishes seriously when this trust has been betrayed . . . Accordingly the sinister warnings have been refuted which I had received from many quarters about the uselessness of the training plan in an English school. The English boy takes readily to the one-minute scoring in the evening on what he has done during the day. Of course they all regard the daily filling in of the training plan as a nuisance, nevertheless they are proud of having the training plan and would hate to lose the burden and the honour . . . Of course, the training plan only works if the staff plays the game, that is to say does not misuse it for

the purposes of illegitimate information. The training plan has nothing to do with the confessional system as practised by the Jesuits [. . .] it is the Protestant confession to yourself not the Catholic confession to the stranger.'

This system of trust was surprisingly successful, and it is clear from the testimony of many old boys that the majority of them took it very seriously. 'That acceptance of trust,' remarks Ian Lawson (who taught at Altyre, Forres, and then Gordonstoun), 'provided a basis on which routine and discipline could be based without detailed and intrusive supervision. Breaches of trust were, by definition, rarely discovered, but the occasional lapse served as a strong reminder of the acceptance of certain obligations owed by the individual to the community.' He goes on to quote a case in point: 'The airfield of the Royal Navy's Fleet Air Arm adjoining the Gordonstoun estate did not have much of a security fence. Surplus aircraft were parked close to this periphery prior to scrapping. One day the Commanding Officer visited the school to report that, sadly, it was suspected that pupils were helping themselves to bits and pieces from these aircraft. A whole school meeting was immediately called and the pupils told that if any of them had taken bits and pieces they were to retrieve them from their houses and bring them back to the meeting.

There was a measure of good-humoured scepticism from the officer that anyone would voluntarily surrender such objects, taken at some risk, and identify himself as a culprit. Scepticism evaporated as the boys came back and the pile of returned souvenirs grew and grew.'

Jeremy Sale is one of several participants who have vivid memories of the incident: 'I always loved planes and there were some great old Mosquitos, Seafires, Avro Ansons, Rapides, etc. Plus a few tired old jets, Sea Vampires and Scimitars, mostly. It was in a pretty remote part of the airfield so no one seemed to notice. Later we scoffed a few dash plaques, then still later things like airspeed indicators, etc. Anything that looked as if it would make a cool souvenir. Then word got out that some boys had been chased off the airfield by the base police with escalating rumours of dogs [there was one dog], jeeps, planes, gunfire [untrue] . . . and guards on bicycles [true]. That was when the big row started. There was a school meeting and we were told that anyone involved had to come to the upper dining room in Gordonstoun House to confess. (This was one thing I never could reconcile with myself. Gordonstoun didn't have to catch you doing something, all they had to do was ask you to confess! Not fair!) They had you come in the door and march about 100 yards all the way up the room to where the hanging jury including Henry Bear [Brereton] sat behind a long table. [. . .] I duly confessed my sins and was immediately hanged. Well, I actually don't remember what my punishment was but I was made to feel very guilty. The school authorities said we could have killed innocent pilots "as the planes could have been flown the very next day!" Rubbish, even with the pitiful state of the Royal Navy. As my stepfather was in the RAF and knew the planes were going to be junked he didn't seem to mind. So there it is. My life as a criminal.' Another of the trophy hunters recalls that the Fleet Air Arm turned up with two long wheelbase Land Rovers, but such was the quantity of 'cool souvenirs' that a couple of trucks had to be sent instead: 'The deal done with the RNAS was that each person was fined a percentage of their theft to be paid to some retirement charity for ex-RNAS personnel.'

Some ten years later, RAF Lossiemouth invested in substantial new security measures, including new perimeter fencing, and offered Gordonstoun the opportunity to test it by trying to break into the base. Numbers of students made various attempts to scale the fence, tunnel under it or otherwise to force entry, all to no avail. But one enterprising individual donned RAF mechanic's clothing, arrived at the main gate ostensibly for work and was immediately allowed in!

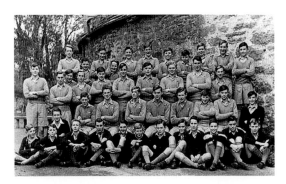

Boys from the Round Square, 1946. Those seated in front are wearing Day Uniform; behind them are boys who had earned their Evening Uniform.

Students at Gordonstoun had two uniforms – Day Uniform and Evening Uniform. On arrival, new students wore only Day Uniform. After a term or maybe more, depending on the student, he would qualify to wear Evening Uniform as well. To do so, he would have demonstrated familiarity with the system and an understanding of the importance of honesty and trust. After the student had gained school uniform, he would embark on his Training Plan. In consultation with his Housemaster, personal goals were set; the Plan contained a few core items such as skipping and rope-climbing with other items to help individuals remedy their own personal shortcomings. Over each week he was expected to record, in a special booklet, such things as extra hours spent on study or 'lates' – occasions when he had been late for class or late out of dormitory, for example. Each day a plus or a minus was registered opposite simple headings designed to produce Plato's ideal of *mens sana in corpore sano* (a healthy mind in a healthy body). Hahn had taken to heart the words of Socrates when Plato is evaluating the relative importance of physical training and the education of the mind and character or soul: 'Have you ever noticed that lifelong devotion to physical exercise, to the exclusion of anything else, produces a tough, uncivilised, uncouth person, while a purely literary and academic training makes people soft, oversensitive and lacking in backbone?' In spite of his frankly unhappy personal experience at Gordonstoun, Prince Charles was clear about the intentions of Hahn (who had, of course, left the school by the time the thirteen-year-old Charles arrived there): 'His whole idea was to produce a physically and mentally rounded human being, who was civilised and self-disciplined.'

The Plan included simple routine tasks concerning hygiene, e.g. cold shower after warm wash, exercise, study and community duty. It was to be kept up to date and to be

The Silent Walk, along which generations of Gordonstoun pupils have approached the Michael Kirk.

an accurate and honest record of the extent to which the goals had been achieved. The student's Housemaster could ask to look at the Training Plan from time to time, but it was made plain that if he were dishonest or negligent in his recording process the student would harm only himself. The elements of a Training Plan were gradually reduced with age to suit the individual; later it developed into a Discipline Handbook. Each boy also possessed a chart on which he recorded a unit or assessment given by a master, alpha, beta or gamma, to denote the quality of his work. This was the only official record of work and boys were expected to keep it honestly and on a regular basis. Bernard Kuenssberg (1962–66) much preferred this method to the educational scoring systems commonly found elsewhere: 'Recording alpha, beta or gamma marks in one's own personal record to discuss with one's tutor weekly rather than the ridiculous positions in each class, i.e. 28th out of 31 or 4th out of 28 and [as a result] sitting in a particular place as at my previous school.' James FitzGibbon, who taught in school for well over twenty years, remembers one occasion when a Training Plan was filled up with pluses for the two weeks ahead.

A boy was trusted by staff to report to his Housemaster or Helper without further checking if required to do so. The only witness to a boy's failure or success was his own conscience. Hahn's intention with this system was clear. In Jocelin Winthrop Young's words, 'To admit to a misdemeanour, to excuse oneself, to accept the punishment, that was not enough. He wanted more, he wanted the full acknowledgement of one's own weaknesses; the conquest of self-deception.' Another sign of the Trust System was that individual lockers of boys in the locker room had no keys or padlocks.

Walking Punishments were handed out for a variety of infractions of school rules and breaches of trust and were imposed by Housemasters or the Headmaster. They ranged from a No. 1 (about fifteen minutes' walk to Duffus village and back) rising to a No. 7 (there and back to Elgin – a round trip of some twelve miles). 'The Punishment Walks', reflects Bernard Kuenssberg, 'seemed so sensible after the corporal beating I had experienced before with gym shoe and tawse.' David Conway (1944–45) reflects that punishment walks were not necessarily a hardship: 'Punishment at Gordonstoun . . . was endured or enjoyed in solitude. Typically, it was self-administered and its correct performance was a matter of honour. The offender was required to rise before the others in his dormitory, at a time which would allow the walk to be accomplished before the daily routine began. Running and any attempt to make the exercise a group activity were forbidden. Solitary meditation on the nature of the sin committed was the order of the day. Heading into wind, hail or rain on a cold dark winter morning made for uncomfortable expiation of wrong-doing. It seems in my long-term memory that not infrequently I walked against the weather in both directions! But, on a clear bright, spring or summer morning punishment turned into pure joy. The scent of wild flowers and foliage was borne on the breeze, the birds sang and small animals scurried across the road from hedgerow to hedgerow. The only other human presence might be the figures of other offenders striding along ahead or behind at a respectable distance.'

In addition to Walking Punishments, there was one other, more conventional sanction available to punish petty offences, and it could be handed out by Colour Bearers as well as by teaching staff. It seems unlikely that Penalty Drill, or PD as it was known, took place in pre-war days, but it was certainly happening in the late 1940s and carried on until 1990. The aim was to use an hour of a pupil's time at an awkward point in the day – an hour before breakfast on a Saturday morning – and it consisted of four circuits of the south lawn, three running to every one walking. Peter Muckle (1951–54) contributes a reminiscence which illustrates how particular Hahn was that the various components of his elaborate system of correction be adhered to: 'I remember one summer's morning doing my almost weekly stint at Penalty Drill when the CB or CBC in charge, one Anthony Fildes, a first-class cricketer, decided to use all this free muscle to roll the cricket pitch for a big game, for that Saturday. He left us to it to attend a call of nature, a window was opened in Gordonstoun House, and a thunderous voice called "Shtop!" We froze in mid-pitch. Again the voice bellowed "Shtop! What are you boys doing?" Ten seconds later, Mr Hahn erupted from the front door, at the same time as Anthony emerged from the side door, and they arrived together. As I recall, poor A.F. got a right rollicking for interfering with the Penalty Drill system, and we returned to our peregrination around the Triangle, deep in thought about our misdeeds which had landed us in trouble. No-one dared use the Penalty Drill culprits again for other purposes.'

School Meetings were held for important announcements to be made, and for infractions of the school's rules and ethos to be investigated and examined, with the perpetrators asked publicly to own up to their misdeeds. It is clear from the recollections of several of those who attended them, that these occasions could be intimidating affairs. Perhaps unsurprisingly, it is the

determination of Hahn to root out any impropriety among the boys that sticks in people's memories: Jimmy Fraser, at the school when Prince Philip was Guardian, recalled 'Great numbers of school meetings, with old Hahn pacing up and down on the platform, hands in front of him pointing downwards, and the fingers of the left hand massaging the back of the right hand . . . "Some Poy . . . some poy . . . has been guilty . . . of . . . a rude . . . LAAAVATORY. . . choke!" '

David Conway provides a powerful evocation of a School Meeting in Wales: 'Nowhere on school premises was there a room capable of holding all the boys. For this purpose the Llandinam village hall was pressed into service and the whole school met there infrequently. School Meetings, like public hangings, were not good news – even for the spectators. I seem to recall that they were held on the spur of the moment. What terrible crime had been committed? Who was the offender? Was it YOU?' He continues:

'One warm summer's day we had all converged, walking or cycling, on the village hall. The chatter of voices ceased without command, as we seated ourselves. Particles of dust sparkled in shafts of sunlight and we all pondered our recent misdemeanours. Were they about to be publicly revealed? After an age, the sound of tyres crunching unseen on the gravel as Hahn arrived in his chauffeur-driven Austin. The car doors slammed and all heads turned to follow the progress of the great man. He walked in silence – head bent, right arm swinging, dark glasses protecting the eyes from sunlight – down the centre aisle to the platform. Now for the moment of truth. Somebody had been "schmoking", indulging in "feelth" (anything from mild schoolboy homosexuality to telling dirty stories and – on one occasion – a boy caught with a naked village girl in the cricket pavilion; he was summarily expelled). "Honourable gentlemen will own up" was the message which invariably followed the announcement of the current crime. Transfixed by Hahn's compelling presence and penetrating gaze, the desire to own up was near irresistible. Anyone who has stood on the edge of a cliff or looked at the electric rail

THE RING OF GYGES

James FitzGibbon draws a fascinating parallel between the Trust System and the story of the ring of Gyges in Plato's *Republic*. Gyges, a shepherd in the service of the King of Lydia, one day found a gold ring. He then discovered that this ring had the power of making the wearer invisible. With its help, he seduced the Queen, attacked and murdered the King and then seized the throne. Socrates goes on to say that a truly just or moral man in possession of Gyges' ring would be steadfast in doing what is right, even though he knows he can probably escape detection and punishment.

from an Underground platform will recognise the mesmeric urge to jump. A long silent pause broken by the scrape of a chair as the first offender rose to own up; followed by another and another. Some were regulars – old lags of the schmoking habit. Others – shock, horror, disbelief – were pillars of the establishment, Colour Bearer Candidates, even Colour Bearers. The rewards for "honourable gentlemen" were demotion or some other punishment, usually the cane and the knowledge that one had taken an active part in the Gordonstoun system.'

Perhaps Hahn's most original innovation and one that sets Gordonstoun apart from other schools was the constitution he devised for the school community and his method of selecting leaders. Hahn would have been aware of Eton's 'Pop', a self-electing body of prefects, and it is also very likely, as James FitzGibbon observes, that the influence of the Rule of St Benedict (which had been freely drawn on at Salem) can be seen: 'As often as any important business has to be done in the monastery, let the abbot call together the whole community and himself explain the situation. And having heard the advice of the brethren, let him do what is appropriate. Now the reason why we have said that all should be called to council, is that God often reveals what is better to the younger.' This last phrase touches on something that was of great importance to Hahn – the relationship between older and younger boys. According to St Benedict: 'The juniors shall honour their seniors and the seniors shall love the juniors.' By adopting this simple

precept, Hahn transformed the suspicions and phobias that had constantly bedevilled the lives of public schoolboys into a relationship of friendship and trust. One of the most remarkable characteristics of the school was that the care and interest shown by older boys for their juniors have always been a prerequisite for promotion to responsibility, not a barrier. There would be no room for the 'fagging' system of conventional public schools. Instead of tasks for a senior boy, every boy had a duty of service to the community, starting with humble chores, but increasing in responsibility as he rises in status.

Satisfactory management of a Training Plan meant that the Housemaster could advance the student to the rank of a White Striper. A White Striper was given a degree of authority over other students and entrusted with certain responsibilities, mostly house-based: for example, ensuring that the boys were out of the dormitory on time, that laundry had been collected, cleaning done. They were expected to get others to do as they should by using the force of their own personality, by positive pressure – never by recourse to threats or punishment to younger students who failed to do their allotted jobs.

Equating roughly with prefects in other schools was the body of Colour Bearers. The title 'Colour Bearer' was chosen by Hahn because, as mentioned earlier, he was concerned that in public schools the highest honour bestowed was generally the award of 'Colours' to those who displayed outstanding talent in sports. He, by contrast, believed that

Penalty Drill in the late 1970s.

THE RULE OF SILENCE

A painting entitled *The Gordonstoun Boy* by Dr Erich Meissner, who had a deep respect for the Rules of St Benedict, used to hang in the Silence Room of the Round Square. It depicted a pupil in monastic habit with his hand to his mouth urging silence. St Benedict says: 'Monks should practise silence at all times, but especially at night.' Also, 'After the sixth hour, having left the table, let them rest on their beds in perfect silence; or if anyone wishes to read by himself, let him read so as not to disturb the others.' At rest groups, pupils would lie on their beds for half an hour after lunch for rest or reading. In the evening a silence bell was rung when all

movement in the house and talking stopped for five minutes, and there was silence at the beginning of meals. Silence was also observed when going to and from worship at the Michael Kirk. Colour Bearers were obliged to go for a walk each week and meditate in silence. 'All our boys', noted Hahn in his report to the Governors in 1935, 'approach the Anglican Chapel in a silent walk of ten minutes, leading through a beautiful wood; even though not all go in, all have shared in this silent worship.'

Rest Group supervised by Norman Pares on the North Lawn, late 1930s.

the honour of bearing the school colours should be given to those who embodied the overall values of the school and gave responsible leadership. They won their position because of their training in character, not because of their pre-eminence at sport. 'We have dethroned team games', Hahn remarked. He was determined that his Colour Bearers would indulge in none of the excesses and abuses of power sometimes observable among prefects in other schools. His determination that an atmosphere of care be fostered is clear. When Colour Bearers elected their peers, the first question asked of a new candidate was whether he got on well with the juniors.

Paul Meyer was dubious about the rightness of the Colour Bearer system: '[Hahn] inculcated in his school what I can only call an elaborate espionage system – remember his definition of a Colour Bearer as one who hears the grass grow – that violated the privacy of the individual to a high degree. On the other hand,' he continues, 'I can vouch for his system when it comes to the subject of bullying. In my experience and in that of all those I knew, no bullying was ever countenanced in Hahn's schools, and when this offence was committed, there was a very effective punishment meted out to the culprit – on one occasion my cousin – he was made to box against an older and stronger boy and thus given a dose of his own medicine.' Clive Holland, at Gordonstoun in the late 1940s and early '50s, also remembers this corrective measure, though it clearly didn't always work quite as expected: 'If a boy was found guilty of bullying, the punishment was to box a bigger boy. On one occasion the bigger boy was beaten up by the bully. The fights took place in Cumming House in the big room above the arch. Every boy in the school would try and watch the fight by climbing on the roof and hanging down on sheets etc., etc.'

Jocelin Winthrop Young has also voiced his reservations about the Colour Bearer system: 'Is there not something a little smug about pupils of seventeen, who decide that some of their fellow pupils are not worthy to sit in assembly with themselves on grounds of character? [. . .] Surely there should have been a higher rate of resignation from the Colour Bearer body if self criticism is one of the principles of the school?' And he drew attention to the tension inherent between two of Hahn's principles – education for responsibility and education for democracy: 'the more responsibility is to be delegated to students, the more likely it is that a gap will grow between those responsible and the rest of the school.'

A Housemaster could advance a student no further than the rank of White Striper; for further advancement a student had to be nominated, usually by his Housemaster and two or three Colour Bearers. The Colour Bearers met regularly, and Housemasters and certain other members of staff attended their meetings, but their powers of voting were limited so that the pupils were responsible for actual decisions. The suitability of the candidate was discussed and finally voted on for advancement to the status of Colour Bearer Candidate. If made a CBC, the student was given greater responsibility and entrusted with more serious leadership tasks and responsibilities; he was also permitted to impose certain punishments. By the same process – that is, by nomination and by vote at a Colour Bearer meeting – a Colour Bearer Candidate could advance to the rank of Colour Bearer, who would then be entitled to wear a small purple stripe on his school pullover.

Although the powers of the Colour Bearers were restricted, the Headmaster could appoint Helpers and Guardians only from the self-elected Colour Bearers and had therefore handed over to them part of his power. Through this limited form of self-government, the whole school was represented by their fellow pupils in the formation and administration of the fundamental principles of the school. Hahn thus successfully blended the ideals of Cistercian communal life and Athenian democracy.

The reality, was of course, not always identical to the ideology, and Ekke von Kuenssberg and Bex Richter, in conversation with Ian Lawson in 1985, recalled that while Kurt Hahn 'consistently affirmed his belief in a democratic form of school government, in practice he worked a managed democracy . . . Everything was stage-managed to ensure that the correct democratic decision (that is, the Hahn solution) was reached.'

Hahn decided that the head student should be known as the Guardian, again a direct take from Plato's *Republic* where the Guardians, the philosopher-kings, were the rulers of the hypothetical state. Heads of Houses or Services were to be known as Helpers and were chosen by the Headmaster from the ranks of Colour Bearers. Once more, the title Helper was borrowed from *The Republic* where the Guardians have bodies of Helpers to assist in the running of the state. It was important that these positions be more than positions of 'name only', and so all pupils who held offices of responsibility had specific tasks allotted to them (for example, Captains of Guests, of District, of Exams, of Assemblies, of Chapel, etc.), rather like ministers in a government being handed particular portfolios.

Jim Graham remarks, 'The system had flaws and did not always operate as well as Hahn no doubt wished. Regular counselling and supervision was needed at all stages of

Kurt Hahn towards the end of his tenure at Gordonstoun.

has talked about Hahn's talent for reading young people, divining their aspirations and identifying their potential, and cites his response to Mark Arnold-Forster, with him at the start of the school, as an example: 'Mark Arnold-Forster was a great grandson of Thomas Arnold, the famous Head-master of Rugby. The Arnolds were intellectuals and Mark is, in my opinion, probably the most brilliant student Hahn ever had. He was slightly built, not a bit tough or strong. He decided that the academic teaching in Gordonstoun was not satisfactory and left in the lower sixth form to study elsewhere. But after a year he returned to Scotland and Hahn appointed him Captain of Seamanship. He had seen the man of action, where we had seen a boy who was not interested in sports. Mark became a very distinguished journalist after the war. But at sea he was one of the most decorated and distinguished young Naval officers.'

Hahn had the great gift of making people feel very important for suggesting something with which he, Hahn, disagreed. Jim Orr gives a flavour of this persuasive technique: ' "I think you are entirely right", he would say, and then go on to give his own view and make his visitor think that it was he, the visitor, who had suggested it in the first place . . . He had an extraordinary modesty, almost humility . . . When he addressed the school, each boy felt that he was being talked to personally. His penetrating eyes seemed to bore into one's very soul; all rather frightening if one had a guilty conscience, which one often did . . . Hahn's concentration on the person to whom he was speaking was remarkable. He was able to switch off completely except for the matter in hand, a wonderful encouragement to those seeking his advice as I so often did. He always made allowances for those boys who made mistakes.' Hahn had an unwavering belief that it was the responsibility of a teacher to help a recalcitrant or unsuccessful pupil to perform and roundly upbraided any member of staff who blamed a child for failing. He spoke admiringly of a riposte made at a meeting of educationalists by Dr Carl Reinhardt: 'One schoolmaster made the remark, "I have no faith in this boy." Dr Reinhardt said to him, "Then you have no right to educate him." '

Hahn's work was his life. He literally never took a day off. 'My only complaint against life is that it all passes too quickly', he would say, and, 'I'm an old man in a hurry'. He never wasted a minute of the day. If he was travelling to London, an associate whom he wished to see would accompany him to Elgin; someone else would be summoned to the train at Aberdeen and so on to King's Cross and Brown's Hotel in London where he would have at least one working breakfast.

development through the system . . . but I would have to say that I found it to be a most effective system for developing in students a real sense of responsibility.'

Hahn was physically imposing with a huge personality that was impressive, sometimes intimidating, and certainly, on occasion, eccentric. The many myths, legends and stories that have grown up around him sometimes verge on the burlesque, and the figure that they conjure up can seem forbidding and intimidating. And yet, many of the personal memories of him paint a picture of a kind, warm, intuitive man. 'His wisdom, compassion, enthusiasm, drive and sense of humour permeated the whole school', wrote Jim Orr. 'His judgment of people, after the briefest of meetings, was uncanny.' Ian Farmer (1941–47) remembers being very nervous at his interview 'with this big man exuding suppressed energy who seemed to be able to read my thoughts before I uttered a word'. Jocelin Winthrop Young

Path running through the estate near the Round Square.

'He was large and somewhat clumsy', remembers Jocelin Winthrop Young. 'The head slightly bent forward, giving the appearance of a stoop. The head was round and there was a thin covering of hair at the back. A large prominent forehead. The hands looked clumsy and he was unable to shave himself. He was shaved daily at Salem by Herr Wolfensberger and later by James Black in Elgin. His legs were powerful and he was proud of his own agility in the High Jump. At the first modern Olympic Games, the Greeks included the standing High Jump, believing that this was one of the events at the original games in Olympia. There are photos of Hahn showing him performing this event at Salem.'

His colleague Godfrey Burchardt wrote of him, 'Kurt Hahn was a master of words in his adopted language yet he never spoke it with an entirely English intonation. In particular the vowel "o" was treated in his own way. Mother rhymed with bother, the "o" in wonderful (a favourite word) with that in gone.' David Conway notes that Hahn presented a perfect opportunity for schoolboy mimicry: 'Impromptu performances of the way in which he walked and talked took place everywhere . . . Following him into the dining room one day, I adopted his manner, measured tread, right fist closed with arm swinging to shoulder level and head down. In fact, my head was so far down that when I caught sight of his shoes they were very close – toes pointed towards me! The great man gazed down at me as I quaked in anticipation. "Not very good Conway" came the perfect squelch.'

Jocelin Winthop Young again: 'Hahn's skin was exceptionally white, both from its nature and from its intentional lack of exposure to the sun. His eyes were glacier blue and unforgettably impressive. His tailor-made suits, worn loosely, were ordered in London, as were his shirts, and, until he was about fifty, he had a penchant for plus fours. His shoes had thick crepe soles which squeaked as he moved fast along the passages and warned us of his approach.'

Generations of old boys and staff who knew Hahn at Gordonstoun have dined off stories of his eccentricities. There was the boy called Max Selka who was at the school in the very early days before Gordonstoun House had been adapted to school use. To get to the study he shared with two other boys, he had to walk through the Headmaster's bathroom. One day Max marched into the bathroom and halted when he saw that the bath was occupied. A deep voice sounded: 'Get out you silly ass. Can't you see the door is locked?' Jim Orr talks of being with Robert ('Bobby') Chew, a later Headmaster, when there was a 'phone call from London. 'There was a pause, "I expect it's Mr Hahn trying to put half a crown into a shilling slot", said Chew.

He was most impractical and would always push a gate or door when it said "Pull". He'd pick up the 'phone and say "Come in". His hand would miss his inside pocket when money and papers were deposited and everything would crash to the ground. When explaining something, he would say, "there are three fundamental points, Point A, Point C and Point Five", and he would still be convincing.'

The endlessly-pouring-coffee incidents crop up several times in old boys' reminiscences. David Conway remembers being invited to breakfast in Hahn's study after having endured a punishment beating: 'There were two other guests – parents of a prospective pupil. The coffee cups were grouped together and Hahn rose, coffee jug in hand, continuing his flow of animated conversation. Without looking down he poured the coffee without pausing to move the stream from cup to cup. The liquid flowed, unchecked and unnoticed by the host over the table cloth. The parents gazed at him like rabbits at a stoat.' And Paul Meyer, who himself hailed from Berlin, relates an incident which shows that Hahn was eccentric, not to mention fearless, even as a boy: 'My father, who went to the same Gymnasium [grammar school] at the same time used to tell us how Hahn had been called to the formidable principal because he had inadvertently – he must have been absent-minded even then – donned another boy's overcoat. We were told that when the principal hinted that the coat he had taken was of better quality than his own, young Hahn offered to box his ears!'

'Hahn's wit or humour are unforgettable and helped, at times, to soften his severity', writes Jocelin Winthrop Young. 'His most frequently used quotation, from *Tom Jones*, was "Human nature is very prevalent", and he used it on many occasions when things had gone wrong and the man responsible was feeling very upset. "At thirteen years old," recounted Hahn, "I read a book about the atrocities of Belgian colonial rule in Africa. I was horrified and soon after was staying with my family at a Hotel in Wiesbaden, where the King of the Belgians was also a guest. One day he was sitting just outside the hotel and all who passed him took off their hats. I resolved to protest and passed close by him *without* removing my hat. Nothing happened. I turned and marched past him again without lifting my hat. And he raised *his* hat to me!" ' Hahn had a developed sense of humour and a charming smile, although he seldom laughed. Prince Philip, another pupil at Gordonstoun in 1934, who had also attended Salem (he was a nephew of Prince Max) speaks warmly of his erstwhile Headmaster whose company he clearly greatly enjoyed: 'Hahn undoubtedly made an immense contribution to education in its broadest sense,

and, inevitably, this makes him sound like some zealous and dedicated reformer with barely a shred of humanity or humour. In fact, of course, his heart was even bigger than his brain and a twinkle was never far from his eye. He had a fund of entertaining and illuminating stories with which he larded his speeches, and an impish sense of humour would transform a rather sombre countenance into a child-like chuckle and delightful expression.'

At Salem, just before the arrival of two loyal and enthusiastic friends of the school who were nevertheless always highly critical during their visits, he instructed all the children to hide their toothbrushes in their lockers, and produced a large toothbrush with a huge handle which was then fixed to a chain secured to a basin. When the arrangement was queried, he blandly replied: 'The toothbrushes used to disappear and are rather expensive to replace, so we found that one toothbrush could do for the lot of them.'

Hahn was famous for his end-to-end meetings on railway journeys. Jocelin Winthrop Young recalls that if Hahn heard that he was travelling to Inverness, 'he would phone me and check which train I was on and suggest, "I will join the Euston Express at Perth and we can solve the problem by the time I leave the train and the car meets me at Aviemore." ' One of his greatest talents was what would now be called networking, especially among rich and influential people who might be able to help him with the many projects and causes he espoused at any one time. It was said that his telephone bill was the second largest in Scotland after that of Willie MacLean, a bookmaker in Glasgow. In Brown's Hotel in London, or at Gordonstoun, he would frequently entertain guests to breakfast, but this would take place in two separate rooms simultaneously and he would divide his time between them, punctiliously excusing his absences during the meals.

It is a testament to the power of Hahn's educational philosophy and his remarkable persuasiveness that he both attracted parents, who had plenty of opportunity to make other choices, to send their children to his schools (in both cases – Salem and Gordonstoun – establishments with no history, no track record) and that staff who were disillusioned by conventional attitudes to education and convinced by his strikingly different ideas came to work with him in a far-flung corner of Britain for next to no financial reward. Olivia Campbell, who – with her husband Keir Campbell – taught at the school for many years, summed up his philosophy, which clearly would have had huge appeal to those who had watched the awful unfolding of history in Europe in the first half of the twentieth century: 'Hahn never thought only of

Detail of the Silent Walk.

Gordonstoun but kept thinking of people and nations and how to build men who would take responsibility for their country and encourage honesty, unselfishness, compassion and determination. He was deeply disturbed that only one member of the House of Commons had stood up for the truth about the Katyn murder [the murder of Polish military officers at a Russian prisoner of war camp carried out by the Soviet secret police in 1940].'

A few of the staff from Salem followed Hahn to Gordonstoun: initially only Frau Richter and Bex Richter, but soon Dr Erich Meissner, who had for a short time acted as Headmaster of Salem until he too had to flee the Nazis (he was helped to escape via Switzerland by Norman Pares, an Englishman teaching at Salem at the time). Bobby Chew had also been with Hahn at Salem as a young man, and after serving as an army officer in the war came to Gordonstoun to work once more with him. Bex Richter was to remain at the school until the mid-1970s except for a period of internment in Canada during the war, when his mother went back to the family home in Berlin. After the war, she returned to Gordonstoun, remaining active in school life until her retirement in the early 1950s.

Henry Brereton, who joined the school in its second year as Director of Studies, recalled that the place was desperate for money, but that there was no capital apart from a few small gifts from friends who were not wealthy. Godfrey Burchardt, who came to the school at the same time, told Jim Graham, that having worked for a term at Gordonstoun, he was paid enough to purchase a rail ticket home for Oxford, but he had to borrow money from his parents to return to Gordonstoun at the end of the holidays. Norman Pares revealed that for the first few years he was paid ten shillings a week, plus keep.

Erich Meissner was a keen painter whose work still hangs in various places around the school. Humphrey Taylor (1948–53) refers to him as 'a fine Housemaster', and Alan Bush (1946–49) enjoyed Meissner's humour. He recalls that many of his pronouncements were prefaced with 'Ah', thus: 'When we were eating oat cakes with syrup on them, he rang the bell for silence, and said to Fryer, our House Helper, "Ah Fryer, I observe that you are a member of The Finger Licking Society, please resign".' And again: 'When Halliday was doing something particularly silly and aggravating, he said, "Ah, I think you must be the village idiot". Halliday answered, "I don't live in a village sir". "That is why you have gone so long undiscovered", said Dr Meissner.' Bush also recalls Meissner's dog – 'a large cheerful poodle called Ponto, after Hilaire Belloc's lion, is my guess.' When Bush revisited the school in the late 1950s, Meissner took him to see the newly

THE SCHOOL MOTTO

Antonin Besse, possibly the most important benefactor of Gordonstoun, suggested the motto that fitted so well with Kurt Hahn's belief in individual challenge and self-evaluation shortly after the school returned to Moray from Wales at the end of the war. He had noticed the words carved into the stone lintel of a doorway leading into what had been the home of an eminent nobleman in Bruges, Belgium, called Lodewijk van Gruuthuse (1422–92). The aptness of the motto reflects Besse's belief that the school's educational aims and achievements were truly significant, a conviction that led him to give the then huge sum of £65,000 to Gordonstoun at a moment when it was in dire financial need, thus allowing the purchase of the estate from the Gordon-Cumming family.

renovated Round Square and while showing him round the library remarked, 'Ah. It is like, Ye Olde Tea Shoppe'. Kurt Hahn clearly valued his old associate from Salem, while finding him at times extremely difficult to deal with, at one point remarking with exasperation: 'I want it written on my tombstone "He worked with Meissner for twenty years".'

Norman Pares joined the school from Salem in September 1935 and became Housemaster of the preparatory school at Duffus. In autumn 1938 he was made Housemaster of the Round Square. In Wales he was in charge of the central house, Plas Dinam, and after the war he was Housemaster of Gordonstoun House for a while before moving to Wester Elchies as a Housemaster in 1954 from where he returned in 1963. He retired in 1966. 'Norman Pares', writes one old boy, 'was my idea of a loyal, honourable erudite man who did not seek the limelight or material gain. He was always immaculately dressed and he knew how to draw people out.' And Ronald Gilchrist concurs, remembering him being 'a wonderful reader of P.G. Wodehouse with his old Harrovian drawl . . . He was an elegant and caring man, always prepared to listen. In his flat, second floor, directly above Kurt Hahn at the west end, he held court for friends, and drinks and music were worked on. From his flat you could feel the warmth of companionship and good fellowship.'

Accounts of Kurt Hahn's withdrawal from his role as Headmaster of Gordonstoun are generally partial and unclear. It is probably the case that three or four factors came together to make inevitable the end of his tenure at the school that he had created. Hahn had always been a man who spent large tranches of time away from the school, finding support for both Gordonstoun and the many other enterprises with which he was involved, and leaving the running of the school in the hands of capable lieutenants such as Bobby Chew and Henry Brereton. He referred to himself unselfconsciously as a 'midwife of ideas', happy to delegate their development to others whom he trusted. No matter how visionary his ideas or inspiring his personality, this must have placed strains on those working around him. When he was well, his energy and the force of his personality quite possibly made potential problems fall away. But it is now known that, apart from the problem that had forced him to protect his head from the sun for so many years, Hahn also suffered bouts of manic depression, and it seems very likely that one of these episodes had struck when, in 1953, at the age of 67, he announced his retirement. The clearest statement about this event and what followed immediately afterwards can be found in a speech by Sir Iain Tennant (Chairman of Governors 1957–71) at a Gordonstoun Association dinner in 1987: 'On the 30th April 1953, Mr Hahn finally decided to retire from being Executive Headmaster, due to ill health, after nine months of indecision. It had been a stormy nine months – very stormy at times. The stability the school maintained over those nine months was largely due to the splendid work of the Colour Bearer body.' And he goes on to describe 'the hazardous way' in which Hahn's successors were chosen: 'The telephone rang continuously. All the Governors rallied round their telephones, but each seemed to want something different. On behalf of the Board, I think I asked Mr Brereton to be Headmaster and Mr Chew to be joint Headmaster one morning – then, in the afternoon, I asked Mr Chew to be Headmaster and Mr Brereton to be Warden – then, even later in the day, I asked Mr Brereton to be Joint Headmaster and Mr Chew to be Joint Headmaster-cum-Controller, which was the way the whole thing ended. Both men showed infinite patience. The result was miraculous and, although you could never find two more different characters, they were both on the same side, and the combination worked almost totally harmoniously for some twelve years.'

Hahn remained involved in school affairs for some years after his retirement, though sadly, but not surprisingly, his relationship with those who were now in day-to-day control of the school and, in particular, in charge of its appeals (and contact on behalf of Gordonstoun with potential patrons) was not always easy. For the impassioned Founder of the school to loosen his grip on his creation must have been deeply painful. Soon, his involvement in the school became more sporadic. As before, he spent considerable amounts of time based in London at Brown's Hotel or travelling, directing his still considerable energy towards founding institutions or enterprises of national and international significance. In 1955 he was approached by Air Marshal Sir Lawrence Darvall, Commandant of the NATO Defence College in Paris with the idea of setting up a pre-college school where students from all over the world would be enrolled for a six-month course to promote international understanding. The first of these – Atlantic College (now United World College of the Atlantic) at St Donat's in Wales – opened in 1962. The Duke of Edinburgh's Award Scheme was initiated in 1956, the Trevelyan Scholarships in 1958, and in 1964 Hahn was awarded the CBE, the same year in which his last major achievement, the Medical Commission on Accident Prevention, came into being. Hahn's sister-in-law, Lola Hahn, lived at Burnside, less than a mile away to the north of Duffus village, and it was here that Hahn stayed whenever he was in Scotland. He had, after all, lived away from Germany for twenty years and he had spent time and lived in Moray for over 40 years. David and Mary Byatt remember Hahn staying in the old Bruce House in the early 1960s during summer vacations, and entertaining old friends to musical *soirées* there. Latterly, he lived in semi-retirement in lodgings at Hermannsberg, the junior school for Salem.

Josh Miner (who joined the staff of Gordonstoun in 1950 and left to set up Outward Bound in the United States) describes meeting Hahn in 1968 on what turned out to be his last trip across the Atlantic: 'Greatly concerned about the worldwide violence generated by youthful rebellion and racial conflict, he visited universities and ghetto areas on the continent. As always, he was seeking ways to harness productively the fighting spirit of the young. Throughout that grueling safari, his old sun-induced affliction was heavy upon him. I drove him to Boston airport in a car I had blacked out with blankets. He wore dark glasses, his broad-brimmed hat and an arrangement of green felt to shield the back of his neck. At the plane's door, his hand came up in the familiar farewell gesture, and, as so often before, I felt a clutch of apprehension. Might this be the last time? It was. That year he was knocked down by a car in Piccadilly Circus and never fully recovered. He died at Hermannsberg aged 88 in December 1974.'

Mark Arnold-Forster, one of the first pupils at the school, summed up Kurt Hahn in terms that still resonate: 'To Hahn, as to few other people, enthusiasm and determination were the same thing. Hahn has always been alarmingly impractical, yet for him, ideas would turn into deeds, plans into practice, castles into schools.'

Kurt Hahn wearing one of the broad-brimmed hats he always donned when out-of-doors.

2

A PLACE TO
CALL HOME

'. . . to the north the challenge of the sea, and to the
south the challenge of high hills' KURT HAHN

A group of boys, possibly Colour Bearers, c. 1961. Once girls had arrived at the school in 1972, boys were allowed to opt for long trousers rather than shorts. One master at school in the 1980s remembers a few pairs of shorts, passed from generation to generation, being proudly worn as retro garments.

THE STORY OF KURT HAHN'S arrival in Britain in 1933 to found a school is best related by one of the two thirteen-year-old boys who came with him from Salem, the school in Germany that he had been forced to quit: Jocelin Winthrop Young, son of Geoffrey Winthrop Young, an ardent supporter of the educational project set up by Hahn and Prince Max von Baden.

Jocelin Winthrop Young, together with Mark Arnold-Forster, arrived at Aviemore station one day towards the end of September 1933, where the two were picked up by Jack Ross of Dulnain Bridge (Hahn's chauffeur) in an Armstrong Siddeley and driven to the Doune, Rothiemurchus, a large house that Kurt Hahn had rented. 'The Doune made a tremendous impression on us with the Spey running north past the house as we looked over the open ground to the south. The Cairngorms looked magnificent with the Lairig Ghru dominating the scene.' Accompanying them was Alastair Hill, the nineteen-year-old nephew of Lady Cumming, who had been at school in Pangbourne and whom Hahn had apparently wanted to

Above: Gordonstoun House before World War II. Note the pitched roof, which was destroyed during a fire while it was occupied by the army during the war.

Opposite: Part of a seventeenth-century chimneypiece incorporated into the Garden Gateway to the west of Gordonstoun House. It was moved from one of the manses near Elgin cathedral which was part of a portfolio of property acquired by the school for staff who could not be accommodated on the estate.

make Guardian of the nascent school, 'but Alastair had no intention of wearing shorts and being bound into a routine with us'. Instead he worked hard with his private tutor, Mr Blyth Martin (who also taught the other two Latin and French). Lady Cumming (widow of Mansfield Cumming, aka 'C', the first head of the British Secret Service), also lived at the Doune, accompanied by her maid Anne, as did Frau Lina Richter, who taught French and Politics, and her son Bex Richter, responsible for biology, field study and maths. Non-resident staff comprised Miss McLean, secretary to Hahn, and Jack Ross; Mr Hunter, rector of Grantown Grammar School, taught Maths, and a Miss McBain, who did nature study. Jocelin Winthrop Young remembers her as 'a cheerful, friendly person who knew the Cairngorms like the back of her hand and was most informative about flora and fauna. She seemed to be a popular character who was greeted by hoots of laughter when we met gillies or others on our walks.' The walks came to an end after only a couple of weeks, however, when Hahn, informed that she was a poacher, moved quickly to avoid any damage to the reputation of his embryonic school.

Winthrop Young relates a vivid memory of the vigour with which Hahn enforced the cold-bath element of the regime followed by the boys. Having cracked a bone slipping on a spiral staircase, he had landed up in Grantown hospital with a foot encased in plaster: 'On the third day, there was a terrific row, for not only had I skipped the very

The Doune, home of the Laird of Rothiemurchus, 2010.

cold and very unpopular bath; but I had failed to register this in my Training Plan! . . . I will never forget having to stand in the tin bath with the plastered foot propped on a chair alongside, while Hahn poured cold water over me from a porcelain jug.'

Later that autumn, Sir Edward Dunbar (who was working in London at the time) received a telegram from his factor and lawyer in Elgin to the effect that a Lady Smith-Cumming, four boys and a tutor wished to lease Duffus House for the winter. According to his son, Sir Archie Dunbar, Sir Edward agreed to this, thinking that a mother, her sons and a tutor were a family party – little did he know that the tutor was Hahn! Duffus House stands in its own grounds, of garden, woodland and parkland, half a mile away from Gordonstoun House, just outside the gates of the estate.

Duffus House, 1938.

THE GORDONSTOUN ESTATE

It is thought that a building of sorts has occupied the site of the present house since at least the thirteenth century. The earliest recorded owner of the estate, then known as the Bog o' Plewlands, was Simon de Hogestoun who died in 1240 (the estate stood in the former parish of Ogstoun from which the family derived its name).

The estate remained in the hands of the Ogstoun family until 1473 when it was sold to the Innes family who were neighbouring landowners. In 1616 it passed to George Gordon, First Marquis of Huntly, who invested time and money in upgrading and shaping the estate and rebuilding the house. The present wings, with their steep French roofs and conical turrets, were of his making (c. 1620–1630) and were probably complemented by a central, tall, fortified and turreted keep.

Huntly's son was troubled by debt and sold the estate to his cousin, Sir Robert Gordon, in 1638. He and his family were responsible for improving and extending the estate, and in 1642 the newly enlarged estate was recognised as a barony and renamed Gordonstoun.

Sir Ludovick Gordon, who inherited the estate from Sir Robert and became the Second Baronet (1625–85), had the boglands drained, created the present lake and laid out the lawns and avenues to north and south in the classical style.

Gordonstoun House apparently remained unaltered until 'Ill' Sir Robert, the Fourth Baronet (1696–1772), redesigned the central section in the Georgian style during the period 1716–30. Externally, the house has remained unchanged since the eighteenth century, although the original sloping roof on the central section was destroyed by fire during the period of army occupation in the war and has never been replaced. The house remained in the hands of the Gordon family, and their descendants the Gordon-Cummings, until it was purchased by the school in 1948.

Far left: The south-east corner of Gordonstoun House.

Left: The North Lawn Gates, originally from Charters House, Hancocks Mount, Sunningdale, Berkshire, and presented to the school in 1962 by G. Scott.

In November 1933 Alastair Hill left, and at Duffus, two more pupils – Bill Richmond and Francis Noel-Baker – joined the school. A Mr Ross arrived to teach English and History, and Dr A.C. MacDonald was appointed school doctor. 'We have moved to Duffus House', wrote Winthrop Young in a letter home. 'This place is not a patch on the Doune, of course, no hills, no river, no moons, no deer, but it is warmer, two miles from the coast and lots of seabirds . . . the house is much too full of portraits. All the walls are covered with Dunbar ancestors. We have only one bathroom for twelve people.' He also notes that there was nowhere to play hockey, because the fine meadow beside the house 'was reserved for cows' (though he records that Hahn and Bex Richter played for Elgin in a match against Inverness).

There were no mountains close to the new school premises, and it was at this point that Hahn's plans for providing adventurous outdoor activity for his young charges began to take in the idea of the sea. Mark Arnold-Forster and Winthrop Young already had some sailing experience, but initially, as there was no-one to supervise the new activity, they were sent to work in Alexander Findlay's boat-building yard in Hopeman, where their first task was helping to build the *Braemou*, a seine-net fishing boat. The boys were driven there and back to Hopeman by Jack Ross in the Armstrong Siddeley. 'On one occasion the car did not appear and all five of us started walking back to Duffus. Just before the Burnside turn, we were overtaken by Mrs Gordon Duff, a great character and good friend of the school, driving her Baby Austin. She stopped and we all piled in. When she dropped us off, she remarked, "Some day it will be a fact worth recording that I drove the whole school in my little car!" '

By April 1934 more boys had arrived and Duffus House was no longer large enough to accommodate them. Another lease was signed (at £100 per annum), this time with the Gordon-Cumming family for Gordonstoun House. Numbers of boys and staff continued to increase, and in the autumn of 1935, when the school roll had swelled to 45, Duffus House was again pressed into service. Sir Archie recalls staying there for the family's summer holidays in 1935: 'I have a vivid recollection of Hahn and Walter Laffan [the school's Bursar] inspecting the drains prior to signing the lease . . . My brother and I then played at being them, lifting the drain covers and sniffing!'

The Gordonstoun estate, which consisted of little more than a strip of land between two lodges, with a large house in the middle, had been neglected since before World War I. The owner had apparently even contemplated taking the roof

THE ROUND SQUARE

The Round Square was built around 1670 by Sir Robert Gordon, the Third Baronet (1649–1704), as an estate 'square' or farm steading. Its circular form is highly unusual: a handful of semi-circular steadings exist in Scotland, notably in Aberdeenshire, but the only other entirely circular example was built some 70 years later in Ireland on the estate of Sir William Burden.

Legend has it that while he was a student in Italy at Padua University, Sir Robert Gordon, in return for great scientific knowledge, sold his soul to the Devil (to be claimed at a later date). He became, among other things, an alchemist, and the mysterious experiments he conducted at Gordonstoun on his return added credence to this tale and earned him the nickname 'The Wizard'. When a year had passed, goes the story, the Devil returned for Sir Robert's soul, but Sir Robert persuaded him to take his shadow instead. Twenty-five years passed, and when the stables on the estate needed replacing Sir Robert designed the estate square (now known as the Round Square) in the belief that he could evade the Devil and thwart his intentions if there were no corners in which he could be trapped. Perhaps the plan would have worked had he stuck to it, but Sir Robert lost faith in it, and once he believed that the Devil was finally on his way to exact payment, he quit the steading and, on the advice of his friend the Parson of Duffus, attempted to find sanctuary at an ancient Christian site, Birnie Kirk. On his way to Birnie, the Devil caught up with him, and was said to have been seen riding away with the body of Sir Robert across his saddle. Of course, it is most likely that the design of the Round Square was influenced by Sir Robert's knowledge of Italian architecture, and the truth is that Sir Robert died in his bed.

off the house (a not uncommon move to avoid paying taxes on vacant property which was expensive to maintain). All the buildings were suffering from neglect and in need of repair.

From September 1934 Gordonstoun House itself was used for dining, for classrooms and for staff accommodation. The Round Square was soon in commission as a boarding house, too, though it had not been renovated at all. The washing facilities were reached by walking round the outside of the building, so one was cold long before submitting to the obligatory cold shower. Joseph Pease (1938–40) slept in 'the Barn Dormitory' on the first floor: 'The Round Square had no passages. To get

from one room to another on the ground floor, you had to go outside and in again to the required room; on the first floor, you just walked through rooms until you got to your destination.' Okill Stuart (1938–39), who slept at Gordonstoun House, remembers stabling his horse at the Round Square. There were also classrooms in the Round Square: a Maths Room and a Geography Room on the north and east sides. It was not until the 1950s that the much-needed restoration of this extraordinary building was undertaken (see page 63).

By 1938, in Gordonstoun House, the English Room was in what is now known as the North Room, while the South Room was used by Hahn as his study, with a long carpet runner leading to his desk at the far end – a daunting walk for any miscreant, well-remembered by several old boys. Food was cooked in the old kitchen at the east end of the ground floor of Gordonstoun House, with the dining room next to it in the centre of the building. The French Room was on the north-west end, and Classics was taught in the gun room. Somewhere there were laboratories for sciences.

During the war, when the main school was evacuated to Wales, Gordonstoun House was requisitioned by the army. Careless use and a chip pan fire meant that once the school reclaimed it, the building needed much work. Just a couple of terms after the return from Wales, Gordonstoun House was sufficiently renovated for the old dining room on the ground floor to be put back into use. It was very draughty, and a thin partition wall was put up (which exists to this day), isolating the main stairs to the west.

When Altyre, Forres, was amalgamated with the main school in 1960, Gordonstoun House was once again needed in its entirety as dining rooms for the whole school (except Duffus House). And so it remained until September 1975, when the new Refectory opened, and space was again available to provide a modest amount of boarding accommodation, at this point for thirteen- and fourteen-year-olds who had moved from the east wing of Hopeman House when the whole building was needed for the ever-increasing numbers of girls. Then in 1983, Gordonstoun House became home to about 40 girls, who stayed there until the new girls' house, Plewlands, was ready to move into in 1987. It subsequently became a third-form girls' house. From 1997 to 2001 the House was not used for boarding purposes, but it is now home to 22 sixth-form boys.

From the time when Kurt Hahn first moved into Gordonstoun House in 1934 until 1966 when the Headmaster's House was built, the Headmaster's accommodation was always in this building, and the

IN THE EARLY years of the school, a steady trickle of German boys arrived at Gordonstoun, and Vernon Stone, then under his German name, Werner Schilling, arrived in 1936. The oldest surviving old boy, he writes:

'I was by then seventeen years old and had actually finished my schooling in Germany, and, of course, we were against the Nazis. My mother tried desperately to get me out of Germany, and Gordonstoun came to the rescue. One of the governors put up a scholarship for me, and Mr Hahn accepted me as an ordinary pupil.

'On the academic side Gordonstoun enabled me to prepare for the Edinburgh University bursaries competition. In other respects I learned a terrific lot. The daily discipline of cold shower, morning run and the Training Plan, which was confidential between you and the headmaster so that there was no point in cheating, were all of great benefit to me.'

Founder's Room remains the Headmaster's study to this day. When John Kempe vacated the rooms in the west end of Gordonstoun House, they became staff accommodation and offices. As well as giving the school flexibility in providing a small number of boarding places in addition to those in the main boarding houses, Gordonstoun House contains the main administrative offices and the Sixth-Form Centre.

DUFFUS HOUSE

A school prospectus dating from around 1938 records that from 1935 to 1937 Duffus housed the preparatory school. Norman Pares, newly arrived from Salem, became Housemaster at Duffus in September 1935, although Brereton and his wife and family also lived there after they arrived at the school that autumn. (Henry Brereton was destined to become Meissner's successor as Director of Studies in January 1936.) Initially, only three of the boys were juniors, but by December 1936 there were 27 pupils, including a few girls (usually with brothers in the school) in Duffus House, many of them of preparatory-school age. Colin Crole, who arrived at Duffus in 1936, reports that while the senior boys went to Gordonstoun House for classes, the younger ones stayed at Duffus: 'My clear memories of that year were 1. John Paton sliding down the banister and falling on the stone floor at the bottom. 2. The lovely Easter Day (it was early that year, clear and blue) spent searching for Easter eggs. 3. I was knocked down by the Hut by Hamlet the Bloodhound and could not get up. I still think of the horrid smell of the hound. Hamlet was alleged to have eaten Miss McKim's hat.'

Pares remained at Duffus until the arrival of Pat and Dolly Delap who took charge just before the junior school moved out to Wester Elchies, near Aberlour in September 1937 (see page 91). After the departure of the juniors, Duffus House became the third boarding house for the main school, accommodating 30 boys (who went to Gordonstoun for lessons and other activities) with Bobby Chew as Housemaster. The prospectus also mentions 'a Kindergarten Department . . . for day children between the ages of four and ten.' Norman Pares now became Housemaster of the Round Square, while Commander John Lewty was Housemaster of Gordonstoun House.

Michael Stary sums up his memories of being at Duffus in the late 1940s: 'Mr and Mrs Chew. Fell in love with Eva Chew. Village postman slowly cycling . . . Small boy late for class: "Have you got the time?" Postman extracts pocket watch, looks at it, puts it back and replies "Aye".' Peter Oakley reminisces about a series of tender encounters – and their consequences – in the summer of 1949: 'A friend and I met two young girls wandering around St Peter's Kirk in Duffus. We rapidly made ourselves known and spent a happy hour kissing behind tombstones. The next weekend as agreed they returned with two more friends, as did we. Three weeks later, there were some 30 of us all having a fine yet innocent time when Mr Chew's head appeared for a moment looking over the wall at us and then quickly vanished. At supper that night after the sweet course, he stood up, and with his customary "just one point" said, "Will all those I saw in the churchyard this afternoon come to my study after supper". Some of us did and I was amongst them when he told us that we could have a girl friend but that in future we should bring her to this house for tea. Nobody ever did or dared.'

Anthony Craig recalls that in the mid-1950s one of the Duffus House boys, John Steiner (who went on to become an actor), produced *The Lady's Not For Burning* in Duffus village hall. 'He later did a production of *Pygmalion* in our house, stressing that this was the real thing, not to be confused with *My Fair Lady* which was a West End hit at the time. My memory is that these efforts were put on entirely by Steiner and other boys – I don't remember any staff involvement.' Jasper Brinton, also at Duffus House in the '50s, remembers building and equipping a darkroom in the attic, hanging drapes from the rafters to block out the light. 'The school had no facilities for those of us interested in photography then, and at first arrangements were made with the RAF base nearby to take out their aerial cameras – these had lenses three or four inches in diameter and were barely portable. We washed the film in buckets – even once we eventually had a darkroom!'

Top and above: Duffus House, c. 1955, and a study, c. 1959.

Below: Students relaxing in Duffus mixed common room, 2011.

Opposite: Duffus House photographed in 2009.

If you spent time in Duffus House in 1974, you had the privilege of wearing a unique tie – depicting both the Duffus bull and the Windmill Lodge windmill, marking the moment when all the boys at Windmill Lodge, together with their Housemaster, James Thomas, and tutors, chivalrously evacuated the House for it to become the second girls' boarding house. At that time Duffus had its own catering facilities overseen by the legendary Maver Sutherland, Gordonstoun's Head Housekeeper for nearly 30 years. This changed when, in 1975, the Refectory opened, and the whole school could be fed in one place. Much-needed space was released in Duffus.

The house has, since the beginning, prided itself on challenging expeditions, and no hill has been too tall (Ben Nevis, Ben Macdui), too far north (Ben Klibreck, Ben Hope) or too far west (Beinn Eighe, Beinn Alligin) to be tackled. The Duffus men have always been up for the challenge and able to appreciate the beauty and savour the majesty of their surroundings.

From the mid-1990s onwards the Duffus Housemaster was also the master in charge of rugby – first Steve Brown for twelve years followed by Andrew Lyall, himself a former Duffus boy. In spite of the best efforts of the school to avoid a particular house becoming the 'drama' house or the 'cricket' house, it was almost inevitable that rugby would become a major feature of the house. Of course, Duffus is not all about rugby, and its alumni have gone on to many universities, including Oxbridge and MIT, and demonstrated the variety of interest and flair so characteristic of the school as a whole to become actors, artists and musicians as well as hedge-fund managers, engineers, entrepreneurs and vets.

The current Housemaster, Andrew Lyall, remarks on how little Duffus has changed since he was a schoolboy there 25 years ago, 'although there is now carpet on the stairs and the outside of the house is no longer white. There is no morning run or House Penalty Drill! There are curtained cubicles in the shower room but the two baths still look very familiar. The cold shower has gone – not even an option now – unless the boiler isn't functioning as it should. Duffus is still the only house to have a third-form dorm – but only nine boys sleep there now by contrast with the large numbers who were accommodated in the '80s and before . . . I still, at times, find it surreal that I have crossed the fence, especially when the house has been put to bed and I find myself wandering around in the pitch dark still remembering which doors squeak and where not to tread! "Poacher turned gamekeeper" was how our landlord, Sir Archie Dunbar, greeted me on my return!'

There has always been a good relationship with Duffus estate and the Lairds – first Sir Edward and now his son, Sir Archie Dunbar. In spite of various practical jokes over the years – from brewing beer to doctoring the milk order (leading to the delivery of twenty pints not two!) – Duffus and Sir Archie and Lady Dunbar live cordially side by side and it is difficult to imagine Gordonstoun without Duffus.

Those who have spent time at Duffus tend to feel that it has a special atmosphere – much to do with its location outside the gates and the fact that it is a beautiful country house with spacious grounds. During a visit to Duffus in the 1970s, HRH The Duke of Edinburgh talked wistfully of time spent cleaning the cobbles by the stables with a toothbrush during the early horse-riding days!

GUSTAV MOHN (Duffus, 1948–49) visited the school in August 2009 when he and his wife brought their thirteen-year-old grandson to the Summer School. He was impressed by the improvements in both buildings and facilities at the school. Wishing to revisit his old haunts, he asked to see Duffus: 'Surprise, surprise! Very little had changed – the bath room, the dining room and even my old dormitory were as I left them in 1949. My wife Greta couldn't believe such simple austerity could still exist. But we met a few of the boys and lodgers there, and they all, unanimously, declared themselves very happy with Duffus. They were proud of the house and wished no change.' He then visited the old stables nearby – 'I could almost see Dr Saloschin, his wife Traudl, and even their famous poodle Putzi, standing in the stable door. Thanks! A wonderful experience! Please leave Duffus as it is!'

RIDING AT GORDONSTOUN

The school was barely a year old when riding started up as an activity. From the start, it was treated seriously, as more than a hobby, and by the late 1940s the standard was equivalent to that achieved in the foremost schools of equitation in the country. At first, riding was controlled by Captain Behrens; the first instructor was Mrs Douna Rogers, wife of the Chaplain Henry Rogers, assisted by Captain Gordon Duff. The activity was voluntary, and boys were charged between £1 1s and £4 4s per term according to ability to pay. By January 1936 there were 25 riders and eight horses, some of which were owned by boys at the school. A hunt was staged using bloodhounds belonging to a Mrs Sadlier.

Kurt Hahn, having by now decided that riding was character-building, made it compulsory in the summer term of 1936. Horsemanship, he argued, contributed to co-ordination of mind and muscle, requiring observation, vigilant concentration and rapid decision-making. Classes of fifteen to twenty boys were divided among riding, stable management, lectures and attention to saddlery. His decision resulted in some aversion to the activity, but the core addicts remained and an open gymkhana was held.

The lack of a proper riding school, however, meant that Hahn's dream of allowing his young charges to learn the skills of professional horsemanship could not really be sustained, and by the autumn term of 1936 senior riding had been suspended (although juniors still rode). At this point there were four horses, plus three ponies owned by boys. Lord Davies gave the school two unbroken Welsh ponies which became known as Lord and Lady and were later passed on to Wester Elchies.

Trees were felled in the area now known as the Parade Ground in order to form a riding school, but the work of clearing the branches and extracting the stumps was left to boys. By March 1937 a total of 367 boy-hours had been expended on the job in one-and-a-half-hour

Riding camp at Culbin Sands, 1938.

stints on four afternoons a week. A crab winch and wire ropes were lent by Mr Findlay of Hopeman, and Mr Milne, the Duffus blacksmith, forged a special hook for grabbing stumps. They were dragged out by the school's 36 cwt Bedford lorry and then moved away using sleds made from double stable doors from the Round Square.

The name 'Saloschin', forever bound up with riding at Gordonstoun, does not appear until June 1937, when Traudl Saloschin was invited by Hahn to visit the school; she joined the staff in October 1937. Traudl was a highly qualified rider, the only woman to hold the Golden Whip of Berlin's official Government School of Equitation, an honour won in competition with military personnel. An Aryan, she could have remained one of Hitler's golden girls, but her husband, Dr Victor Saloschin, though a talented cavalry officer, was a Jew and had lost all his status and wealth to Nazi Germany. He too needed employment. Hahn,

with the requisite permission from the Home Office, appointed him from 1 January 1938, asking him to come to Britain a month early so that he could acquaint himself with British riding at the two foremost schools of equitation, Weedon and Kingston. The Saloschins were paid, at first, by the education of their two sons at Gordonstoun.

Riding in Victor and Traudl's hands became steadily more sophisticated. In the twelve months to December 1938 a total of 1,500 lessons were given, and a groom, Jack Macdonald, was appointed. The riding school was completed and the cobbled floors of Duffus stables were removed and replaced with cement for easier cleaning. Saddlery was brought over from Germany and the first riding expedition – to Culbin Sands – took place in June 1938. Later in the term there was a cross-country competition round the school grounds with eighteen jumps.

When World War II broke out, 'Enemy Aliens' were interned and the Saloschins were no exception. By August Traudl had been released and was working for the Land Army; Victor was kept captive for several more months. Meanwhile, Gordonstoun and the two best horses moved down to Wales and riding was somehow kept going. Traudl was given back her job as riding instructor, but, on his release, Gordonstoun could not afford to employ Victor. A year later he was back in

Moray teaching riding at Wester Elchies, and soon riding became a major activity there. By 1944 there were twelve horses plus an unbroken yearling and two foals. The children did all the stable work and took care of the ponies under the supervision of their eminent instructor. Each year there was a riding competition with a cup awarded to the best rider.

By the summer of 1945, the Saloschins were instructing together again at Gordonstoun. Sixteen boys opted to ride and set about whitewashing the stables at Duffus and painting the doors. The pre-war riding school had been used as a rifle range by the army and its surface was ruined, so they set about repairing that too. Riding took place every afternoon, and by the beginning of 1946 the number of riders had doubled. An extra duty for the riders was exercising the bloodhounds, which were kept in the Duffus House kennels. David Byatt remembers Traudl Saloschin driving a trap with himself and three other boys to Gordonstoun House to take greetings to Kurt Hahn on his 60th birthday, 5 June 1946. That summer a gymkhana was held in the school, which started with a procession of all the horses from Duffus stables to Gordonstoun, including a foal, two yearlings, a trap driven by David Byatt and a decorated float driven by Donald Munro, an ex-army heavy-weight boxing champion who was

The stables at Duffus, c. 1949.

good with recalcitrant horses and (from November 1946) was employed as stableman. There followed four years of ever-increasing professionalism in riding.

As in Wales and at Wester Elchies, boys took care of the horses and would get up very early to muck out the stables and to catch the horses and lead them in from the fields for grooming. One of them, Tim Forsyth, recalled, 'Getting out of a lovely warm bed at 6.15 am and walking into the stables to a temperature that felt well below zero tended to wake one up a little too suddenly.' One boy found asleep in a class blamed it on 'too many stables'. Boys were also very much involved in constructing

the permanent jumping lane where horses were trained and with making jumps for events.

Each summer half term there was a three-day riding expedition; destinations included Calcots Farm east of Elgin, a farm near Pluscarden and Darnaway estate. The horses would be ridden over to the camp site and other riders would join them on bicycles. Traudl Saloschin cooked for them. Summer terms always ended with the Gordonstoun Riding Competition, an event which soon took on a more formal structure and ended up with three parts: dressage, cross-country and jumping. The modern three-day event is said to have been modelled on it. The cross-country course in 1949 was six miles long, and the show jumping arena that year had twelve jumps, all built by boys. Outsiders would take part in the competition and horses were also entered for the Elgin Show and the Highland Show at Inverness. An outstanding display of horsemanship was put on in 1949 at a fête organised to raise money for community projects: a village hall for Duffus and the King George Playing Field. The fête was opened by HRH Prince Philip, who had just announced his engagement to Princess Elizabeth.

By the summer of 1950, it was clear that riding was too expensive an activity for the school to support, and it was suspended in the spring of 1951. A brief period of outstanding horsemanship at the school was over.

Charity fête organised in 1949 at Gordonstoun in which eight riders performed a quadrille to music. Resplendent in eighteenth-century dress, they were led to the arena on the North Lawn by a trumpeter and four pages on ponies from Aberlour House. Four of the eight riders were ladies riding side-saddle; the four men were all Gordonstoun boys – Prince Max von Baden (grandson of the co-founder of Salem School), Tim Forsyth, David Byatt and Toby Coghill.

CUMMING HOUSE

In 1938 the first new school building was constructed at Gordonstoun. The architect was George Kennedy, a friend of Hahn from his Oxford days, and the house was named after the late May Cumming who had been such a help to Hahn when the school started. Remarkably for a timber building in Britain, Cumming House is still in use and in good condition over 80 years later.

The building was to have been the estate square for the use and accommodation of maintenance staff, its arched entrance designed to be tall enough to allow large vehicles to enter. But Kurt Hahn saw the opportunity to provide a flat there for the Second Master, Henry Brereton (who was then in Duffus House), so that he could be closer to the centre of things – hence the rather well-appointed flat occupied by the current Housemaster. More accommodation was needed for boys at the school, and so it was suggested that the first floor be developed as dormitories. As the school at that time had no hall where plays could be performed or examinations sat, the space above the arch was given over to this purpose, and rooms on the ground floor would provide accommodation for domestic staff (or maids as they were then called). This was all too much for the architect, George Kennedy, who was also a member of staff, and he is reputed to have sent a letter to Hahn spluttering with rage, claiming that what Hahn wanted was a glorified Noah's Ark!

Once he had calmed down, George Kennedy adjusted the plans as requested, with the idea that the square would be completed when more money became available. Brereton is said to have greatly enjoyed the sunny, south-facing aspect of his new flat, so much so that the projected

completion never happened (though there were probably also financial considerations). Ronald Gilchrist remembers the building as being 'stark, unfinished and gaunt' in the 1940s. But he also remembers (presumably in contrast to other buildings on the estate) that the timber building was warm. The families of Brereton and Keir Campbell both lived there, their presence having, according to Gilchrist, 'an ameliorating influence on the house'. He also notes that one Sunday a month a barber from Hopeman was in attendance to cut hair in the large assembly hall, an event which was often preceded by various of the house's inhabitants finding important activities to pursue elsewhere on the estate.

In 1966 one of the wings was provided with additional bedsits and a common room thanks to a donation from Billy Butlin, whose son was in Cumming House. A new shower block was also added at this time. The wing has been known ever since as 'Butlins', leading some to make arch remarks about the holiday mood that can prevail here and the lightness of its inhabitants' attitude to study.

Given that it is built entirely of timber, Cumming House has lasted surprisingly well. Much of its success is said to be due to the design of its walls which slope outwards at the top in the manner of a Swedish barn, and its covering of cedar shingles. Instead of soaking into the walls, rainwater drops from the bottom edge of each shingle and falls clear to the ground, thus preventing rot. The building is set a few feet above ground level on a brick and cement plinth, which was initially intended to keep out rats, but also helps prevent rising damp. In the 1990s there was a serious problem with bees, and a nest was discovered that covered most of the end wall of the Butlins wing. Its full extent was realised only when the last of the shingles was

CRYSTAL SETS

'YOU COULD BUY one, or you could make one with the cardboard core of a toilet roll, some fine insulated copper wire, a variable condenser, a crystal and a cat's whisker and a pair of headphones', recalls Joseph Pease. 'The secret of listening in after lights out, without getting caught, was to take one earpiece off the headphones and slide it in between the pillow and the pillowcase; you would then pretend to be asleep if the House Helper came round to check. I was in the shower room one morning, and was whistling a catchy signature tune from a late-night radio programme: "Where did you hear that tune Pease?" asked the House Helper, "Oh it was just a tune that came into my head". I was more careful in future!'

Opposite: Cumming House on its completion in 1938, before the exterior had been stained and weatherproofed.

Above: The interior of Cumming House, just above the archway, where examinations were held and plays performed in the early days.

Below: The same room as in the photograph above, still used as a hall, but now equipped with an open seating area, 2011. Below right: Cumming House, 2010.

removed. Sadly, the honeycombs had been tainted by the fumigation process.

Richard Rowe, who arrived at Gordonstoun in 1988 from a comprehensive background, describes the 'shock to the system' of arriving at a school set in such extensive grounds to board, but he was pleasantly surprised by the experience of living in Cumming House: 'As a teacher's son, and therefore living nearby, it was suggested that I board for at least the first term. It was something I loved to bits, somewhat to my surprise; the camaraderie of the dormitory is a surprisingly familial affair. The dorm was big and bright, and my schoolhouse was a wooden galleon of a building that creaked in storms, but was always warm and welcoming.'

The first Housemaster of Cumming House was Freddie Spencer Chapman, who had made quite a name for himself as a mountaineer at home and abroad in Greenland and the Himalayas and had a distinguished career operating behind Japanese lines in Singapore and Malaysia during World War II. School life didn't fit easily with Chapman's adventurous outlook, and he left teaching soon after the end of the war. When the school returned from Wales in 1945, Keir Campbell became Housemaster, supported by his wife Olivia. (He is also said to have been briefly in charge there in 1939 after Spencer Chapman was called up and before the move to Wales.) Campbell had been at Gordonstoun since its inception, having had a magnificent career in the army during World War I. He is reputed to have been an utterly dedicated schoolmaster and a man of stature, respected by all. He retired in 1950 and was succeeded by Godfrey Burchardt, who soon married Miss Macrae, also on the school staff. In 1952 Mr and Mrs Burchardt and the boys from Cumming moved to Duffus House, and the former inhabitants of the Round Square, together with Housemaster Roy McComish (Art master at the school since 1949), moved into Cumming during the renovation of the Round Square. In 1959, when McComish left, Jack LeQuesne took over and presided over the house until his retirement in 1972. He was succeeded by Peter Larkman who was Housemaster until 1983. Then came Richard Hadfield, who was succeeded by Tony Gabb. During Gabb's tenure, the dormitories were converted into bedsits – fitted with high beds to accommodate study areas beneath them due to the very limited space available. Ian Lavender took the reins in 1998, and Andy Collins is the current Housemaster.

THE SCHOOL IN WALES

When war with Germany was declared in 1939, the school leased the large Victorian mansion, Glen of Rothes, from Admiral Dunbar-Nasmith and an 'elderly kindergarten' was sent there under the Revd W.P. Young MC, assisted by a few older boys who were involved in unloading trucks and vans of school equipment. For a few months during the phoney war, Gordonstoun remained a secure home, although boys and staff alike went to work digging air raid shelters. But in

1940 the invasion of Norway and the apparently imminent fall of France spread fear of invasion throughout Britain. Not only was Gordonstoun placed between two air stations and therefore at great risk should they be bombed, but the sandy beaches of the Moray Firth provided ideal landing grounds for an invading army, and the decision was taken to move the school south to Wales where Lord Davies, a parent of two boys in the school, had offered the use of two of his houses, Plas Dinam in Llandinam and Berthddu, both near Newtown, in what was then Montgomeryshire.

There was another stimulus to move the school away from Moray for the duration of the war. In the feverish, suspicious atmosphere of 1940, its proximity to both Lossiemouth and Kinloss airfields, its clear German connections and the fact that Hahn's 150 pupils were openly trained in navigation, climbing, sailing and exploring all contributed to a wave of virulent spy mania and anti-German sentiment aimed at Gordonstoun and its inhabitants. 'At the beginning of June 1940,' recalls Jimmy Fraser, 'there was a succession of perfect, cloudless sunny days. Buses arrived one morning and a huge swathe [of boys and staff] were swept off to internment.' Eleven pupils and five members of staff were interned, initially at Duff House, Banff. Among the internees was Bex Richter, who was sent to Canada, but returned once the school was in Wales, as did Dr Meissner and Dr Zimmermann. The Saloschins were sent to the Isle of Man. It emerged many years later that the

One of two or three rehearsals by juniors for the bicycle ride which was to be the first stage of their evacuation to Wales.

Left: Letter from Kurt Hahn to the parents of all boys at Gordonstoun in June 1940 announcing the school's evacuation to Wales.

Below: Wester Elchies, where the junior school remained during the war while the rest of the school was evacuated to Wales.

GORDONSTOUN SCHOOL,
ELGIN,
MORAYSHIRE.

STATION-
ELGIN.

TELEPHONE-
HOPEMAN 271 & 272.

June 14th. 1940.

Dear Parent,

By next Thursday, the whole school, ex-cluding Elchies, will be re-assembled at Plas Dinam, Llandinam, Montgomeryshire, Tel: Caersws 217. The two mid-term expeditions now at Laggan and Loch Rannoch, 32 and 12 boys, leave for Wales to-day; 32 boys are already there. The School Certificate and scholarship class will not leave Gordonstoun until Wednesday after-noon so as to avoid any break in their studies.

Laggan House will not now be kept open. The parents of only one Gordonstoun boy availed themselves of our offer to keep boys resident in the north of Scot-land at Laggan. They had good reasons. His father is, as yet, stationed near here, and wants to see him when he is on leave. This boy is now in Elchies.

I shall be in Elchies several times during the term. At this juncture I feel sure that we should not dislocate the preparatory school.

The enclosed address was given at a meeting of Gordonstoun parents in London on Tuesday, May 28th, before Lord Davies made his generous offer, and we accepted it. For obvious reasons it should be treated as a very confidential document, and should, on no account, be sent abroad. I should be grateful if it does not leave your study, or even better, if it were destroyed. This address will be embodied in a White Paper containing the sequence of events that led to our deci-sion, but I thought it right to send you this statement in advance as only about twenty parents were able to be present at the meeting in London on the 28th. May.

Plas Dinam, the main school building in Wales.

The view from the Headmaster's window at Plas Dinam – boys helping on a neighbouring farm.

then Scottish Secretary, Ernest Brown, and the Lord Advocate, Thomas Cooper, believed fervently that Hahn should be arrested, much to the exasperation of MI5 and the Home Office, for Hahn had substantial supporters in government circles.

Gordonstoun's first motto was 'Live always as if you were about to make a journey' – good advice for those about to make a great trek. Gordonstoun as a home was thoroughly disrupted by the lengthy move to Wales which took place in several stages. Kurt Hahn was concerned to get the junior boys away first, and early in June 1940 they were sent south on bicycles to two Scottish houses – Carron House on the river Spey not far from Aberlour and Innerhadden at Kinloch Rannoch. Some senior boys remained behind to offer their services to the Home Guard, but were refused because of the school's German connections. A few went straight down to Wales with W.P. Young as 'pioneers' where they helped to unload school equipment from various trucks and vans.

ON ONE OCCASION, Kurt Hahn and Henry Brereton took a taxi to meet Lord Davies's train south. 'Negotiations began, without preliminaries, in Lord Davies's sleeping compartment at Aviemore station and ended at Newtonmore fifteen miles down the line', relates Brereton. 'My contribution was to leap from the train at Kincraig and again at Kingussie to persuade an exasperated taxi driver, exhausting his rationed petrol, to go one station further where we would join him.'

One party of boys, in the care of Keir Campbell, Housemaster of Cumming House, took almost three weeks to reach Pitlochry, where they began their journey by rail to Wales. The first night was spent at Wester Elchies; the next day the party of fifteen juniors set off south for a 30-mile ride to Newtonmore, where they stayed in a hotel for the night. From here they took a train to Dalwhinnie, avoiding a long uphill cycle ride, and then rode downhill all the way to the turn-off for Kinloch Rannoch. Innerhadden, which had been lent to the school by the Revd Lancelot Fleming, one of Hahn's many Oxford friends, was really too small to house fifteen boys plus the Campbell family, and after a week some of the boys moved to the nearby Bunrannoch Hotel. The boys filled their time by working on farms (Jeremy Chance remembers helping with harvesting) and doing housework at Innerhadden. Two weeks later they cycled 22 miles to Pitlochry, where they boarded the night train south, together with some senior boys from Gordonstoun. Chance recounts that they arrived in Aberdovey 'where we lived in seafront B&Bs until there was room for us (in garden "dormitories" in prefabricated chalets) at the main school at Plas Dinam.'

Plas Dinam, the main school building (now under the charge of Norman Pares), was a rambling, half-timbered Victorian mansion, a challenging place in which to run a school (Olivia Campbell remembered teaching History in a passage there), while Berthddu, the second of Lord Davies's generous loans, was a compact, sandstone dower house three miles away, probably not unsuited to being a boarding house. When the boys first arrived, some of them were accommodated in large marquees erected on the lawn at Plas Dinam as temporary housing, but on their first night a violent rainstorm caused the tents to leak, and bedraggled boys crept into the house to sleep on the floors for the rest of the night. Somehow the tents were made waterproof and were used for a while longer. The boys washed in the nearby river and, to begin with, spent their days fishing and helping with the harvest.

In Wales the school largely escaped the mistrust and suspicion that it had experienced in Moray and was welcomed by the local community, integrating with it rather better than had so far been the case at Gordonstoun. A number of senior boys joined the Home Guard; boys attended services in the local church and at Christmas performed their traditional nativity play there. Michael Stary remembers Ma Davies's shop at the bottom of the drive for Plas Dinam: 'I'd love to bake you boys more, but I canna get the fats'. He also remembers the ex-Navy stoker who was Lord Davies's boilerman: 'If you must smoke in my ___ boiler room, at least put your fag end in the ___ boiler!'

'Also evacuated to Aberdovey in 1940', recalls Jeremy Chance, 'was a girls' school from Switzerland – Chatelarde – which occupied a nearby property, now a hotel. One of the boys had a sister or family friend there, and set up assignations on the sand dunes or golf course when we could all escape from school. In those days, being naïve, shy and inexperienced, we dared not come closer than for a chat and giggles! On one occasion after "lights-out" some of us escaped to approach their school after dark. We flashed torches at their dormitory windows. What a treat when some of the girls appeared in their night dresses, waving!'

Some boys started their school career with Gordonstoun in Wales, among them Ian Farmer, who arrived for his first term at the tiny station of Llandinam after a long and tiring journey from London: 'We had to stand in the corridors most of the time as the trains were packed, mostly with soldiers. Two other eleven-year-olds arrived with me at the station where we and our luggage and bicycles were loaded onto the back of an open builder's lorry – I was thrilled at the start of this great adventure, never having been on the back of a lorry before. We were then taken to Berthddu, an elegant, large grey stone house five miles away situated between two farms with a field in the middle that we used for games and athletics . . . When we arrived, we were greeted with great hospitality by our house parents, Captain and Mrs Campbell . . . and shown a very

Berthddu, one of the two houses occupied by the school when it first arrived in Wales, before numbers rose and others were loaned by Lord Davies.

homely dormitory including the fire escape, which was a rope hanging from a window!

'There was a large stable block about 30 yards down the drive, the ground floor of which was used for most of our lessons whilst the first floor was used for a master's bedroom and another dormitory when the main house was full. Although we were the first influx of boys, over the first few weeks more arrived in dribs and drabs so that by the end of the year the place was full – about 20 boys in all. I think there were about 90 in the whole school when I first arrived. Every Sunday we cycled to the main school for church services.'

As always at Gordonstoun, there were duties to carry out: 'I can remember being in charge of the boiler to make sure there was enough hot water for the afternoon showers. This meant finding and chopping sticks and wood and to avoid using the coal which was in short supply. There was also housework to do, taking turns to wait on tables at meal times for a week, digging in the vegetable garden under the ferocious eye of the gardener, picking potatoes to help the

THE EFFECTS OF RATIONING were felt by the boys as by everyone else. Michael Brownson remembers the shortage of jam for bread at tea time 'which encouraged some to see if tooth paste would do as an alternative'. He continues, 'Our food generally was very good and in one instance we were particularly fortunate; due to Hahn's close friendship with Lawrence Holt, head of a large merchant shipping company and father of a pupil at the school, an arrangement was agreed where Chinese cooks from his merchant ships who had been rescued after being torpedoed and required some shore leave to recuperate before returning to sea came to cook for us for a few months. This meant we had excellent food and often superb Chinese dishes which most of us had never tasted before.'

local farmers, training with our fire-fighting equipment (a very efficient small scammel pump which could be carried to the nearest stream by two boys), log-cutting and a great variety of activities to keep the place running smoothly. We were a very happy family unit separated from the main school but following the main school rules and curriculum.'

Among the tasks given to the boys was the operation of the main telephone switchboard at the school. Shortly after his fifteenth birthday, Michael Brownson was on duty alone when a call came through for Dr Hahn. 'As instructed, I asked the name of the caller before putting the call through. It was a man, saying that he was calling on behalf of my mother on a very urgent matter. I put the call through, but then stayed on the line. I heard him saying that my father had just died. This came as a total shock and I was uncertain about what to do or whether to admit that I had overheard a private conversation. So after completing my hours at the switchboard that evening, I cycled back to Broneirion and went to bed. Next day, after breakfast, Dr Meissner asked

me into his study and gave me the news. I did not feel that I could tell him that I already knew. It was not a good day, but he said that I need not go into lessons and suggested I help the man in the boiler room, which I did.'

Another new arrival in Wales was Maurice Seddon, whose German mother, a concert pianist, was a close friend of Kurt Hahn. Seddon founded the Wireless Club at the school and joined the Engineering Guild and the Motor Guild there. He recalls that Dr Richter, after his return from Canada on a snowy night in 1941, was arrested for allegedly signalling to the Luftwaffe using a torch (he was actually looking for moths). It seems however, that Kurt Hahn, who was said to have helped British intelligence to monitor German radio traffic during the war, was able swiftly to arrange for his release.

Dr Zimmerman, newly arrived from internment in Canada, developed an imaginative scheme for promoting fitness and resourcefulness, and Olivia Campbell remembered Hahn, 'undaunted by the awful muddle and mess of the move of that summer term', organising a display to be held in August at which twenty army recruits, boys from London clubs and some Gordonstoun seniors were put through Zimmerman's courses.

It was not long before Kurt Hahn embarked on a variety of characteristically unusual projects. Four of the best horses and nine bloodhounds were sent down from Gordonstoun by train and installed in stables and foxhound kennels at Plas Dinam. Soon after, six more horses followed.

Plas Dinam, 1942. Above left: the first stages of construction of the timber building, The Hut, designed by George Kennedy and built by the boys to provide extra accommodation. Above: Prize-giving at the end of a summer term at Plas Dinam, with Revd W.P. Young presenting the awards.

Exercising one of the bloodhounds near Tyn-y-Maen, Llandinam.

Entry from 'The Bloodhound Diaries', 1940, which was kept by the boys 1936–56.

The cutters: the *May Cumming* and the *Mansfield Cumming* in Hopeman harbour.

'We always had a considerable amount of physical activity,' recalls Michael Brownson, 'cross-country runs following the school bloodhounds, athletics under the instruction of Dr Zimmermann and games of all sorts . . . One training run I did with another boy was the half marathon distance of 13.5 miles around Lake Vyrnwy (when staying at the hotel there over the Christmas holiday). We were surprised and pleased to hear that our time had beaten that of an army commando group – though they probably had heavy packs to carry.'

In due course the two sailing cutters, the *May Cumming* and the *Mansfield Cumming*, arrived at Caersws station. The *Mansfield*, its gear damaged by fire, was out of action for some months, but the *May* was taken up on a timber drag to a small lake in the hills and provided opportunities for a limited amount of sailing.

By the autumn term of 1940 the junior boys were on the move again. Keir Campbell was put in charge of 30, now housed some distance away at Aberdovey in an old café and a boarding house (one small bathroom and 'no noticeable hot water'). Michael Brownson arrived at Aberdovey in January 1941: 'I remember it as a very cold winter. Lasting memories are of the morning run, stripped to the waist, in all weathers, when it was still dark, followed by a cold shower where one had to kneel in the bath and pour a bucket of cold water over oneself. Of course, the

weather improved and life became really good at Aberdovey with sailing, seamanship, and expeditions to the surroundings hills.' The lake to which the *May* had been dragged had proved too small for meaningful seamanship, and she was soon brought down to Aberdovey, followed in February 1941 by the *Mansfield*. Now, at weekends, senior boys travelled to Aberdovey for seamanship training.

Soon after this, Hahn was approached by Lawrence Holt, head of the Blue Funnel Line. Holt was becoming increasingly concerned at the large numbers of seamen on torpedoed vessels who survived the attacks only to lose their lives because of a lack of survival training. Unlike the older, more experienced sailors, who had trained on sailing vessels, these younger men lacked the experience to survive severe weather conditions on board ship. Hahn proposed that they start a new kind of school, one with a course of dinghy sailing, orienteering by map and compass, rescue training and an expedition at sea. Holt provided the finance and staff, and the Aberdovey Sea School started in October 1941, becoming the first Outward Bound Sea School early in 1942.

Erich Meissner was Housemaster at Berthddu until Keir Campbell and 41 juniors came back from Aberdovey in the summer of 1941 to stay there. It is on record that at this point Meissner and his boys occupied the billiard room at Plas Dinam. By the summer of 1942 he was Housemaster at Bronfelen, a house with no electricity, some three miles away from Plas Dinam in the opposite direction to Berthddu. Then, in the winter of 1942, Meissner and 30 boys were moved to Broneirion, another of Lord Davies's houses, in the village of Llandinam just across the valley from Plas Dinam. Kurt Hahn himself was Housemaster at Bronfelen by September 1943, though as he was generally away on other business Mrs Whitworth was in charge. Peter Whitworth (whose twelve-year-old brother had come down to Wales from Gordonstoun with the school) remembers arriving there with his mother after his father's death at Dunkirk: 'Mother was a firm believer in what Kurt Hahn was trying to do for education and took a job to help the school in what was a chaotic time [. . .] Bronfelen was an exciting place for us to be and it was here that my mother started a Kindergarten to which various Gordonstoun masters' children came each day plus some other locals. To me it was a very happy time, no electricity, tadpoles coming out of the taps, paraffin tilly lamps and steam trains to watch in the valley below at Caersws Junction. Every so often Kurt Hahn would visit us at Bronfelen to see that it was being run properly. A Mr and Mrs Watkins came each day to help my mother, she did the cleaning and he filled all the paraffin

lamps and cleaned the outside lavatories; he only spoke Welsh and was a large, frightening quarryman.'

At the start of 1944 the juniors were dispersed from Berthddu amongst the other houses, and Keir Campbell remained Housemaster at Berthddu with seniors as well as juniors. Just as there had been at Gordonstoun before the war there were now five houses: Plas Dinam, Berthddu, Broneirion, Bronfelen and 'The Hut', a wooden building designed in the grounds of Plas Dinam by the architect George Kennedy with most of the construction carried out by the boys.

Montgomeryshire was safely away from most enemy action, but the boys were not cut off from news of the war and old boys came to visit and talk about their experiences. One of the boys' war duties was to deal with the blackout, making sure that every window was covered at night so that no chink of light escaped to draw the attention of German pilots. On one occasion a bomber crashed in bad weather on the hills above the school, killing all the crew. Brownson takes up the story: 'Always keen to find souvenirs, some of us cycled over there on our next afternoon off. The main part of the plane had been removed by then but pieces were still strewn over a wide area, pieces of metal, perspex, etc. One boy called from a distance, "I've got a boot", and someone replied, "nothing special about that", to which he answered "this one's got a foot in it!" '

Above: 'The Watchers', made up of Conway boys, in a semaphore class. The prefabricated building in the background provided schoolrooms for Conway classes, May 1945.

Right: 'The Hut', built by the boys in the grounds of Plas Dinam to provide extra sleeping accommodation, May 1945.

Below: Broneirion, near Llandinam.

THE RETURN TO GORDONSTOUN

The fire that broke out on the top floor of Gordonstoun House while it was in use by the army during the war caused grave damage. The building was gutted, and its fine plaster ceilings were lost. In April 1945, a party of boys travelled up to Moray from Wales with Kurt Hahn to clean up the house after the departure of the army. A letter to his mother and sister from one of them, Toby Coghill, tells the story and reveals much about Hahn's attitudes towards his young charges when it came to responsibility, safety and adventure:

'The first few days were spent washing walls and ceilings to be painted or distempered. Or we were digging in the rose beds which are now in good shape, all except for the ones the tanks destroyed. They are going to plough up the lawns and make new ones as the present condition of them is irreparable.

'After about five days of alternate jobs, Mr Corlette, my Architecture master, turned up and set me to measure up and plan out the East Lodge. It was great fun and work I enjoyed, and once I had measured it up I was given a proper drawing table and instruments with which to plan it. I felt very important sitting with a whole lot of weird looking objects in my hand, drawing out a house like a "professional" architect . . .

'Mr Hahn has been extremely good to us. He gave us permission to drink cider while working. (He is strictly against alcoholic drink.) But after a day he changed his mind and bought us some crates of lemonade and only let us drink cider whilst working outside. He also bought us a wireless as he thought the war was at a climax. He took us on a long walking tour of the river Findhorn, relating all the time the history of the district, surrounding clans and river, dating back to about the thirteenth century. It was very interesting and he showed us the historical spots on the river and without caring a damn for anyone or anything trespassed right under the nose of the present land owner; right across the lawns and through the stables and God knows where . . .

'The state of the school estate is deplorable but Mr Hahn said it was not as bad as he had expected. The house itself is a massive, domineering looking building (Georgian) which before the army burnt it used to be like a rabbit warren. The wings still are, and not having been down a rabbit warren I should say worse. It is being slowly re-done, and the fire has given Mr Kennedy [George Kennedy, architect and member of staff] and Mr Corlette a chance to let fling with bright ideas. There is only one thing that anyone has against it and that is that there is a dormitory

for 50 boys. There is still a hell of a lot to be done, both inside and out, and one person expressed the opinion that we would be camping out in September. The Round Square still has a lot to be done to it and instead of being a sleeping house it's going to be an entirely school work building. The grounds are covered with Nissen huts and latrines. Wherever you go you see either Nissen huts or a latrine or sometimes both.

'The sea front is lovely, or what we saw of it, as a good bit of it is restricted as it is a practice ground for trainees in the army and there are a lot of unexploded bombs lying around. There are hundreds of caves and cliffs to explore and climb, but I fear that Mr Hahn will make a Safety Rule concerning them. There is very little [sea] traffic except for the occasional lobsterman.

'It is a terrible thought that I have got to go back to Wales for fourteen weeks after being at the original home of the school, as it is so incomparably nicer than the bleak rain-soaked grimy hills of "Coal Land Wales".

'Mr Hahn got a hold of a mountaineer to take an expedition of boys to the Cairngorms. He would not let me or two other boys go as we were too small. He had to find somewhere to board us as there would be no-one left at Duffus. So he asked a friend who has a boy at the school who lived near at hand to put us up, so here we are, except that one of the "wee ones" went home to Inverness.

'[*Written from Dell House, Nethy Bridge*] The weather has broken. When we arrived here it was snowing and there is about an inch on the ground. All the puddles are frozen over. This morning we walked to the school's mountaineering hut, about two and a half to three miles away, called Lyngarrie. Walking home through a blizzard we saw and heard a cuckoo. We leave for Wales tomorrow.'

Ian Farmer talks of the move from Wales: 'Volunteers were asked to work two weeks of their holidays at the end of term or two weeks at the end of the holidays in order to load and tidy up and prepare the place for the start of the new term. I volunteered with about twenty others to work the second shift. When we arrived there was plenty of work to do

Hahn's study in Gordonstoun House, now the South Room, as it was when in use as a country house (left); as Hahn's study (centre); as it was found after the army's departure at the end of the war (right).

Aerial photograph of part of the Gordonstoun estate showing the Nissen huts left behind by the army.

Highland dancing with girls
from local families, 1952.

containers on the lorries were then put on trains for onward
transportation to Gordonstoun. When the school returned
from Wales, boys and staff were fed in the NAAFI, a Nissen
hut on the main drive beside Cumming House. 'We needed
immediate accommodation for 190 and not for only 135 –
our numbers when we left', wrote Henry Brereton. 'We were
reduced to the expedient of converting unattractive army
huts for classrooms, workshops and even living quarters.'
Memories of the labour involved in reclaiming the estate are
keen. 'We cleaned, whitewashed (ourselves as well!), moved
desks and beds, dug high and long jump pits, marked off
distances along the long drive for two-, one- and half-mile
events, etc. I particularly remember going up and down one
field that was going to be used for rugger, picking up
stones, sticks and rubble left by the army. It took ages.' And
he reflects on the school's facilities at the time: 'There were,
of course, no sophisticated amenities at the school: the sea
(the Moray Firth) was our swimming pool, as the river
Severn had been in Wales. That just meant that we learned
to make the most of what we had and use our initiative to
find ways around any problems.'

'Adjacent to and parallel with the west drive about
100m from Cumming House were two Nissen huts', writes
Ronald Gilchrist (1946–50). 'By 1948 these, along with all
the other Nissen huts on which the school depended, were
in poor condition and also very basic, no insulation, heated
by coal or wood stoves and bitterly cold on winter evenings.
In one hut was located Roy McComish's Art studio, always
full of activity and also the Latin classroom where we were
taught Latin successively by Messrs Holmes and
Bannerman. In the second was the school clothing repair
room staffed by local ladies who sewed on buttons,
renovated tears and holes and generally put things back
together again. Also in the second hut was the Maths
classroom where Major H.J. Downton presided. Frequently
we had to light the stove of an evening, and by the time it
got going and began to emit heat the class was over.

'The Nissen huts were rusting and had been sprayed
with a bitumen mixture to help preserve them. Rather
unfairly I decided to find out whether a Nissen hut could
be opened by a can-opener, not the type with a winder
handle but the type where you dug the point into the can
and levered it open. I selected a point low down on the
side of the hut and nothing could have been easier – no
hesitation at all. The corrugated iron was rotting away.
When I left in 1950 Nissen huts were still in wide use all
over the estate. From the fire station to the laundry, to the
engineering guild to Charlie Fraser's carpentry room and
numerous classrooms.'

under enthusiastic friendly supervision. Life continued busily
and advanced very happily over the next few years full of
variation. I joined the Highland dance club with a few others
and on Tuesday evenings in the summer we would
congregate on the flat roof of the main house to learn the
intricate steps of the various dances. Local girls would be
bussed in from the local villages and countryside which made
it much more fun for us; I think the girls enjoyed it as well. In
1945 four of us were returning one afternoon from one of the
many expeditions. We arrived in Forres tired out and decided
to rest our legs in a local cinema before continuing our
journey. We fell asleep but were awoken by a tremendous
noise. Outside we found the streets crowded with cheering
people, bands playing, horns blowing fireworks and a general
hullabaloo. The end of World War II had just been
announced. We joined the celebrations and even indulged in
a forbidden drink or two. We arrived back later in school but
nothing was said of this momentous occasion.'

Peter Whitworth recalls the removal men arriving with
steam-powered lorries to pack up and load the school's
belongings for their long journey to Scotland. The

HOPEMAN LODGE

Hopeman Lodge, a large white house on the cliffs overlooking the beach and harbour of the fishing village of Hopeman, was acquired from the Gordon Duffs by the school in 1945 and used as a boarding house – 'lovely in summer, but very cold in winter', remembers Ian Farmer, who was despatched there on his return from Wales. 'Term started on time though there was still much practical work to do. As in Wales, Captain and Mrs MacGregor were my house parents. I was glad to have Captain Mac as my Housemaster. He was strict but kind and fair with a twinkle in his eye. We lived in fear of Mrs MacGregor who was a strict disciplinarian, very house proud and played hell if the housework we were allocated wasn't done properly. The result was that the house was immaculate and very clean in spite of small boys running riot morning and evening. I remember the time she nearly went mad when she caught us hypnotising her chickens by grabbing them and holding them so that their beak pointed down a wooden board. When a chalk line was drawn on the board running away from the beak the chicken would stay transfixed. The competition was to see whose chicken would stay transfixed the longest. I didn't think it helped their laying abilities and I can't really blame Mrs Macgregor for being furious with us nasty little boys. I shall always remember Captain MacGregor coming into the locker room whilst we were cleaning our shoes for the next day, taking off his

metal leg and polishing it whilst standing on the good one. (I was told that he had lost his leg after being torpedoed at the beginning of the war.) Unfortunately, the house had no showers so we had to sit in an empty bath and pour a bucket of cold water over ourselves before setting off on the morning run stripped to the waist.' The boys housed at Hopeman cycled the few miles to and from Gordonstoun each day. 'Of course we all wore shorts all of the time until we left the school for good, which made the cycle ride in the winter to the main school for lessons very cold and invariably I had chaps on my knees, thighs and backside. Even gloves were easily penetrated in the cold east wind.' Michael Stary (1944–48) recalls the ride too – 'wind against you both ways'.

Captain MacGregor was Housemaster until his death in 1955, when he was succeeded by Robert Whitby until the amalgamation of Altyre with the main school in 1960, at which point Major John Downton took over. Hopeman Lodge was small for a boarding house and at something of a distance from the main school. The compensations were quieter weekends, away from the main school, summer dips in the sea in lieu of cold showers, and the benefits to its inhabitants of living in a small community. It acted as a holding house for new boys when they had to wait for a place in their allocated house until 1968 when Hopeman House was built and the occupants of the Lodge moved onto the main school grounds.

Above: Dunkinty, one of the houses that were used as the school roll increased after the war. It opened in 1948 but closed three years later when Altyre House (Forres) was leased.

Hopeman Lodge in the late 1940s.

PLEWLANDS, DUNKINTY AND LAVEROCK BANK

In 1948 Dunkinty, a large mansion lying to the south of Elgin (and seven miles from the main school), was bought, followed by Laverock Bank in Lossiemouth in 1949, both used as main school houses. (Just before this, Plewlands, a farmhouse a little to the north of the estate was briefly rented by the school, its Housemaster the Revd W.P. Young, but it was too small to be viable and was closed down.)

Neil Mackintosh, who began his school life at Laverock Bank, remembers that each morning, set up by a 300-yard run, a cold shower and a cup of cocoa, he used to cycle round the perimeter of Lossiemouth airfield to reach the main school – a practice that was apparently banned after the Revd Young followed the same route in his car, terrifying a pilot whose aircraft was just taking off.

By 1949 there were 270 boys scattered through the various boarding houses that comprised the school. Those not housed in the main grounds had to be transported into school each day by bus. This inconvenient arrangement lasted until 1951, when Dunkinty and Laverock Bank were replaced by Altyre, Forres, with the space to accommodate 130 to 150 boys.

KITES AND PLANES

In the 1980s, thirty years after the Revd Young alarmed pilots at Lossiemouth, Seren Irvine and her friend Fiona van Buren also unwittingly unnerved personnel at the airfield. Fiona's father made kites of all shapes and sizes, some of enormous power, and the two girls had decided to fly one particular kite with a very long string on the hockey pitch: 'Since the kite was showing signs of lifting us off the ground, we decided to reel it in – a task which took much longer than letting it out . . . We realised we could be in a spot of trouble when Mr Byatt drove his car onto the pitch. He got out and said, "You have done as Hitler failed – you have grounded the RAF – get that thing down!" And then we remembered the two jets which had seemed to be circling immediately overhead earlier . . .'

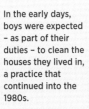

In the early days, boys were expected – as part of their duties – to clean the houses they lived in, a practice that continued into the 1980s.

The Round Square was in sore need of restoration from the time the school first took on the estate, as can been seen in the photograph top left, dating from c. 1945. The other photographs show the building undergoing renovation in 1952.

THE ROUND SQUARE

After the school's compulsory requisitioning by the army during the war, the Round Square, which was in any case in need of thorough renovation, was left in a very sorry state. The refurbishment of Sir Robert Gordon's late seventeenth-century circular estate square took place in several stages during the 1950s. It was re-roofed in 1951 with traditional heavy stone tiles and a retaining grid installed all the way round to protect anyone walking below should a tile come loose and fall. The removal of the old cobbled garth within,

The Round Square, photographed 2006.

the sowing of grass and the laying of the circular walkway of Caithness slabs round the inner edge were all done by boys in 1952, under the guidance of Commander Armand Smith. Plans for refurbishing the building itself were drawn up by the school architect, George Kennedy, and approved by the Gordonstoun Board of Governors in February 1953.

Gordon Shiach was at the house from 1948 to 1954 (except for a brief period on exchange at Salem School in Baden, 1951–52): 'Round Square, with its outside staircases, was almost a history lesson in itself. The "wake-up" boy on duty had to complete a vigorous round with his call of "Time to get up" or, in seriously inclement weather, "Time to get up; no morning run". This could be amplified on occasion – once, after the US Presidential election, it included the call: "Eisenhower is President". Lights out at night would, as a concession, be allowed later on a Saturday than on weekdays to enable us to listen in bed to *Saturday Night Theatre* on the radio.

'The old fashioned boilers in Round Square were stoked by an elderly boiler-man who would vary his greeting as he passed in the morning, from "Ay!" to "Ay, Ay!" Although laconic, he was much respected. On occasion, the boilers leaked fumes, to the extent that the dormitory above had to be evacuated. We would then move mattresses and bedding temporarily to another dormitory, and sleep in the narrow spaces on the floor between the beds. Few would complain. There was always the wonderful warm wash –

and dash through the cold shower – to look forward to in the morning.

'Meals for Round Square were in our own dining room on the ground floor of Gordonstoun House. Dr Meissner would preside at lunch and supper, with a hand-bell. Each meal would start with a few minutes' silence, ended by a ring of the bell. A further ring would renew the silence for the closing minutes of the meal. At the end of a meal there might occasionally (and unpredictably) be an "augeas" – named after Hercules's task to clean the Augean stables. It involved answering a general knowledge question, set by the duty Helper, which was whispered to each boy in turn. If a boy gave the wrong answer, he had to undergo a hand inspection, with an appropriate penalty if his hand or nails were dirty.'

The renovation of the Round Square was funded to the tune of £10,000 by the Scottish Council for the Preservation of Historic Buildings, £1,000 from the Pilgrim Trust and many donations from friends of the school. Edward Lightowler had been appointed in July 1951 to take charge of the school's works department, and it was he who oversaw the renovation of this unique building. His drawings, archived at the school, reveal that the whole design, including all the fitted furniture – the curved bookcases of the library and the seating in the alcoves of the reading loft – were his conception, skilfully executed by the school's joiners. By December 1957 the first-floor library

and reading loft were nearing completion, accessed by a new stair from the cloister to the west of the main archway. Work was finally completed in 1966. The carpet woven with the school's crest was donated by an old boy, Gavin Morton, of Blackwood, Morton & Sons of Kilmarnock.

A first-floor Housemaster's flat was constructed to the east of the archway, accessed, as it is now, by an outside stone stair. In the southern section of the Round Square lay-lights were inserted into the roof, and the apple loft was converted into a dormitory and study for twelve boys. The names of dormitories created in the 1950s recalled the school's wartime stay in Wales: one was called Plas Dinam, another Lady Lowys, a third was called Churchill.

In the mid-1970s Angus Scott – Housemaster at the old Bruce House – had introduced a small number of bedsits for sixth formers (in the face of considerable disapproval from some of his colleagues). In the 1980s, when the Round Square was the first house to undergo a major refurbishment, this lead was followed and a substantial number of bedsits were installed. Some senior staff felt that bedsits eroded vertical integration (the mixture of ages which allowed older children to help and support the younger ones), but the need to improve study conditions and to protect individual privacy, together with the

demands of the market, carried the day. In 1987, a purpose-built new house, Plewlands, opened to cater for the increasing demand for girls' places at the school. The need to match these new standards in the boys' houses was clear, and the other boys' houses followed in the steps of the Round Square.

Round Square pupils enjoyed their bedsits and the generally improved standard of their accommodation. The tone became markedly more civilised, and the need to order one's private patch was a good preparation for life beyond school. The structural alteration that probably did most to improve the ambience was the removal of the old-style locker room. This had been a spartan place in a prominent position on the ground floor where every pupil had his own locker (which ironically could not be locked). The boys changed there in the morning and at bedtime and for games and other pursuits. It was a haven for 'borrowing' and other nefarious activities. New beds were made which were fitted with drawers, and clothes were now kept in bedsits and dormitories. The old locker room became a mixed common room, equipped with table tennis and pool tables. It was also used for house dances.

The Round Square has always prided itself on its expeditions. In the 1980s these generally involved camping

The Lady Lowys
dormitory and study
on the first floor of the
Round Square,
probably late 1950s.

at Derry Lodge in the summer and at Roy Bridge in the autumn. The southern Cairngorms, Mamores and Grey Corries were the most frequently tackled mountains. Sports were also taken seriously and the house had some outstanding skiers, mostly from Badenoch and Strathspey. Highlights on the arts front were a co-production with Hopeman House in 1981 of *Guys and Dolls*, directed by John Lofthouse, and two film musicals, *The Boy from New York City* and *Frankie and Johnny* (both in the mid-'80s), incorporating songs from the '50s and '60s and created and produced by David Spooner and Ron Pickering (house tutors). The world premieres were black-tie occasions in Gordonstoun House.

In the 1960s, '70s and '80s, the Round Square had only three Housemasters, each of whose tenure was substantial and corresponded approximately to a decade: Michael Jenkins (1962–72), Anthony Jones (1972–80) and Angus Miller (1980–91). For almost all of this period, Bob Waddell served as resident Assistant Housemaster, and he too made his own considerable impact on the house.

Round Square is now home to some 60 boys. Sitting at the centre of the school campus, it is squarely in the public eye and thus under a certain pressure not felt by other houses; and it has certain idiosyncrasies, like its very small windows and a rather temperamental heating system. Nonetheless, Luke Tattersall, Housemaster 2005–10 and variously associated with the house for the last 22 years, remarks that 'the building itself seems to exude an aura of calm which somehow transmits itself to the boys'.

MOVING AROUND

From the foundation of the school until the early 1960s it was common for both boys and staff to move between houses from year to year, even from term to term. Much of this stemmed from the school's rapid rate of growth and from the fact that the stock of boarding houses was constantly shifting, with hastily acquired extra houses that were not necessarily ideal for their purpose being abandoned once a better alternative had been found.

In Wales, despite the great generosity of Lord Davies in lending various of his properties, it had still been very difficult to find efficient solutions to the practical problems of housing and schooling the boys. Colin Crole was not untypical: in 1940 he went to Wales to be with his two older brothers (evacuated from the main school), having arrived at Duffus House in 1936 and moved to Wester Elchies in 1937. June and July 1940 were spent in Plas Dinam, followed by the autumn term in Aberdovey, 1941 to 1942 at Berthddu, and 1943 to 1944 in the main house, Plas Dinam, with Norman Pares, moving to Bronfelen with Mrs Whitworth in summer 1945. Even once he was back in Scotland he found himself first at the Round Square under Meissner for the autumn term of 1945, then at Cumming House under Keir Campbell; by summer 1946 he was back at Duffus, and he finished his school days with Bobby Chew at Gordonstoun House in March 1947. This peripatetic style of boarding was a common experience in the early years of the school. Anthony Craig (1956–60) remarks that although the integration of Altyre into the school in the autumn of 1960 caused some redistribution between houses, 'I was never clear why numbers of boys were shifted from one house to another.' Practical considerations notwithstanding, Kurt Hahn is said to have deliberately moved people around in an attempt to discourage the formation of cliques.

In spite of Hahn's desire to avoid certain houses becoming associated with certain pursuits (which would inevitably cramp efforts to improve on a child's weaker points and limit ambitions to promote as broad and rounded an education as possible), the personalities of Housemasters and natural grouping together of people of like mind have, over the years, meant that particular interests have become seen as part of the character of particular houses. Anthony Craig, for example, remembers being aware that 'Godfrey Burchardt aimed to get the academic boys for Duffus, Meissner grabbed the sporty types for Round Square, Dr MacKnight took the psychos for Cumming, McComish got what was left for Gordonstoun House and so on. Whitby was out at Hopeman Lodge and I can't remember who was at Windmill – such is the

Pen and ink drawing by Roy McComish, who taught at the school 1949–58, showing the locations of the various houses acquired by the school before and immediately after the war. This illustration appeared in many issues of *The Gordonstoun Record* in the 1950s.

restricted territorialism of an adolescent boy.' And accounts from former inhabitants of all the various houses bear out the reality that, however successful these communities are in accommodating broad mixtures of people and interests, history builds upon itself and success breeds success.

THE GROUNDS

The estate had been badly neglected during the war, with no management of the woodland carried out. Ronald Gilchrist remembers that Keir Campbell, Housemaster of Cumming House and a keen forester and woodsman, began, within a couple of years of the school's return, to clear the estate woods of quantities of dead and decaying timber, using all the hands he could muster. 'Of course, it had to be dried before it could be used, and wood does not heat water as does coal, but this kept us going within reason until the coal famine came to an end, which was that summer (1947).' Towards 1950, Keir Campbell began in earnest the repair of the damaged forest estate, planting a nursery to the north side of Cumming House from which seedlings were transplanted into the woods.

In 1951 the school employed its first gamekeeper, a local man called David Gordon, after complaints from neighbours about the quantity of rabbits running wild on its estate. He subsequently became the school's woodsman as well as working with the boys training the school's bloodhounds (see page 151) and those who bred pheasants for the school's shoot. Gordon remembered that shortly after his arrival he had to fell massive beeches along the Silent Walk which had become unsafe with nothing more than a hand saw. In 1953 a storm force gale took down many ancient broad-leaved trees on the estate and destroyed the woods. Replanting was enabled through a grant from the Forestry Commission, which in turn led to the woods becoming part of the Forestry Commission's Dedication Scheme. When the woods had to be thinned in 1975, it was Gordon who oversaw the felling.

Clearing the copse on the north side of the estate in order to enlarge the cricket ground.

This doocot was converted in the eighteenth century from a windmill, hence the name of the neighbouring Windmill Lodge.

GORDONSTOUN'S DOOCOTS

Of the four doocots (dovecotes) built by the Fourth Baronet, Sir Robert Gordon (1696–1772), two (at Balormie and Smithfield) were destroyed by the Jacobite army as it passed by in 1745, and two survive. The beehive doocot that stands on an artificial mound close to the Round Square is a fine example of its type. Birds flew in and out of the domed chamber through the two-metre-long splayed funnel at its apex. Inside, concentric rings of about 1,000 stone nest boxes line the walls. The second doocot at Gordonstoun, next to Windmill Lodge, was originally a windmill, and was converted by Sir Robert, probably in the 1730s, to extend the estate's pigeon-breeding capacity. Both doocots contain a 'potence' – a revolving ladder that enabled easy access to the nests.

The beehive doocot in 1949 in dilapidated condition, its domed roof covered in ivy, and, opposite, in its renovated state today.

GAME SHOOTING AT GORDONSTOUN

Moray is a shooting county, and virtually every acre of arable and woodland is home to a shoot. Some are small family rough shoots; some are grand driven shoots with all shades in between. Kurt Hahn was a keen hunter in the days at Salem and tutored the boys in the art of shooting and deer stalking. The Gordonstoun estate in the early days of the school was a haven for wild game, especially after the neglect it suffered during the war – poor farming equals great game cover! Game shooting took place at the school from the 1930s, and as the Gordonstoun estate developed it became more formalised. Alistair Paterson, Art master at Altyre and then at the main school, led the shoot. James Thomas remembers Gordonstoun being 'renowned for the tremendous woodcock shooting towards the end of the season, with 27 being the highest daily total – given good weather and heed to conservation. Wood-pigeon shooting in the snows of January and February could also be really testing and some good bags were made with a team of club members distributed around the grounds and along the Silent Walk and into Shempston.'

'In the mid-'60s', recalls Thomas, 'there was a rearing project involving both boys and staff and led by Alistair Paterson and David Gordon. A hundred or so pheasants were reared under bantams, an activity that required good discipline and dedication as the feeding and exercise regime had to be carefully maintained during incubation and when the chicks were hatched – there was always great pride taken in a hundred per cent hatch and the bantams became well cared for pets. Ruaraidh Adams-Cairns, Jamie Cameron, Henry Page, Philip St C. Tisdall and Richard Pickup were early enthusiasts – Richard Pickup now runs a thriving shoot in south-west Scotland rearing around 50,000 birds each year!' Tisdall recalls Henry Page and himself being caught in the pens by James Thomas, feeding the birds when they should have been in their studies: 'We were put on a Pink Card for two weeks which meant that every class or free period had to be signed by a master. We felt that the punishment was a bit harsh as we were looking after the pheasants that he would enjoy shooting.'

The birds were released into the grounds at the end of the summer term for the end of season and for Christmas shoots of which there were three, the first two for local alumni and friends of the school with the staff leading the beating teams as walking guns. And at the start of the winter term in January the boys were allowed the third day to round off the season.

As the school developed and buildings sprang up across the estate, shooting became less viable at Gordonstoun. Various local landowners who had either been at the school themselves or whose sons had attended it generously hosted shoots for the club over many years, but in 2006 the club finally came to an end.

Game shooting at Shempston, c. 1980.

Cricket in front of
Altyre House,
1950s.

ALTYRE, FORRES

In 1951 Altyre House was leased from Sir William Gordon-Cumming to replace several smaller outlying houses (Dunkinty and Laverock Bank, in particular) that had been taken up piecemeal as the school recovered from the upheaval caused by the move to Wales during the war and as its numbers began to rise. Sir William went to live in Blairs House near the loch of the same name on the estate. Altyre House lay three miles north of Forres and about twelve miles from Gordonstoun.

Although it was always part of Gordonstoun School, Altyre enjoyed a surprising degree of autonomy, and to staff and pupils alike it felt, at times, almost like a separate school. The decision to set up Altyre House so far away from the main campus might now seem curious, but it was a closer reflection of one of Kurt Hahn's stated intentions than one might imagine. Back in 1935, in his report to British Salem Schools Ltd on the progress of Gordonstoun School, Hahn expressed his hope that the influence of the school would be felt beneficially in the surrounding area and went on to voice his belief that when the numbers at Gordonstoun and Duffus House exceeded 140, 'we should take another beautiful house ten or twenty miles away, and then another on the sea, or on the hills, until there are five or six health-giving centres, spread over this favoured district in the north-east of Scotland.' The leasing of Altyre was, perhaps, the first decisive step in this over-arching plan.

John Gillespie, fresh from university, applied in 1952 for a temporary one-term appointment at Gordonstoun School (but in fact stayed for eleven years): 'To my surprise, I found myself at Altyre House, a dozen miles from Gordonstoun House, an improbable, probably unique arrangement to enable the school to expand. It was typical of Gordonstoun's pioneering spirit that it worked. Altyre proved to be an ideal place to start teaching. Connected to the main school, but far enough away to develop its own identity, in a lovely large house, in the most idyllic, secluded surroundings. There were about 100 boys, and a young staff who made up in enthusiasm what we lacked in experience.'

In 1951 Bobby Chew, who, at the time was financial controller for the whole school, was appointed Housemaster of Dunbar House, one of three houses at Altyre (followed by Ian Lawson in 1957). The other two, Bruce House and Comyn House, were presided over by John Downton and David Snell, respectively. In 1953, on Kurt Hahn's retirement, Henry Brereton and Bobby Chew were made Joint Headmasters of the whole school, with Brereton staying at Gordonstoun and Bobby Chew still based at Altyre.

Immediately after he graduated from Cambridge, Bobby Chew had briefly been at Salem with Hahn and subsequently worked with him at Gordonstoun until the war. As Colonel Chew, he had led British troops into Bergen and taken the German surrender, and it was here that he met his future wife Eva, whose husband, a flying instructor in the Norwegian air force, had lost his life while training aircrew in Canada. Later in the war, Bobby Chew had played an important role at the Highland Field Craft Training Centre in Glen Feshie. (Its Commandant, Lord Rowallan, later gave his name to Rowallan Company at RMA Sandhurst, set up in 1977 to address the high failure rate of officer cadets on the the Regular Commissions Board.) Among the instructors at Glenfeshie were John Downton and Adam Arnold Brown (who was to become the first Warden of the Outward Bound School at Eskdale). Glen Feshie's task was to help young men to overcome their failure to win a commission and to try again. Its success rate was high, due mainly to the exceptional quality of the instructors. Their guiding principle was to instill and develop self-confidence, quietly, but profoundly, so that each person learned to develop, to the full, their potential – an intention which clearly had much in common with the fundamental aims of Hahn. The physical distance of Altyre from Gordonstoun, the strength of Bobby Chew's personality and the independence he was allowed meant that from the beginning he ran Altyre almost as a separate establishment.

The obstacle course at Altyre, 1954.

The front of Altyre House showing the porticoed entrance to the Assembly Hall.

'The Chews were both remarkable people', remembers John Gillespie. 'His natural authority stemmed from complete integrity, devotion to duty, practical wisdom, and also humility – he was totally unpretentious and unassuming . . . There was an atmosphere of civility and harmonious zest pervading Altyre, which owed much to the Chews, and to the two senior men among us: John Downton, the embodiment of upright modesty, who had served with Chew

during the war, and, especially, David Snell, Chew's deputy. He was only a few years older than us beginners, and his fine spirit and breadth of mind influenced everyone.'

Others among the young members of staff selected by Bobby Chew were similarly impressed by the couple. John Ray remembers Eva Chew thus: 'Tall, regal and yet friendly and concerned, she inspired awe in us young bachelor masters whom she undertook to civilise. Most of us were in first jobs and loved the place. We enjoyed good comradeship and a lot of laughter. It was like a large family, with a lot of fun, adventure – and a few ups and downs. I guess I was not the only one who, when I later got married, brought my wife to meet the Chews rather as if they were parents. And what does it say about the atmosphere that Bobby Chew's nickname among his staff was "our Father"?' Ian Lawson remarks on how well the Chews complemented each other: 'They made a good team. Who else but Mrs Chew could lower a handkerchief on a piece of string from her sitting room window to warn the Big Study below that the noise level had become unacceptable and that Authority was on his way downstairs. Instant and prolonged silence would follow.'

Schoolboy memories of them are similarly warm. Donald Fairgrieve's fond recollections are typical: 'Bobby Chew was well suited to the role being an accomplished athlete, climber and racquet player with a personality and intellect which commanded respect . . . His wife Eva did much to create a "family" atmosphere at Altyre. I remember well the delightful smell of freshly ground coffee wafting from their kitchen at the top of the back stairs, as we returned from our morning run. Bobby Chew has been a strong influence on my life and I count myself fortunate to have spent most of my school days in his care.' Tim Saville echoes this fondness: 'We were in awe of that wonderful man, FRGC, seemingly distant to us but with such a warm smile and we were in love with his elegant wife.'

These sentiments are seemingly almost universal among Altyre old boys, though the adoration of Eva Chew was certainly not shared by John Shackles, who recalls an encounter with the lady one mealtime in chilling detail: 'Once, when it was my turn to be in charge of the waiters [boys took turns at this duty], Eva Chew walked past a dining-room window during sweeping up. She paused and looked at the sausage skin of a mealy pudding that we had had for supper which was lying by the window. It looked horribly like a used condom. She pointed at it and looked quizzically at me. She knew what it looked like and I knew that she knew. I am sorry to say that instead of laughing, I was intimidated by her supreme bearing and

The Car Club, 1950s.

The dining room at Altyre, resplendent with the trophies shot by one of the house's erstwhile inhabitants.

sophistication and so I turned, po-faced, to call a boy over to tell him to clear it up.'

Ian Lawson, another 23-year-old teacher who arrived in 1951, remembers how tight-knit the community of boys and staff was from the start: 'Every member of the teaching staff turned out to play rugby on that very first games afternoon – including Mr Chew the Headmaster who imposed his personality right from the beginning by some very decisive tackling. During the game, the boys treated us with some courtesy: the occasional "sorry sir" as grievous bodily harm was being committed at the bottom of the scrum – which, of course, was never penalised by John Downton, our impartial referee. Some years later, playing club rugby against Ross Sutherland, a certain Angus MacDonald (later to become Chairman of the school's Board of Governors) would show the same courtesy that he showed on that first afternoon, with a polite "sorry" as he knelt on my face with his bony knees.'

The respect commanded by Bobby Chew and the extent to which he could hold the boys in his thrall is clear from many accounts of him. Douglas Gibbon remembers 'Chagger' Chew's Hush Puppies 'that caught so many of us out. I think we called them "creepy crawlies".' John Shackles gives a powerful evocation of an imposing figure: 'He was a large man with something strange about one of his eyes. The boys said that it was a glass eye, but I don't think this was true. He had an unsettling way of looking at you that

made you feel guilty of something. It was a false impression, for he was a kindly, fair-minded and wise man. He was a good teacher too . . . However, when angered, he could be truly terrifying. He did not rave or raise his voice but his contained wrath and immense presence commanded full attention and obedience.'

On the ground floor of Altyre House were marble corridors, a panelled assembly hall and the huge dining hall. Upstairs were mainly dormitories, a library, studies, offices and a sanatorium presided over by the Matron, Sister MacDonald. The grandeur and style of the house's architecture were not lost on the boys. 'The Dining Hall was a magnificent room lit by full-length sash windows looking east and facing the drive which was flanked by several huge Wellingtonia trees', writes John Shackles. 'The walls were hung with full-length oil paintings of the Gordon-Cumming family: the men, looking grand with magnificent whiskers and dressed as highland chiefs, the ladies posing demurely in silk gowns, examining roses or dead birds. Next to this was the Assembly Hall. Massive oak doors, studded with nails, opened out to a portico that formed the main entrance, which was seldom used. The Hall itself was very grand. Oak panels lined the walls up to the clerestory, which was covered in hunting trophies, claymores, targes, spears, crossbows, fans of flintlock pistols and antique Arab rifles. Facing the entrance was an Irish elk's head with a massive spread of antlers fixed above the mounted heads of a moose and an American bison. Lion skulls were all over the place as were the heads of assorted Cape buffalo, antelope and gazelles. All these things made a pleasant diversion to gaze at during morning prayers or stuffy Sunday evening services.'

Some 50 boys were transferred from the main school to Altyre and were joined by 60 new boys. Humphrey Wakefield remembers that 'much of Duffus came over, but not the Germans and not those who had been rioters with me. I went to Altyre as Mr Chew was a great friend to my explorer uncle amongst other reasons. There was a very strong "ethnic" Scots bunch.' The Gordonstoun boys regarded themselves as refugees from Gordonstoun proper, chosen apparently at random for transfer and not always willingly. But they found Altyre a pleasant surprise. Michael Newton (first Guardian at Altyre) remarked at the time: 'Most of the refugees find Altyre vastly superior – there are wonderful facilities here – tennis, squash, curling, a skating rink and eleven acres of playing fields. There are many expeditions to the Cairngorms, Ben Nevis and elsewhere.' Altyre's pleasant, rather innocent atmosphere is neatly evoked by Newton's description of the festivities in December 1951: 'Our first term ended on a merry note. The staff challenged the school to a football match and beat them in a very nice and friendly game, 3 to 1. In the evening, we had a wonderful Christmas party, with the usual dormitory plays and general gaiety' – which included David Snell driving a Baby Austin 7 into the panelled

Assembly Hall, followed by Mr Chew, in cap and gown, on his Vespa scooter.

The 60 new boys were to be at Altyre for a year before returning to Gordonstoun for the remainder of their time at the school, taking with them, no doubt, recollections of scuttling in all weathers across the open, cobbled courtyard, after the famous Altyre Basin Bath (John Shackles, in Comyn House, has vivid memories of 'the dash from locker room to washroom dressed in nothing but a towel, in full view of the kitchen maids'.) But loyalties developed and soon the transfer back to Gordonstoun after one year at Altyre was stopped, and Altyre began to feel more like a school in its own right, rather than an annexe of Gordonstoun.

As Altyre matured it developed its own personality, and rivalry with Gordonstoun intensified. Ian Lawson remarks that people from Altyre would sometimes return from the main school, 'pretending to be suffering from severe cultural shock at what they had seen over there – boys playing rugby in dungarees and Wellington boots. But I never felt it was more than the assertiveness of a younger brother seeking to prove himself.' Recollections of pranks played against Gordonstoun, however, are legion, and never far from the surface when you speak with Altyre old boys. 'We at Altyre certainly felt part of the school but there was also a great rivalry between the two halves', recalls one. 'In my last year,' recounts Gordon Currie, 'the news broke that in the middle of the night I'd been kidnapped to Gordonstoun but had made my way back to

Every day, first thing in the morning and at dusk, as at Gordonstoun, the Guardian of Altyre raised and lowered the flag on Altyre House. Michael Newton remembers the perilous-sounding ascent: 'you climbed out of a window, walked up the side of the roof, planted a foot on each side of the roof's ridge and saw to the flag'. At the end of each school year the flags of Gordonstoun and Altyre were taken down for the summer holidays, the whole school attended a Flag Service and the flags were handed to the Chaplain for safekeeping.

Altyre boys preparing for a hill-walking expedition.

Right: The Altyre Pipe Band, 1950s.

A group of Altyre boys at the foot of Ben Rinnes, March 1955, about to board the ex-army bus that figures in the memories of many old boys.

Altyre, before getting-up time. Chew said to me, "If some of you wish to respond in some way the keys of my Land Rover are on my desk and I don't check the mileage", and a day later added, "better let me know before you go as I sometimes let the diesel run very low". We didn't use Chew's car, but a retaliation was organised.' Several of the most senior Altyre boys 'borrowed' a couple of masters' cars to pay the Elgin campus a 2 am visit. Michael Foulkes takes up the story: 'There were perhaps ten of us in the raiding party. We drove from Altyre to Gordonstoun, parked the cars. With extreme stealth and precision, one group entered the kitchen. We took piles of the largest white plates and used them to spell out ALTYRE in large letters on the front lawn. There was moonlight, which made it easier to get around and the plates reflected perfectly. Group two expertly removed the green carpet from the front stairs and in minimum time we exited like commandos, silently, slipping back to the cars and away. An entire school and its staff slept through it all. Back at Altyre, the cars were returned and the carpet on our front stairs was removed and replaced by the newly acquired one. The following morning we watched Bobby Chew ascend the stairs and pause, look down and with a smile of satisfaction continue on up. The three drivers all had licenses and the owners of the cars were quick to forgive. There was a brief, official telling off, token punishments meted out and everyone was happy. Kurt Hahn would have been delighted.' Other Altyre old boys remember the plates spelling out PLUS EST EN NOUS!, but perhaps this was the result of yet another escapade.

Humphrey Wakefield was Captain (House Helper) of Dunbar House and Guardian during his last term, and remembers that the Altyre and Gordonstoun Guardians were called Joint Guardians of Gordonstoun and that there was a Court of Honour, elected from the House Helpers and Heads of Games and Services from both establishments. 'I revelled in the Guardian visits to Gordonstoun to discuss this and that and the exchange of ideas and occasional nights too . . . We had joint Colour Bearer meetings at Altyre or at Gordonstoun. We always felt they distinctly looked down on us . . . We stole their flag and I have it now.'

It was not long before the very different natural environment of Altyre led to a significant distinction in the nature of the outdoor activities pursued there. 'Perhaps the greatest pleasure of all', reflects John Gillespie, 'was to be found in the mountains. Outdoor adventure is fundamental to the idea of Gordonstoun. The main school had the sea and seamanship. Far from the sea, we turned to the hills and Expedition Training. A remarkable man, John Ray, was appointed to run it. Under his leadership countless boys found *plus est en vous* in the wild. Eventually we had a fully operational Mountain Rescue Service to match Gordonstoun's Watchers and Fire Service.' John Ray himself is unequivocal in his remembered enthusiasm for Altyre's embracing of outdoor activities: 'I loved the place. Fancy being paid (not very much!) to take lads up mountains! Hahn's sense that, while adults might falter, boys would give their utmost, was so true. He was very right in believing that it was vital to engage the enthusiasm and passion of a boy before adolescence. Same with girls, I'm sure. Every week, on Dava Moor or in the Cairngorms, I bet my job (so to speak!) that *this* group of boys, with *this* leader, in *this* weather, having been dropped at some map reference in the morning, would actually reach the pick-up point in the evening . . . John Gillespie and I twice took groups of sixteen-year-olds in summer, fairly racing across Austrian peaks and glaciers.'

Tony White, who arrived in 1953, also a new graduate, describes the experience of teaching at Altyre as 'varied and happy beyond anything I had imagined. I was the only resident Music teacher, though the staff included several competent amateur musicians, whose skills were very valuable. We all had to be versatile. I soon found myself driving the famous green bus to and from mountain expeditions – a rebuilt army truck, whose crash gearbox was familiar from my national service days.' And that green bus (an ex-army twenty-seater) surfaces in the memories of many.

'Very early on,' recounts Ian Lawson, 'Andy Clelland and I were allowed to start a Mountain Rescue Service. This had been discussed, but we heard nothing more until ten minutes before the first Services afternoon when we were told: "Right, you can start your Mountain Rescue. We'll send you all those not required by John Downton for the ACF and who do not want to join Alistair Paterson and David Marshall in the Scouts." ' And that was the beginning of what was to become one of the most prominent Services at Gordonstoun after Altyre had amalgamated with it.

The freedom to roam around the substantial grounds and woodland of the estate is remembered by many. Tim Saville recalls: 'We cycled all around the locality, through the Altyre Estate forests – climbed the towering Wellingtonia trees, looked down upon our familiar world. We splashed through streams and rivers, abseiled from railway bridges with the thrill of the challenge and the joy of achievement.' While, generally, great benefit appears to have been drawn from this *laissez-faire* attitude towards boys exploring outdoors, often alone, it is arguable that it also contributed to the sad events of October 1951. 'I remember most clearly being summoned from bed to a meeting in the front hall at night', writes Humphrey Wakefield. 'Mark Hobhouse, a co-Englishman whose family I knew, had been digging a cave with my cousin Tiggy Birkbeck and they had not returned. Donald Munroe had found the fallen-in cave, guided by the stricken co-digger Birkbeck who had run back to report. Donald M. had dug out the suffocated Mark Hobhouse. When we were assembled and quiet, Brereton arrived and was silent too. He then just said, "The child is dead", and we all knew who and why and how. We went off to bed and he could not have said it better . . . Mark Hobhouse's father most gallantly came to talk to us at Chapel in the front hall, with all those animal heads looking down. He calmly told us not to dig into sandy caves. I am sure none of us have. Maybe, since OGs spend their lives pushing their luck in the hills, he saved some lives.' From then on, relates Tim Saville, there was a 'tea check': when the boys gathered for their afternoon sustenance, each had to be marked present. 'David Marshall's recollections of how he had noticed that the boy who sat by him at lunch had not been there at supper had left an indelible mark.'

If you talk to Altyre old boys about the end of their beloved home, one word is often uttered with a wry grimace: 'pheasants'. 'Those who pay large sums to shoot stags or pheasants', as John Ray observes, 'tend to be unhappy when a trail of boys scatters their prey at the vital moment.' Multiple reminiscences testify to the open hostility towards pheasant shoots shown by the denizens of Altyre. Michael Foulkes's memories of close encounters with the laird on this matter are typical: 'There were of course the famous pheasant shoots finishing across the front lawn, the dogs driving the hand-reared birds off the grass so the rented guns could blast them with an easy shot. The irony of it being "not sporting" to shoot a bird on the ground was not lost on school boys who were being trained to real standards of sportsmanship.' Gordon Currie remembers a master called Dougal Greig rampaging towards the guns shouting, 'Murder, bloody murder'! 'Oh the joy', continues Foulkes, 'when a pheasant made it through the barrage of smoking twelve bores and cleared the fence where the boys were gathered and who spontaneously cheered and clapped.' Contrary to popular belief, however, the reasons for the demise of Altyre were almost certainly more prosaic.

The original lease for Altyre was to run for ten years. When Hahn tried to renegotiate for a longer lease, this was not forthcoming, probably because the outgoings on such a large property made it unattractive to its owner as a continuing commercial proposition, and it was decided that the school should leave as soon as was practicable. Ian Lawson remembers that by 1957 Altyre boys were already being bussed to Gordonstoun for A-level Science and Physics lessons, and it was clear that it would not be possible to develop a fully effective sixth form without enlarging the existing buildings to allow numbers to increase. That was clearly a non-starter without a secure long lease. Minutes of Gordonstoun's annual meeting of Governors and Council make it clear that the dilemma was already under discussion in 1958: 'Our biggest worry is Altyre. Here is a thriving and lively community, comparatively newly born, yet warned that they must leave Altyre House in seven years time [it turned out to be only two]. This might be enough to shatter the morale of any concern, but not Altyre; here the people – although no

The impressive results of two boys' Projects: handmade canoes, one of which was sold by its maker, Rhett Anchor, and subsequently used by its new owner to cross the Channel.

doubt nervous of the future – live in the present . . . Here is, in fact, a most healthy atmosphere for any boy to be educated in, but your Board has much to think about on their behalf.' There was a thought that other premises could be found for the denizens of Altyre, and the Dall House on Loch Rannoch in Perthshire was identified, but after sending three Altyre masters (Pat Whitworth, John Fleming and Dougal Greig) to investigate it, Gordonstoun decided not to pursue the matter, leaving it to them to set up a new school which developed its own story and traditions. Mr Chew left Altyre a year before it closed to take over as Headmaster of the combined schools. David and Delphine Snell took over at Altyre for a challenging, but successful, final year. 'All too quickly,' writes Ian Lawson, 'the last year slipped by. Soon it was time for the farewell party in the panelled hall – from which all trophies had been removed to pre-empt souvenir hunters. Then there was the final Flag Service for both schools, held at Altyre for the first and last time.'

The Laird wasted no time in having the house unceremoniously demolished, much to the dismay of those of its erstwhile inhabitants who occasionally ventured back. (Ed Lightowler used some of the stones to build himself a cottage at Hopeman which he called Little Altyre.) By the late 1990s the site of the original house was occupied by a large cattle shed, many of the mature trees had gone, and the only remaining original building, the stables, was occupied by craft workshops and flats. Altyre existed for only nine years, but its memory inspires ferocious loyalty among alumni. The request for reminiscences sent out for this book produced more and fuller accounts from Altyre old boys than from any other group at Gordonstoun over the 75 years of its existence.

In 1953 Henry Brereton and Bobby Chew had been made Joint Headmasters of the whole school. Once the amalgamation of Altyre with the main school was underway in 1959, Bobby Chew returned to Gordonstoun as sole Headmaster, and Henry Brereton became Warden of the school and went to live in Elgin. Almost all of the Altyre masters were appointed to the main school, many as Housemasters: David Snell went to the Round Square, John Gillespie to Bruce House, John Downton to Hopeman Lodge and Ian Lawson to Altyre House, one of the two new timber blocks built specifically to accommodate the intake from old Altyre, the other being Bruce House. David Marshall went over to teach Geography, Alistair Paterson taught Art, along with Bob Waddell who also taught Pottery, and Tony White taught Music. The calibre of the staff at Altyre had certainly been recognised.

NEW BUILDINGS, COURTESY OF THE ADMIRALTY

In 1957 timber barracks at RNAS Evanton on the north side of the Cromarty Firth became available for sale. Ed Lightowler, the school's Clerk of Works, and Colonel W.S. Baird went to inspect them on 21 June 1957, and the school then purchased from the Admiralty 50,000 square feet of prefabricated wooden buildings as well as piping, radiators, boilers and handbasins for £2,840 10s. The school's joiners travelled there with the school lorry, dismantled the buildings and transported them little by little to Gordonstoun, where they were stored for two years under tarpaulins and in a wartime hangar on Sweethillocks at the east end of the estate.

When the decision had been made to quit Altyre House, Forres, the materials were already to hand to build the necessary accommodation for the now-enlarged school at Gordonstoun. Lightowler assembled a considerable labour force of local tradesmen who constructed five new buildings to his design. The first to be built was Windmill Lodge, completed in 1959. Next, starting a pattern of naming buildings on the main school grounds after latterday houses in the surrounding countryside, came Altyre House in 1960, which is still in use today. Its mirror image, Bruce House (named after the house of the same name at Altyre, Forres) was built at the same time, though its name was appropriated when the new Bruce House opened in 1990. Old Bruce House was then turned into Drama studios and renamed Ogstoun. Impressively inventive deployment of the Evanton timber also yielded the Estate Workshops, the Bank Block Classrooms and Domestic Block and the two cricket pavilions.

Also in 1960, though not using the Evanton timber, the Services Centre for the Rescue Services was constructed, housing the Coastguards, Fire Service and Mountain Rescue

Some of the RNAS Evanton huts just before they were demolished.

The Services Centre, the ground in front of it strewn with bicycles after a Fire Service call-out, c. 1970.

Left: Altyre House, 2011.

Below: Students setting off from Bruce House for afternoon activities, 2011.

on its ground floor, with, on its first floor, a hall large enough to accommodate the whole school. This provided the much-needed large space for gatherings of pupils and it functioned variously as an examination hall, a venue for drama productions and film showings, and the forum for sixth-form lectures as well as the school assemblies that the tiny Michael Kirk, serving as the school's chapel until St Christopher's was built in 1966, could not accommodate. Around that time, the Headmaster's house was built in the same neo-Georgian style.

ALTYRE HOUSE

Altyre House is possibly the house that has changed most radically in recent years. From its opening in 1959 until 2000, it followed the traditional lines of a Gordonstoun boarding house and was home for 50 to 60 boys between the ages of thirteen and eighteen. In May 2000 the Housemaster, John Whitaker, held a dinner for all staff, both past and present, to mark the closure of Altyre as a boarding house, in order for its interior to undergo extensive remodelling and refitting. For the next two years it was largely empty, although a few staff were housed there.

In 2002 it reopened as a mixed sixth-form boarding house. This was, of course, a radical departure from the traditional houses, and indeed Altyre remains one of the few mixed sixth-form boarding houses in Britain. To signal its new start, the original house symbol of a boar's head was replaced by a phoenix. The new Housemaster, Peter Thomas, accompanied by his wife Julia, was at the helm for this new venture. Inevitably, in a mixed house, the role of the Housemaster's wife becomes much more that of a Housemistress; Altyre also has both an Assistant Housemaster and an Assistant Housemistress.

In 2007 Peter and Julia Thomas moved on and Angus and Eileen MacEwan took over, returning to the school after sixteen years (Angus had been Assistant Housemaster at

Altyre 1986–91; Eileen was the first Assistant Housemistress at Plewlands). Unsurprisingly, Altyre has a very different atmosphere from other houses. Generally each term a Head of Boys and a Head of Girls are appointed, but occasionally when there is an outstanding student there is a single Head of House. Twice in recent years, this role has gone to a girl student, who has had the difficult task of trying to get the boys to clean the kitchen!

The house is at present home to sixteen girls (all in single rooms) and 24 boys (in a mixture of single and double rooms). In the central part of the building, where the students are free to socialise and relax, are the common room, TV room, games room, kitchen, office and Matron's office. One wing of the house contains the girls' studies and the other the boys' studies. It is, of course, strictly against the rules to stray.

Peter Thomas established the tradition of the Altyre Leavers Exped, which continues to this day. This involved a walk in the Culbin Forest, a boat trip across Findhorn Bay and dinner in the Kimberley Inn in Findhorn village followed by a bonfire on the beach back in the forest.

BRUCE HOUSE

Bruce House opened in 1959, built at the same time as the new Altyre House from timber sections reclaimed from the Fleet Air Arm base at Evanton. The house symbol is the spider which appears on the house tie. The first Housemaster was John Gillespie who was married to Susie Lachman's daughter, Ruth. He was followed for short periods by Norman Pares and Robert Greenshields. Angus Scott took over in 1968 and remained in post until 1983, when he left to teach in America.

Angus Scott was a tall, gentle, quietly spoken man who was both determined and competitive. He won Blues at Cambridge for both athletics and rugby and competed for Great Britain in the 400-metre hurdles at the Helsinki Olympic Games in 1952. He regularly sported his Hawks' Club tie. He was liberal in his approach to discipline and ran the house in ways which did not entirely conform to the prevailing pattern at that time. A particular departure was the conversion of a wing to bedsits for the senior pupils. Inter-house sport was a prominent feature, and Scott and his charges took this unusually seriously. After Gordonstoun House opened as a waiting house for third-form boys in 1976, gifted athletes were encouraged by him to consider Bruce as their first choice. This competitive spirit extended to house expeditions when small groups of boys would be dispersed in different directions from a base camp and Scott would return to report that his house had conquered some enormous number of Munros. 'With the fantastic Mr Scott,' recalls Per Gwalter (1979–83), 'we did such house expeds as climbing Tower Ridge on Ben Nevis carrying his little white Scotty dog that came everywhere with him.' Alasdair Gordon-Gibson, who joined his brother in Bruce House in 1968, remembers Angus Scott being nicknamed 'Bozo' because of his resemblance to a circus clown of that name who sported similarly long, bushy side-burns. He also recalls two West Highland terriers, Sally and Polly, 'who normally accompanied the nightly Housemaster's rounds of the dormitories and bedsits, shortly before lights out.'

Per Gwalter recounts, with only a trace of remorse, that, in his last term at school, his entire year in the house was demoted to junior rank 'as a result of overenthusiastic extracurricular activities': together with a friend, Chris Heyes, he had established an efficient method of brewing beer in a space beneath the floorboards, accessed from above through their wardrobes. Part of the proceeds of the beer sales financed meals out with young ladies at weekends.

Scott left in 1983 and was succeeded by Ben Goss, who remained in post for thirteen years. Goss had been a good rugby player when he was younger, and for many years was the master in charge of rugby, as Scott had been. Also like his predecessor, he was liberal in matters of discipline. After Ben Goss had left the old Bruce House, it was discovered that certain of its denizens had made further use of the space beneath its floors, constructing a facsimile of his office directly beneath the real thing!

Expeditions continued to be a strong Bruce tradition, though they became somewhat less focused on mountains and bagging Munros. Gairloch was a frequent destination, with canoeing around Longa a favourite activity. The Bruce Carol Service in the Michael Kirk became an important event in the house's calendar. Goss, a great enthusiast, threw himself wholeheartedly into all that he did.

The building (in 1987) of Plewlands as a girls' house had set new standards in boarding accommodation and exposed particularly the poor condition of several of the boys' houses. Plans were drawn up for a new Bruce House in the woods just to the north of Plewlands. It was built to the same high standards as Plewlands and was officially opened by the Duke of Edinburgh in 1991.

When Goss left the House in 1996, Richard Devey succeeded him as Housemaster until 2003. The current Housemaster is Robbie Hamilton.

Above: Setting out on a Bruce House expedition in 2005.

Left: Chris Heyes and Per Gwalter checking their latest batch of home-brew made below the floorboards in (the old) Bruce House, 1983.

Article in regional newspaper, 24 November 1970; and, far right, posing for a press photograph.

The Press and Journal

223rd Year   No. 36,160   THURSDAY NOVEMBER 26 1970   7d

GORDONSTOUN BOYS VOTE FOR GIRLS

By BRUCE TAYLOR

THERE has only been one topic of conversation among the 400 boys at Gordonstoun School the past few days—girls.

The board of governors' decision that the school go co-educational after September, 1972, could mean about 130 girls on the roll after the first four years.

And yesterday the majority of boys I spoke to seem to favour the change.

The school, founded in 1934 by Dr Kurt Hahn on the lines of the Salem School in Germany, is noted for its strict discipline and character building.

Peter Whitworth (14), from Yorkshire, who will be at Gordonstoun when the changeover comes, said that most of the boys in his form were in favour of having girls

PETER ROBINSON "An improvement"   RUARAIDH ADAMS-CAIRNS "More interesting"   DAVID DUNN "Difficult but . ."   PETER WHITWORTH Looking forward   ANDREW THOMS "A challenge"

GIRLS ARRIVE AT GORDONSTOUN

Largely thanks to the enlightened approach of the Headmaster, John Kempe, girls began arriving at Gordonstoun in 1972, a relatively early development for a boys' independent school. Initially there were ten sixteen-year-old girls embarking on A-level courses. The following year saw an intake at both junior and senior level. 'If Gordonstoun gets over the problems of co-education,' remarked the then Guardian Andrew Thoms in 1970 in a newspaper article, 'we could lead the public school system.' Another boy pointed out that their sister school in Germany was co-educational 'and it has worked all right there'. 'The school has been getting a bit stale lately,' remarked the seventeen-year-old Ruaridh Adams-Cairns, 'and the introduction of girls should bring in a new point of view.'

By 1975 Hopeman House (originally all boys) was composed half of junior boys accompanied by a few seniors from boys' houses and half of a growing population of girls. Windmill Lodge, also originally boys only, was now full of girls (the boys having transferred to Duffus), with many more waiting to enrol. By 1977 both houses were populated entirely with girls aged thirteen to eighteen. Rivalries ensued between the two girls' houses and partisanship between them in sport matched the boys' inter-house rugby competitions in ferocity.

During the late 1970s and through the 1980s there was a considerable increase in the school's intake of children from families resident in Scotland, many of whom were keen that all their children should be at the same school. Furthermore, both Kempe and the governing body were aware of the academic and social benefits of co-education as well as the financial incentive.

By the late 1970s even the most conservative members of staff had come to acknowledge that co-education was indeed the way forward. There were still relatively few female teaching staff, but after the admission of girls, the numbers gradually started increasing, with a number of young women who had recently graduated among the first

arrivals. Housemistresses lived with their charges in the girls' boarding houses. Three female members of staff lived in the top east corner of Gordonstoun House, and by the spring term of 1976 'The Bungalows', just up the hill from Hopeman House, had been completed and were ready for occupation by female staff and the Catering Manager.

By 1980 demand for girls' places had increased significantly, and in 1983, under the relatively new Headmaster, Michael Mavor, the top floor of Gordonstoun House became home to sixth-form girls who were joined not long after by junior girls. When the third girls' boarding house, Plewlands, opened in 1987, the students from Gordonstoun House were among its first inhabitants, along with some from Windmill and the year's fresh intake.

HOPEMAN HOUSE

In 1970, with the school expanding and the arrival of girls imminent, Hopeman Lodge was sold to part-finance the building of a new boarding house within the school grounds, Hopeman House. Initially the girls were accommodated in just half of the house, the structure of which – two separate wings linked by a staff corridor – lent itself to housing both boys and girls. By 1975 the school had its first female Guardian. These early pioneers paved the way for an expansion to the three current houses for girls.

Left: A school magazine meeting, 1975.

Housemistresses Diana Witts and Pat Johns – the latter remembered by Jane Hewitt (1975–79) for her two rather fierce corgis and a very characterful old car – saw through most of the first decade, while Windmill Lodge, converted from a boys' house in 1973, was established under Judy Cowx. Angela Clutton reflects on her time at Hopeman in the 1980s: 'The role of Housemistress was clearly influenced by Gordonstoun's tradition of enterprise and innovation. There was a stimulating degree of autonomy allowed in the day-to-day running of each house, enabling an individual character to develop, though the Headmaster's overview and vision ensured adherence to the school's first principles. Housemasters and Housemistresses at Gordonstoun had a teaching timetable only marginally reduced from that of a full-time member of the academic staff. This, along with commitments to one of the Services, activities, Projects and expeditions made one quick to appreciate that the school motto *plus est en vous* applied equally to staff and to pupils: it helped to be an extremely dedicated, unshockable insomniac . . . Life was hectic, at times bizarre – never dull! Being *in loco parentis* to upwards of 70 teenage girls meant creating a family atmosphere where each individual could thrive socially and academically: a secure base as well as a springboard to get the best out of work and play. Offering an open door to the Housemistress's study and flat, and being an accepted presence in the girls' part of the house, afforded the opportunity (sometimes) to pre-empt problems before they developed into anything more serious. Older girls played a crucial part in looking after younger ones; a good House Helper was indispensable. With an Assistant Housemistress and supportive House Tutors the house was provided with a strong adult team.'

The 1980s was a period when the number of pupils, especially girls, was rising; in Hopeman a temporary building provided extra study space and increasingly imaginative use had to be made of every corner of the House. The main house was laid out in the shape of an H and – in the 1970s at least – was referred to as 'H Block', after the infamous prison in Northern Ireland. The corridors on each side of the building flanked a mixture of single rooms for older girls and 'horseboxes' remembered by Jane Hewitt with affection: 'I loved them. They gave us our own little spaces with fold-down beds, a desk and wardrobe, but with open shelves giving views through into the adjoining horseboxes. They were rather cold, though – I recall sleeping in layers of tracksuits and jumpers which made it convenient for the compulsory morning run each day [. . .] I remember the difficulties we sometimes had in explaining to new pupils, especially those with foreign royal

One of Hopeman's 'horseboxes', c. 1980.

connections, just why we simply HAD to get out of bed and run round the rugby pitch.' The private study bedrooms were allocated to girls in examination years; the horseboxes – four adjacent rooms with half-height connecting walls – housed a senior girl at one end with three junior girls in the other three. This provided each girl with her own bit of personal space, while preserving her from isolation once her room door was closed. During the '80s, the horseboxes, ever popular, were still extant, but in the '90s, the low partition walls were extended to the ceiling to create individual rooms, providing more privacy for the occupants.

'There was no tradition of Matrons in individual houses at the school,' remembers Angela Clutton. 'It was incumbent on Housemistresses and Masters to note signs of well-being or otherwise: to recognise and distinguish, in someone operating below par, between social or work-related difficulties or a health issue. It was at this time that it was arranged for the girls to be given access to a female doctor. All houses operated a self-help system with duty rotas so that everyone had some responsibility for the smooth running of the house ranging from bed-changing, fire safety and drills to rubbish clearing. Everyone was expected to pull

Below: Hopeman House seen from the south-west. Bottom: Year 13 students relaxing at the weekend outside the main entrance to Hopeman House, May 2011.

her weight and make things work. The excellent domestic staff did all the heavy cleaning and took great pride in it. On one occasion, a very brown stained bath became the focus of consternation, the staining having mysteriously appeared overnight. It transpired that one enterprising youngster wishing to prolong her holiday suntan had used a packet of 72 teabags to "tan" in a hot tub!'

These were the days of morning run followed by Chapel and a full day of study and activity. After evening prep was a time for relaxing for 'brews' before junior lights out. Jane Hewitt again: 'My fondest memories are of late-night brews of hot toast and butter with mugs of tea or hot chocolate.' Older girls often took the opportunity to attend pupil meetings or various rehearsals for music and drama. A long but fruitful day! The girls accepted all of the challenges in and out of the classroom already established for the boys including Projects, Design and Technology in the work-shops, Duke of Edinburgh's Award preparation, seamanship, expeditions and Services. In the 1980s the school's ATC squadron opened up to girls, giving them the chance to fly with the RAF at Kinloss and Lossiemouth and to learn to glide. Two house expeditions would occur in the first year involving all new thirteen-year-olds along with the more established fourteen-year-olds, their Housemistress and staff more qualified in outdoor activities. As Angela Clutton relates, 'Pupils graduated from the house and form expeditions to more demanding experiences on the hills later on, but those early weekends away gave important opportunities for social integration as well as for developing a vital respect for the weather: its fickle changes of mood on mountains, wind and water. One group of youngsters looked particularly baffled at being asked to carry not just their lunches but cagoules, gloves

and hats in their day bags. It was a blisteringly hot day in mid-June for their climb of Lochnagar. The summit was reached but by then it was all change to a horizontal blizzard . . . A valuable lesson. In contrast, conditions on another expedition were blissful: canoeing down the Spey – boats and barbecues.'

WINDMILL LODGE

The estate windmill was built at some point before the eighteenth century, and on its site Windmill Lodge was constructed. This, together with a gamekeeper's cottage (which became the Housemaster's house) and the kennels (which had once accommodated sporting dogs), formed the group of stone buildings that later became a boys' boarding house. At first a wooden annexe was added to the erstwhile kennels to provide for resident domestic staff, and then, in 1951, it became a small boys' house under an American visiting member of staff, Josh Miner (who went on to head Outward Bound in the United States). Ian Sime followed him as Housemaster until 1959.

Norbert Kampf arrived at Gordonstoun from Germany in May 1956. Kurt Hahn and the Headmaster of Salem had come to the conclusion that he would never pass his final school exams there and that he should therefore transfer to Gordonstoun where he could specialise in his favourite subjects, History and Literature – a good move, as a year and a half later he passed the required A levels. 'In May 1956, I was greeted by a pale sun and temperatures I did not think were spring-like. One could smell the nearby sea and the landscape seemed barren and almost austere compared with the abundant nature surrounding Salem, where I had spent the last six years. I was assigned to Windmill Lodge and given a very small bed in a kind of Nissen hut dormitory

JOHN TAYLOR, at Windmill 1952–57, provides the reason for the blocking up of the doorway to the part of the building that had been the mill: 'Mr Sime ordered us to clear both lawns of stones and dump them in the doorway into the mill. The Navy had made a complaint. One of the boys was operating a radio that was jamming the signals between aircraft and RNAS Lossiemouth.'

Windmill Lodge. Students in standard sports kit emerging for afternoon activities (above); the boarding house shortly after its construction, the doocot converted from a windmill base clearly visible nearby (below); and girls socialising in the mixed common room, 2011 (bottom).

with twenty other boys, all of them much younger than me (I was nearly twenty) . . . I do not know for sure, but I guess I was one of the very few boys who had subscribed to a daily newspaper. As during daytime there was almost no opportunity to read a paper, I and another boy from Windmill, Emerich von Maltzahn, retired in the evening (our age meant we were allowed to go to bed later than the others) into two very old-fashioned bathtubs in the shower room where – in boiling hot water – we read in all tranquillity our papers: Emerich *The Times* and I *The Manchester Guardian*, with tea and biscuits on a board in front of us.'

In 1959 Windmill was entirely reconstructed, using timber sections from Evanton. After considerable renovation work by the estate staff in 1974, Windmill Lodge became the second boarding house at Gordonstoun to welcome girls. By the time Carleen Broad arrived at Windmill as its third Housemistress in 1996, few remembered its beginnings as a boys' house. Her predecessors Judy Cowx and Mary Evans had established a strong girls' house. Over the years various alterations to the accommodation had resulted in all girls having either single or double rooms with a mix of year groups in most corridors. The exception was the Glass Corridor, which was a quieter area for fifth-formers approaching their GCSE exams.

'Each house at the school somehow takes on its own character,' remarks Carleen Broad, 'and Windmill certainly had quite a large number of Scottish girls, together with the many lively and interesting girls who joined us in the sixth form, often from an international background.' Windmill excelled in inter-house sport over a number of years, meeting with particular success in cross-country events and athletics.

'The arrival of Windmill's first Matron was a great step forward,' remembers Carleen Broad, 'and both she and the sensible, supportive and caring ladies who followed her made a significant difference to the lives of everyone in the house, but particularly to the younger girls as they settled in. Every year sees the arrival of a new young Assistant Housemistress bringing different skills and interests.'

Windmill's Dance Show is an initiative that was originally suggested by girls at the house in the late 1990s, and it continues today. Organised and largely choreographed by a talented sixth-former, it presents an opportunity for every girl in the house to be on stage, whether she is performing a solo, dancing in a small group or taking part in a year group piece. The summer term barbecue is also an important tradition: at one time it was held on the beach at Covesea, but now everyone gathers on the grassy banks of the doocot for the meal, followed by a special cake decorated with the names of all the leavers and the presentation of songs or poems to each girl by a fifth-former.

Alisa Rose (1979–83) recalls the feeling of solidarity at the house: 'I lived in Windmill Lodge and the showers were normally cold though the girls were warmhearted. We had outrageous fun. The sweet voice of the third-former on duty waking us and putting on the lights saying "morning, morning run" echoes in my mind, followed by a good dose of Bob Seger, which thankfully was blasted every morning by a sixth-former who knew that's what was really needed to get us out of bed and running! We had many a crazy night brew: shared girl secrets and had few concerns since they were so quickly dismissed by a sense of being invincible because we supported each other so well.'

THE 1980S – A NEW ERA

In the 1980s the educational context in which houses and house staff operated changed considerably. At the Flag Service in September 1979, Michael Mavor announced the immediate abolition of the rank system, a bold move that can be seen to have heralded a new era. A more rigorous approach to academic endeavour was expected. The intake of girls and sixth-formers increased. Within the boarding houses, study accommodation was improved, and dormitories were to various degrees replaced by bedsits. Locker rooms disappeared, and there was an increased emphasis on the protection of individual privacy and property. Housemasters and Housemistresses remained powerful both on their own patches and in the running of the school, but increasingly they were expected to apply common standards to matters such as rules and discipline. House staff became more closely involved in the day-to-day running of their houses so that there was closer supervision of behaviour and interpersonal relations. Initially, senior pupils claimed that this development, in particular, was eroding the Trust System, but the change was gradually accepted.

PLEWLANDS HOUSE

Plewlands was designed by a committee largely composed of members of the school's staff, and its appearance and layout reflect their ambitions for it. Georgina Souter, who was to be the first Housemistress here, a position she filled for twelve years, remembers a long walk through the woods opposite the east end of Gordonstoun House with Michael Mavor when potential sites for the new building were being identified. The name of the house, which opened in 1987, derives from the location on which the Gordonstoun estate had been established, a place formerly known as the Bog o' Plewlands.

It was thought that Plewlands should complement in appearance the Scottish vernacular buildings already on the estate. The aim for the interior of the house was that it should feel spacious and airy, with generously proportioned corridors and a good-sized meeting room on the ground floor. This resulted in the large and prominent faceted room that sits to one side of the front entrance. Dormitories were to be small, with the youngest girls sleeping in four-bedded rooms, and the number of beds per room diminishing with the age of the children. On the top floor were single studies and the Assistant Housemistress's accommodation, sometimes enviously referred to as the 'penthouse flat'.

The location of Plewlands at the centre of the school meant that before long its mixed common room became a popular gathering place after supper and at weekends, and this remains the case. For some years, the annual house dance was a much-anticipated social event. Over the last five years there has been an annual cabaret, and Plewlands has long been used for junior socials. There is also an annual Christmas concert (formerly a pantomime).

In common with the rest of the school, pupils in the house come from a great variety of international backgrounds. Two memorable events which stick in the mind of Georgina Souter are the fall of the Berlin Wall, when a German girl, Kristina Spohr, was woken up at midnight to watch the event and enjoy the brew, and the liberation of Kuwait, when celebrations were led by Sara Al-Sayer, whose family had been exiled by the Iraqi occupation of their country.

Plewlands House, 2011. Students walking back to the house after the end of lessons at 2.45 pm (top); and above, getting together before changing for afternoon activities.

SARA AL-SAYER recalls the traumatic events that preceded her arrival at Gordonstoun, and the support she received while at the school.

'I had been enjoying my summer holiday with my family, as we always did, in Aberdeen. The invasion not only meant we were not able to go home, but also that all of our assets were frozen and we had to rely on the kindness and generosity of our friends. It was a devastating time for my family. As I was thirteen, I was able to comprehend the severity both of our situation, and that of all the people (Kuwaitis and Westerners alike) stuck in Kuwait. As September approached, my parents started talking about finding a school for us to go to. I will never forget my mum telling me – I crumpled into a sobbing heap as I realised that this was not going to be the little issue that would be over in a few weeks. My life as I knew it had changed forever.

'As we went to an English school in Kuwait, and we had once attended the Summer School at Gordonstoun, my parents made an appointment for me and my brother Khalid to meet the new Headmaster, Mark Pyper. We went up to see him before term started,

and my parents explained our situation. My brother and I were asked to take a small test as we didn't have any school records or report cards. Luckily, we both passed the test, and Mr Pyper very kindly agreed to admit us to Gordonstoun without payment until our situation was resolved. We were the first pupils that he had admitted!

'My first year at the school was a blur – I remember bits and pieces of it, like always getting in trouble for handing out "Free Kuwait" badges in class. I remember going to Mrs Souter's office to watch the news with Helen Webster (Appleby), whose parents lived in Saudi when Saudi was being bombed. I remember the stories I heard of the atrocities that were occurring in Kuwait to people we knew. I remember the compassion of the friends that I made at Gordonstoun.

'My life *was* changed forever, but I had a wonderful four years at Gordonstoun, and it made me who I am today. Because of that experience, I believe that no matter how bad things are, something good can come out of anything! Gordonstoun holds a very special place in my heart!'

THE MICHAEL KIRK AND ST CHRISTOPHER'S

The small, open building that had originally been the Gordon family mausoleum had already been turned into a chapel when Kurt Hahn first rented the estate in the 1930s, but its roof was unlined and its timbers were rotten. It was unheated and unlit. Even so, it was always a place with a very particular atmosphere. Norbert Kampf (1956–58), reminisces: 'I loved this place, its remoteness from the bustle of school life, the quiet and ancient graves and the wind-torn lonely trees surrounding the small chapel. The Michael Kirk remained my refuge during my entire time at Gordonstoun.' Many pupils over the years have enjoyed 'the serenity and grace' of this building alluded to by Ed Lightowler (who oversaw the restoration of the church and wrote a book about its history), including Prince Charles who refers to 'the magnetism of the Michael Kirk'.

Not until 1959 was it financially possible to do anything to this historic building which had by then been a place of worship for hundreds of Gordonstoun boys over 25 years. Two Gordonstoun Governors, Mme Hilda Besse (widow of an important benefactor to the school, M. Antonin Besse) and Mr O.A. Guggenheim, provided the necessary funds to renovate the chapel, and Ed Lightowler, the school's Clerk of Works, took charge of the task. The roof was removed and replaced with new timbers and an insulating lining. An electricity supply was installed enabling the chapel to be both heated and lit for services. Three ornamental lanterns were hung in the chapel – one which was already owned by the school and two copies made in the school workshops by

a couple of American pupils, the Williams brothers. Perhaps the most innovative change was the re-orientation of the pews so that the chapel could house a larger congregation. The altar was moved to the west end and the old harmonium to the east so that 60 boys (a complete house) could be seated. The heavy oak reredos (by now sadly riddled with woodworm) was removed, but the carved figure from it of St Michael slaying Satan in the guise of a dragon was retained and placed in the north-west corner. A new lectern was provided, made by Robert Thompson of

The Michael Kirk was originally erected on the site of the old Ogstoun Kirk as a mausoleum for Sir Robert Gordon (the 'Wizard') by his widow, Elizabeth Dunbar of Hempriggs, in 1705. Some 200 years later, Lady Florence Gordon Cumming transformed it into a chapel for the family's summer home. Extensive works included glazing the window traceries with leaded amber glass and installing heavy teak exterior doors where none had existed before. The chapel was consecrated in February 1901.

Kilburn, Yorkshire, well-known for his trademark symbol of a tiny carved mouse. A further generous gift from Mme Besse allowed for the harmonium, hand-pumped by boys, to be replaced with a pipe organ in 1964.

The Michael Kirk was the principal place of worship for the school until St Christopher's was completed in 1966. Anthony Montgomery (Chaplain to the school from 1968 until 1993) describes how well each complements the other: 'While St Christopher's presents the majestic transcendence of God (in its grand scale, its height, its light, the austerity of its architecture and its superb organ), the Michael Kirk could not be more different: here pupils can respond to its eighteenth-century antiquity, to the intimacy of a sacred place just large enough to provide a very special focus for one boarding house on its own; perfect too, for the weekly celebration of Holy Communion open to all denominations; always much in demand for christenings and among staff and former pupils for weddings, and staff services at Christmas time. The churchyard itself remains an active burial ground and here lie the mortal remains of several staff and their families.'

1968, when Anthony Montgomery arrived at the school, was a time of great political and social upheaval internationally, and this was mirrored within the school itself: 'Gone were the certainties of an era dominated by the forceful figure of Robert Chew, Henry Brereton himself and, in pastoral terms, the much-loved figure of W.P. Young and alongside him in W.P.'s final years, Philip Crosfield. But these men left a legacy in its way as revolutionary as the time itself: St Christopher's (which was, deliberately, never referred to as St Christopher's Chapel to mark its multi-purpose intent).'

St Christopher's was built thanks to a generous gift from the Douneside Trust in memory of the late Lady McRobert of Douneside and Cromar who had suffered, by any measure, great tragedy in her personal life: in 1922 when their three sons were still children, she lost her husband, and by 1940 all her sons had died in separate flying accidents. She is said to have remarked: 'I cannot go and be a pilot myself. Had I been a man I too would have flown on such service.' The architect was Patrick Huggins of Murray, Ward & Partners, a Gordonstoun old boy, whose plans were selected from three submissions. The brief specified that as far as possible the building should be one in which members of different denominations 'feel equally at home'.

Although far from perfect – the roof leaked, the acoustics were difficult and there were no toilet facilities – both the uncompromising concrete exterior and an interior conceived in-the-round offered a challenge to the new decade. The eight outside doors to the ambulatory give access to eight widely spaced entrances to the almost circular central chapel, which has a dished floor and raised

St Christopher's, built 1965-66. The original brief to the architect made it clear that conventional ideas of what a church should look like were to be subordinated to religious and practical requirements, not least allowing 600 pupils, staff and visitors to get in and out with the least possible delay. The virtues of honesty and simplicity were to be expressed in the architecture; contemporary materials were to be used, but the building was also expected to complement the ancient mansion house of Gordonstoun. It is no accident that the great curving exterior walls come together in a shape resembling that of a ship's prow.

Below: An informal game of cricket on the North Lawn.

Above: Pupils gather in St Christopher's at the end of the spring term, 2011.

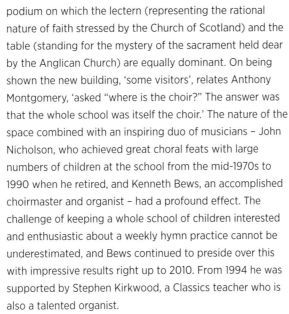

podium on which the lectern (representing the rational nature of faith stressed by the Church of Scotland) and the table (standing for the mystery of the sacrament held dear by the Anglican Church) are equally dominant. On being shown the new building, 'some visitors', relates Anthony Montgomery, 'asked "where is the choir?" The answer was that the whole school was itself the choir.' The nature of the space combined with an inspiring duo of musicians – John Nicholson, who achieved great choral feats with large numbers of children at the school from the mid-1970s to 1990 when he retired, and Kenneth Bews, an accomplished choirmaster and organist – had a profound effect. The challenge of keeping a whole school of children interested and enthusiastic about a weekly hymn practice cannot be underestimated, and Bews continued to preside over this with impressive results right up to 2010. From 1994 he was supported by Stephen Kirkwood, a Classics teacher who is also a talented organist.

So, while St Christopher's was in its way revolutionary, it was also reassuring. 'There were sometimes demonstrations,' recalls Montgomery, 'such as the occasion when Round Square had planned a mass walkout: but it was – much to their annoyance – scuppered by a junior member of the house. He had been reading the works of Karl Marx, and, deciding to take a spot of direct action, threw a "bomb" at the Headmaster. Fortunately, cricketer though he was, it failed to reach the right spot, and, being rather badly constructed, it fell to pieces in front of the altar.'

The ambulatory provided a cheerful, noisy meeting place for pupils and staff alike when they came together for the daily service, but strict silence reigned in the chapel itself. 'This', recalls Anthony Montgomery, 'was not always easy for pupils to handle: discipline was difficult and I well remember John Kempe asking me, "Do you think we should give up compulsory chapel?" I was glad that I felt bound to answer, "If you give it up, you can never get it back."'

Anthony Montgomery remembers being surprised that the numbers presenting themselves for confirmation preparation required three classes a week to cover Anglicans alone; local clergy provided instruction for members of the Church of Scotland and Roman Catholics. More recently, much to Montgomery's satisfaction, the service of confirmation has become an inter-denominational occasion. 'One of the very best aspects of Gordonstoun', he reflects, 'has always been that the staff are encouraged to immerse themselves in whatever aspects of school life they feel able to contribute to: the Chaplaincy is no ivory tower and the Chaplain is fortunate to be encouraged to participate in teaching all subjects, on the games field, in the Services,

within the boarding house, in the Staff Common Room, and to be exposed to school life warts and all; but that is only one side of the coin; the other is that the pastoral dimension is a combined effort of Headmaster, staff and senior pupils.'

From the start, St Christopher's has been much more than a place of Christian worship. The school has always welcomed pupils of other faiths and nationalities and of course people who are not committed to any formal religion or denomination. The emphasis has consistently been on promoting respect for the views of others and enabling individuals to explore their own spirituality. In recent times the vestry has been turned into the Meeting Place, a room set aside for faith group meetings such as the Muslim Prayer Group, the Christian Union and the Faith Inquirers' Group.

Although the daily weekday services have usually contained a hymn, a prayer and a reading, they are the only occasions when the whole school meets together and so also fulfil the role of school assembly. The Headmaster has traditionally presided on one day each week and assemblies on other mornings have been led by the Chaplain, members of staff or pupils. In this way the school as a whole receives feedback on all sorts of activities, including international projects and expeditions.

Outside the morning services, St Christopher's has been used for operas, musicals and both orchestral and choral concerts as well as performances by outside groups such as the Philip Jones Brass Ensemble, Ensemble Bash and Ronnie Scott's Band. In the days before there was a purpose-built Music department, the chapel area and the ambulatory were both used for rehearsals by instrumental groups and choirs, and for a while the ambulatory was used for the weekly lunchtime concert. Enoch Powell, Ted Heath, Terry Waite and other well-known figures have addressed the school in this building. The ambulatory is frequently used as an exhibition space where pupils can browse before entering the chapel area, and for many years now has been the main venue for the annual Services Convention.

Though new developments have been significant, at heart the function of the chapel remains unchanged. St Christopher's is still a place where students are, above all, encouraged to reflect on compassion – on what Kurt Hahn saw as the antidote to William Temple's 'Spiritual Death', a place that values all individuals in a way consistent with its distinctive Christian ethos, encouraging and enabling all to realise their fullest and deepest potential. It remains (in the words of the dedication spoken by the Rt Revd Dr C.K. Sainsbury on 19 July 1966) 'a place of reconciliation and peace . . . the centre of the community [dedicated to] the unity of common purpose in the love of God and Man.'

FOOD AT GORDONSTOUN

From the beginning, no matter how primitive the buildings in which meals were taken, there was an emphasis at Gordonstoun on eating for health. In the early days the diet was simple and wholesome, though as with much else at the school, there was the odd unusual touch. 'What on earth do you call this stuff?' asked Joseph Pease as a new boy in 1938. 'It's muesli, lovely stuff. Please give me yours if you don't want it', came the reply. Muesli was served as a pudding for dinner and fought over at breakfast if there were any left-overs from the night before. 'One of the first things I noticed' (Pease again) 'was that boys waited at the tables.'

Gordon Adams recalls during the war years in Wales, being fed 'very well indeed, although I only recall one dish, and that was fish pie.' He too remarked on the oatmeal and milk mixed with whatever fruit was in season 'with a German name that sounded like "mushily".' Robin Rimmer, however (1956–58), was not as satisfied: 'One of the most important lessons the school taught me was not to waste food. We were growing boys and were constantly hungry. Meals were wolfed down in the remote hope of "seconds" . . . The lake in front of Gordonstoun House was full of small and unfortunately inedible, scaly little fish. But it also contained eels. I only ever caught one, a monster of nearly a pound. Bex the Biology teacher allowed us to cook it in his room. It was barely dead and still writhing slowly as they do. When we put it into the hot pan, it convulsed as the flesh contracted and made a horrible buttery mess over Bex's carpet. But it was delicious. Now I know it should have been cut into short sections. I think Bex enjoyed watching us learning by our

mistakes. [. . .] There were no fat boys at Gordonstoun. We were starved. There wasn't much food about in those days so we had to be creative. I once even ate a fox. It was not fun.'

In the late 1940s, recalls Ronald Gilchrist, the kitchen of Gordonstoun House, on the ground floor at the east end, was responsible for feeding pupils in Gordonstoun House and The Round Square (in the north-facing room on the ground floor) and Cumming House (on the first floor). Duffus had its own kitchen. 'There was some excitement when it was announced that a new Housekeeper had been appointed, who, it was quickly discovered, was young and attractive and dynamic. Hilda Thomson (the brother of a contemporary of mine) stirred things up in more ways than one. She applied professional standards to her job of managing the staff and what were somewhat primitive and basic facilities and in fairly cramped conditions.'

Maver Sutherland was employed as Head Housekeeper in charge of Catering and Housekeeping from April 1954 until 1979. She was given one room facing the lake to serve as her sitting room, bedroom and office. The kitchen was still on the ground floor of Gordonstoun House, and all food

Opposite: The Refectory, built 1975, refurbished in 1991.

Mealtime in Gordonstoun House, 1955.

Breakfast at Duffus House, c. 1955.

Soup service at Plas Dinam, 1942.

ECHT MUESLI

Thanks to David Conway, who in the 1980s asked Gordonstoun caterer Jean Alexander, who asked Maver Sutherland, who asked Frau Berger, Kurt Hahn's housekeeper, we have the recipe for a now-familiar breakfast which seemed so alien when it first appeared at Gordonstoun:

> 1 cup rolled oats
> half a pint milk
> 2 tbsps sugar

Soak the oats in the milk and sugar overnight. Add one grated apple (including skin), the juice and rind of one lemon, one or two sliced bananas (not possible in the war years). Strawberries and other seasonal fruit, cream and nuts may be added.

TWENTY-FIVE YEARS OF CATERING

Jean Royan has clear memories of her long career in catering at Gordonstoun:

'I arrived at Gordonstoun on 15 October 1979. I was 26 years old, and the perfect career move had presented itself earlier than expected. I took over from Maver Sutherland who had ruled over both housekeeping and catering for the previous 26 years. Little did I know that, between us, we would enjoy the privilege of looking after a remarkable spectrum of pupils for over half a century.

'Maver remained a good friend with a great sense of humour until her death in 2008. Many pupils will have their own memories of her, and I know she would have enjoyed her obituary in the *Edinburgh Evening News*, in which her first meeting with Her Majesty the Queen was described by a member of staff in the following terms: "Maver did not meet the Queen – the Queen met Maver!"

'I was very fortunate to spend seventeen years of my time at the school in the bungalow behind Hopeman House. The view from my window – which overlooked the playing fields – was a constant reminder of the changing seasons: girls with duvets round their shoulders going for their morning runs, Summer School activities, even a week of pre-season training for Aberdeen FC, when a young manager called Alex Ferguson reminded his players to keep in mind: '*plus est en vous*!' Perhaps his and Manchester United's future success owed something to this inspiration?

'When I arrived at the school in 1979, the school ethos that a healthy mind needed a healthy body was thoroughly understood and pursued with some vigour. It struck me that both the healthy body and the healthy mind needed the appropriate fuel on which to function. Determined to succeed in this new environment, I challenged myself to reverse common beliefs about public-school catering and instead to create a Refectory experience that was interesting for the pupils and provided the most appropriate for the school regime – all within budget, of course.

'Little did I realise that joining expeditions to the Cairngorms, trips with pupils on *Sea Spirit* and playing the role of accident victim on the cliffs at Covesea would all figure in my job!

'The school management recognised the importance and opportunity of a good Refectory experience, and in 1985 I was fortunate enough to be awarded a Catey Award as UK Catering Manager of the Year, a reflection of the support given to me by the Board of Governors and the late Michael Mavor in my efforts to make the food experience at Gordonstoun an important and satisfying part of life there.

'When I left Gordonstoun in 2004, I took with me a whole catalogue of memories ranging from royal visits, through jubilees, parent days, summer schools and even the 1983 production of *Joseph and his Amazing Technicolor Dreamcoat*.

'*Bon appetit* Gordonstoun! Part of me will always be purple and white.'

was cooked on an open range equipped with narrow flues to lead the smoke outside. These were cleaned by Colin and Isaac, the latter known as 'the prune' because he didn't bother to wash off the soot that came with the job.

After the amalgamation of Altyre with Gordonstoun had taken place in 1960, various alterations both to buildings and to dining routines ensued. The main part of Gordonstoun House was converted into dining rooms, the original ground-floor dining room was converted into store rooms, and food was carried up to the first and second floor dining rooms in lifts. Hopeman Lodge had a kitchen which provided breakfast, but for other meals boys from there joined the denizens of Cumming House in the North Room. Bruce and Altyre used the South Room, and Round Square the second floor. Boys from Duffus House, which had its own kitchen and dining room, ate there until the Refectory was built in the mid-1970s. Alasdair Gordon Gibson (Bruce, 1973–78) evokes the pre-Refectory atmosphere just after the arrival of girls at the school: 'Perhaps the last surviving bastion of the boys school was to be found at that time within the primitive customs of the house dining rooms, in the days before the Refectory was built. Tradition had it that the most junior boys would be designated as "waiters" to the rest of the house. I never discovered the system (I assume that there was one), but two or three young boys would be selected to spend a fraught week bringing food and water from the catering trolleys to satisfy the incessant demands of the remaining 60 plus persons in the house, all of them ravenous, thirsty and impatient. Then, almost before this was completed, were expected to clear the plates, re-load the trolleys and begin again with the next course. I am certain I was not the only one who felt he had scarcely time to eat, during his appointed week as a waiter. Nourishment was obtained from stolen moments snacking on bread and pudding as we wheeled the trolleys out to the catering lifts in Gordonstoun House, where the dining rooms were located in those days. The same rotation of waiters would begin again, a week or two later.'

In September 1975 the new Refectory was ready for use. There was now a cafeteria style of servery, and an outside catering firm was engaged. As payment for their services amounted to ten per cent of the Gordonstoun food budget, this move was not a success, with insufficient money left to satisfy the ravenous appetites of hungry adolescents. All this improved beyond measure with the appointment of the school's own caterer, Jean Alexander (now Jean Royan). Jean Royan retired as Catering Manager in 2004 and was succeeded in the post by Angus Smith.

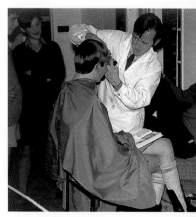

LINEN ROOM AND SANATORIUM

No account of the early years at Gordonstoun should be without mention of Aina Main, who retired in July 1975 after 37 years in charge of the Linen Room, looking after the laundry and mending the clothes of the entire school with her faithful team of sewing ladies from Hopeman. Aina started work in Duffus House in 1938. She had been introduced to the school by Mrs Gordon Duff of Hopeman Lodge who had presented her with a prize for sewing at Hopeman School when she was a schoolgirl. When the school was evacuated to Wales during the war, Aina went along too. She sometimes recounted one of her first experiences there: she and other female members of staff had been given a bothy to sleep in; one night they awoke to a strange rubbing noise and discovered that they were surrounded by a herd of cows!

In 1945, Aina returned to the Gordonstoun Linen Room – a timber extension to a stone building near the old sanatorium, to the west of the Round Square, which, at the start and end of each term, was a hive of activity. Each day at break, boys would come to see Aina about their laundry and mending. Aina could tell a boy's size just by looking at him, and without so much as a tape measure, she would find a uniform to fit. Her office walls were covered with photographs of past pupils. The building once occupied by Aina was finally abandoned in 1991 when a new laundry and Linen Room were built behind the recently refurbished Refectory.

Top left: The Linen Room; top right: submitting to the attentions of one of the barbers who came to the school; both photographs 1969.

Above: View looking west from the Round Square just after the war. The Sanatorium is on the left.

The Linen Room (now known as the Sewing Room) is still in existence, but the days of a band of eight lovely ladies patiently darning socks, turning shirt collars and patching the seats of trousers are long gone. By far the largest sewing task is now labelling uniform and casual clothing – items of the latter having increased exponentially since students were allowed to change into their own choice of casual clothes after the end of activities at 4.30 in the afternoon: 'The array of up-to-the-minute fashion that finds its way to our in-house laundry and Sewing Room', remarks Carol Gabb, 'is the size of Ben Nevis'.

The Sewing Room is annexed to the school shop where all the school uniform can be purchased (no more trips to Edinburgh to visit the school outfitters, Aitken & Niven). The shop also stocks memorabilia and a wide range of student essentials – spray deodorant and mouthwash being the most popular items.

The original Sanatorium had been an old building to the south-west of the Bank Block Classrooms. Ronald Gilchrist remembers it in about 1947–48 being a pre-fab with Sister McGowan in charge. With the advent of girls in 1972, a new Sanatorium was built behind Cumming House with separate accommodation for boys and girls.

UNIFORM

When Gordonstoun first opened, the uniform was simple and uniquely casual for the times. Navy serge shorts and a navy jumper were worn with a grey open-necked shirt in the morning, and after afternoon activities the boys changed into grey shorts and jumper for the evening. Both jumpers were V-necked, and no tie was worn. Socks were thick, grey and woollen and constantly descended to the ankles. David Conway remembers that new boys were recognisable by their lack of uniform, and that the right to wear the grey shorts, shirt and pullover was bestowed at the end of the first term.

Joseph Pease recalls a friend already at the school telling him 'that I would have to wear the daytime dark blue until it was announced that I had "gained my school uniform", by which he meant the grey shorts, shirt and pullover worn in the evenings and on Sundays. The only marks of distinction on the grey pullovers were either a white or purple stripe on the left breast. George [a friend] went on to tell me how the basis of life at Gordonstoun was a system of trust. To an outsider it might seem ridiculous but it did work, instilling self-discipline. It was when I had shown some degree of trustworthiness that I would be allowed to wear the school uniform. Later I would be able to wear a white stripe to show that I had been awarded my

Day Uniform, c. 1970.

Training Plan and could be trusted further. A purple stripe was for Colour Bearers and Helpers, equivalent to Prefects in other schools.' David Conway records that at some point in the first ten years of the school Kurt Hahn apparently announced that the Gordonstoun System was 'in jeopardy' and white stripes would henceforth be worn only by those who had proved themselves to be worthy of the honour. John Pease (1944–47), brother of Joseph, remarked that there was only one back pocket to school shorts, 'sufficient to hold a handkerchief. Pens and combs were kept in your stockings.' John Shackles, at Altyre in the mid-'50s, maintains that the single back pocket was designed to prevent boys slouching around with their hands in their pockets: 'If you ever see anyone walking around with their hand in their back pocket, there's a good chance that they were at Gordonstoun.' In the 1960s Mrs Chew (wife of the Headmaster) had a reputation for throwing packets of garters out of a window of her flat in Gordonstoun House if a boy passed with socks round his ankles.

In 1972, with the arrival of girls imminent, shorts were replaced with long grey flannel trousers, the grey pullover from the Evening Uniform was worn in the mornings and boys were allowed to wear their own clothes in the evenings. An attempt was briefly made to control what was worn, and long dark cord trousers were specified for evening wear, but neither this, nor another move – to replace the fine-knit V-necked jersey with a round-necked heavy knit pullover – lasted for long. At about the same time, a formal 'Going-out' Uniform was introduced: for boys, blazer, tie and flannel trousers with a white shirt. One of the girls who arrived at the school in 1975, Jane Hewitt, remembers wearing a grey flannel skirt, thick knee-length socks, polo shirt and a baggy pale blue jumper for lessons, with a tartan skirt – 'kilts were for men or boys!' – and a smarter jumper of the girl's own choice for Sunday chapel and trips out of school. The casual uniform specified for the rest of the time was baggy cords and plain jumpers. Eventually the socks were replaced by navy tights, and the multi-coloured tartan skirts exchanged for one in the Gordonstoun tartan – a combination of soft colours representing the hills, moorland and sea of Moray. 'Boys with sartorial ambitions', she notes, 'wore knee-length grey shorts or kilts, the less-cool (though undoubtedly warmer!) wore long trousers, with similar jumpers and shirts.'

Today's uniform consists of the familiar V-necked blue/grey sweater, still worn for boys with a grey open-necked shirt (though now of polyester rather than the itchy wool mix of yesteryear) and for girls with a white polo shirt. Capes, duffel coats and puffa jackets are now all things of the past, replaced by wind and waterproof coats. Formal uniform comprises blazers, house ties and smart white shirts with calf-length Gordonstoun tartan kilts for the girls.

Above: Going-out Uniform, 2011.

Right: Day Uniform, 2011.

MATRONS

In the early days there was a Matron for Gordonstoun, who looked after the health and wellbeing of all pupils, as there was for Aberlour. Not least because there were so few female staff at the school, for junior boys especially, Matrons could become important figures when one was so far away from home. And then there was what Robin Rimmer describes as 'burgeoning adolescence'. He continues, evoking feelings that were probably shared by a good proportion of boys over the years: 'In my last term at Aberlour House we had a very pretty Assistant Matron who was much loved by everyone. A couple of hours after lights-out either she or Mr Delap, the Headmaster, would do the rounds of the dormitories to make sure everything was in order. If anyone was still awake, Matron could sometimes be persuaded to tuck them in and give them a peck good night. It was a heady experience. Emboldened by the fact that it was the last night of term, I decided that one little peck was not enough and as Matron stood by the door I rushed over to her and put my arms around her for a final hug. The door opened and light shone in from the passage. I assumed it was she who had opened it, so didn't disengage. Unfortunately, it was Mr Delap and he had seen all. Deeply embarrassed and frightened, I was sent to his study, a sad little figure wrapped in a blanket as our dressing gowns were already packed in our trunks. He didn't seem angry, more curious. "Do you have any deep feelings for Matron?" he asked. "Me, Sir? Oh, no Sir", I replied. Somewhere in the distance a cock crowed, for I adored her with all the passion of a twelve-year-old.'

When Matrons were appointed to individual houses in autumn 1997, Housemistresses and Housemasters were released from much of the domestic work associated with running a boarding house. The presence of Matrons also meant that there was now always an adult presence in the houses to cover for the times when the Housemistress or Housemaster was away from base for some reason or other, as is still the case today. Some of those who had been involved in the school from the early days regretted the move, feeling that taking responsibility for household tasks was character-forming for the pupils and part of the overall ethos of the school, and this was undoubtedly the case to some extent, but the reality was that the staff presiding over houses had for years faced a huge and many-faceted task in organising all of this rather arduous work, often doing much of it themselves.

Top: Cricket on the lawn at Aberlour House, where the junior school was located from 1948 to 2004.

Above: Quiet reading in the Aberlour school library, c. 1950.

GORDONSTOUN JUNIOR SCHOOL

Gordonstoun's junior school started as 'a junior department' in Duffus House in 1935, with Henry Brereton as Housemaster, although there were very few children of preparatory school age until 1936. The first Headmaster was Pat Delap, who arrived in 1937 and, accompanied by his wife Dolly, moved eighteen junior pupils up to Wester Elchies in Strathspey.

Wester Elchies was built in the Scottish Baronial style, with the older parts of the building dating from the seventeenth century. A school prospectus of the time described it as 'situated high on the banks of the river Spey in a romantic setting of mountain, moor, woodland and river. Although it is within twenty miles of Gordonstoun, the immediate surroundings of the two schools form a striking contrast – Gordonstoun in the fertile "laigh", Wester Elchies amidst the high hills. It is an environment calculated to challenge the imagination and enterprise of the boys.' The house had an important early observatory built to house a large telescope (long gone by 1937) purchased from the Great Exhibition in 1851 (it cost the vast sum of £1,000 and all the local bridges along its route to Wester Elchies had to be strengthened). But like many large country houses that were expensive to maintain, Wester Elchies was demolished in the 1960s.

Colin Crole, who was at the school in its first year at Wester Elchies, reports that 'the Delaps ran a happy school with a marvellous chef, John Murray. Teachers included Frerichs, Coutts, Bickerstaff, Diana Pares (sister of Norman

Pares) and Commander Holmes, a splendid teacher who was not entirely approved of by Delap. Most memorable were the Shakespeare plays *The Tempest* in 1939 and *A Midsummer Night's Dream* in 1938.'

Unlike Gordonstoun, Wester Elchies remained open throughout the war years, and by 1939 the school roll had grown to 35. Jimmy Fraser recalled 'digging out the curling pond one winter' that year, 'and on a miserable afternoon in the sleet and snow of November, lifting tatties for a nearby farmer, Ben Rinnes white in the background.' There was no electricity at Wester Elchies and lighting was by means of acetylene gas, made on site in a small brick building with a large carbide dump outside it. Fraser wrote of 'the fearful excitement of evening group forays against the seething mass of roots on the tip in the woods at Elchies, beside the great mound of spent carbide from the lighting plant.' Allan Shiach (post-war) recalls that 'the carbide dump consisted of a white odourless compound, and was Out of Bounds though the rule was never enforced. It provided a playground of the best kind, alternating between the Grand Canyon with hidden Indians lurking and the deck of the *Titanic* with orchestra playing.' Heating of the school was by log fires, and collecting kindling and sawing up wood were everyday activities. A shower consisted of an enamel jug of cold water, administered by Matron McGowan. When a shower, two baths and ten hand basins were installed, Mr Hahn said sadly, 'the pioneering spirit of Wester Elchies has gone'.

Dolly Delap noted that 'the snow was really quite a major factor in our lives at Wester Elchies', and David Byatt (1939–45) remembers being snowed up for six weeks in 1943 and having to fetch stores from the road one-and-a-half miles away 'using sledges drawn by Shetland ponies. My load was a large cardboard box of carbolic soap bars. The sledge overturned and the corner of the box was damaged . . . The wet bars of soap kept slipping out of the box as the enthusiastic pony slithered its way back and it took a very long time to cover the last half mile uphill to the school.'

Food was not short during the war, in spite of rationing: Dolly Delap kept hens, geese and turkeys, and milk came from the local farm. One of Dolly's hens used to go up the back stairs and lay eggs on a bed, even, on one occasion, when the boy who owned the bed was in it having an enforced day's rest. Barty Brereton, who joined the school as a ten-year-old in September 1943, was scared of Dolly's turkeys. 'I was always last out of the side door for the early morning run, past Mrs D's hens and turkeys. The biggest gobbler, with angry red wattles, invariably chased me, pecking at my bare legs.'

The Delaps were known to the children as Mr and Mrs D and formed a much admired team in a very happy school. 'There was a family feeling in it all', recalls Hilary Hamilton Grierson, one of the first girls. 'Mr D was a great listener and when someone talked to him that person was made to feel important . . . Mrs D was the most efficient person one could ever imagine. Every detail of the domestic side was at her fingertips. She worked harder than anyone else.' The Delaps employed German or Italian prisoners of war from the camp at nearby Archiestown and billeted three in the bedroom at the top of the tower. They also housed some of the great many German Jewish refugees to whom Kurt Hahn gave refuge.

Hahn retained close supervision of Wester Elchies, and Islyn Davies (1939–44) recalled that he would pay periodic visits to the school, causing apprehension and concern to various members of staff. 'As a result of one of these visits, we all had to change dormitories because Dr Hahn believed that when everything ran too smoothly it led to compla-cency and therefore some sort of upheaval was necessary.' Hahn's preoccupation with good health at Gordonstoun extended to the children at Wester Elchies, and he instructed the local doctors that any child with a temperature of 102°F or above must be visited immediately. Matron McGowan was an important part of Wester Elchies; to a small boy like Islyn, she was a comforting figure in a starched uniform, smelling slightly, but not disagreeably, of disinfectant. Wester Elchies was very much an outdoor school and Islyn said of it 'one of my most vivid recollections of my time at Wester Elchies was the hours spent in practical work, endeavouring to resurrect the curling pond. It had been neglected for many, many years and was filled up with mud and leaves and overgrown with bushes. The smell of the mud lingers on to this day.' Many will remember the ponies and the riding which took on a professional slant when Victor Saloschin joined the staff in 1941.

Anthony Craig attended Wester Elchies and Aberlour 1952–56: 'School life was an alternative existence – one almost forgot what home was like. The autumn term, especially, was long – thirteen weeks without a break, though sometimes parents, or parents of friends might appear and take one out at a weekend for tea at hotels in Aberlour or Elgin. The compensation was growing up in the country. At Wester Elchies, far from getting away for an October break, we were put to work behind the tractor for a week, tatty-howking on the home farm. In the courtyard of the old house (sadly now demolished) Mrs Delap strangled hens between a broomstick and the cobbles, and John the chef strung up slaughtered pigs, shaved and gutted them. You knew where your protein came from!'

In 1948 Wester Elchies was no longer large enough to accommodate the whole preparatory school, and Gordonstoun purchased Aberlour House on the opposite side of the river Spey to run in parallel with Wester Elchies, where Pat Delap remained as Headmaster with the younger pupils while at Aberlour House, Charles Brereton took charge of the older pupils. Aberlour House Limited was formed to run the two houses.

Anthony Craig remembers the occasion when a violent storm struck much of Britain on 1 February 1953: 'We were confined to the house, watching the trees outside being battered by the storm. The next day we walked around the shattered wood and saw the fallen trees and the trunks of those still standing, coated on the windward side with packed ice and snow. The clearings created by the storm in the woods around Aberlour were put to good use when, in the summer term, the school used them to present its plays. I remember *Toad of Toad Hall*, but especially *A Midsummmer Night's Dream* because in that I had a small part and spent a great deal of time sitting around in the woods during rehearsals.' Robin Rimmer was ten when he first went to Wester Elchies in January 1956: 'It was so cold. My favourite place was the log-room where I could cry quietly for my mummy. But after that first term it was huge fun. I went on to Aberlour House and then to Cumming House with my brother Nigel. Our father died in December 1958 so I had to leave after that spring term.'

In 1963, when Wester Elchies finally succumbed to dry rot, the junior school was combined at Aberlour House with Wester Elchies used for a short time only as a dormitory. A year later, Pat and Dolly Delap retired, Toby Coghill took over as Headmaster, and the name of the school was changed to Aberlour House. In 1973 the former Headmaster's flat in the main building was adapted to accommodate 30 girls: the whole school was now co-educational. Under the leadership of Sir Toby and Lady Coghill, Aberlour continued to expand and flourish.

Per Gwalter speaks evocatively of his time at Aberlour: 'In retrospect, it was tough in many ways, but had a fantastic atmosphere and every day was a kaleidoscope of activity and opportunity. The cane was introduced to my backside on a number of occasions and served to ensure that I never did the same naughty thing twice. One thing that stands out was ensuring one got some time in sitting on one of the few radiators scattered through the main building during the Scottish winters. I also remember the dormitories where the big windows were kept open making it as cold inside as out. There was a time, the winter of '76, I think, when the thermometer plunged to below –20°C.

PHILIP SHERTEN, at Abelour in the 1950s, was put in charge of a dormitory at Aberlour: 'During the holidays I had purloined a copy of one of my mother's ghost story anthologies and devoured it with relish. So on returning to school and being in charge of the dormitory, I decided to tell some of the ghost stories I had read. After a week or so, I had a captive audience of terrified, traumatised boys, some of whom now had trouble sleeping and would suddenly burst into tears for no reason. Alas, I was discovered and hastily demoted. I still love a good ghost story though!'

Above: Bedtime in Aberlour House, 1966.

Below: Performance of *A Midsummer Night's Dream* in the woods around Aberlour, 1953.

Top left: M. Cavalier's French class at Aberlour, 1979.

Top right: Enjoying wintry conditions, 1980.

Above: Morning run at Aberlour, c. 1965.

Classes were stopped (ink froze in our pens) and we were allowed to wear long trousers. I also clearly remember turning up with a continental duvet when everyone else had sheets and blankets. This meant that making my bed in the morning was a very quick exercise indeed, one flap of the duvet and job done! In Aberlour I remember there was always something going on and it was a place where one was given the freedom to plan one's own expediton, draw the food and tents from stores and disappear on our own into the hills at a very young age – it was a source of pride, fun and adventure.'

In 1989, after 25 years, Sir Toby and Lady Coghill retired. David Hanson, long-standing Deputy Head at Aberlour, briefly became Acting Head, until John and Jane Caithness took up the reins in 1992 and he returned to his original post as Deputy Head until his retirement in 1997. When the Caithnesses retired in 1999, Neil and Carol Gardner were appointed Joint Heads, and they continued to run the school until the end of 2003 when it was decided to move from Aberlour House in Strathspey to a new bespoke building on the Gordonstoun campus. Robert McVean became Head of the junior school at the end of 2003 and with his wife Laura oversaw the move to the Gordonstoun campus where the couple has continued to lead the school successfully since.

The transition of Aberlour to the main school was an adventure in itself as the building was not quite ready to move in to at the end of the summer holidays. So while the builders put the finishing touches to Aberlour House, the 60 children and staff went on Outward Bound activities in Perthshire for ten days. On their return from this adventure, everyone was able to move into the new school, with the benefit of the strong friendships forged just before. The girl

boarders lived in the Medical Centre for a couple of days and the boys stayed at Homewood House (behind the sewing room, originally built to provide accommodation for female domestic staff when the Refectory was renovated). To the sound of the pipes and with much excitement, the inhabitants of Aberlour House entered their new home on 22 September 2004.

The school proved to be an enormous success and very quickly was at full capacity. After the first year temporary classrooms were built at the school to cater for the demand. In 2006 Homewood House had to become a Year 8 boys' boarding house, while a new extension of the school was built to double the school's capacity. This extension provided four new dormitories, four new classrooms, increased staff accommodation and a splendid new hall, which was opened by HRH The Princess Royal on the 1 November 2007. Now Aberlour House is a popular junior school, welcoming children from all over the world who wish to embark on a Gordonstoun education, as well as providing many places for local children to be day pupils or weekly boarders. In 2010 the total number of pupils grew again and almost all the boarding spaces are now occupied. The children have access to many of the facilities of the main school at Gordonstoun, among them those associated with outdoor education, the sports hall, the Design and Technology workshops, Art, Drama and Music. True to the school motto, *plus est en vous*, pupils of all age groups challenge themselves in the many aspects of school life. Highlights of the school calendar include drama shows, concerts, expeditions, project activities, team sports, the Junior Highland Games and the ever-popular inter-club competitions.

3

LEARNING AND CREATIVITY

'Education must enable young people to effect what they have recognised to be right, despite hardships, despite dangers, despite inner scepticism, despite boredom, and despite mockery from the world' KURT HAHN

Year 13 Chemistry class, 2011.

AT THE TIME WHEN first Salem and then Gordonstoun were founded, Kurt Hahn's vision of an all-round education for the young people in his charge was highly unusual. Among the early pupils there were not a few who had found it hard to flourish in the narrow and highly competitive context of traditional British public schools, and for whom it was something of a relief to attend a school where the ethos was so firmly based on getting the best out of each child in a very broad curriculum.

In the original school prospectus a distinction was made between 'academic staff' and 'character training staff', as at Salem. But Gordonstoun soon adopted the British public-school model where teaching staff were involved in all aspects of the curriculum. This system allows staff and students to build a rapport not attainable solely in classroom encounters. Today, all full-time academic staff also play a major part in activities and the Services, as well as having a pastoral role. However, increased professionalism in sport, guidelines from national governing bodies and the simple time demands of modern

Above: Year 9 Information Technology class, 2011.

Opposite: *Let's Dance* Show, 2010.

academic courses all now conspire towards the increased specialisation and compartmentalisation of staff roles. The challenge for the future, as this process continues, will be to retain the benefits of the broad spectrum student–teacher contact while maintaining the highest standards of specialist tuition.

Over the 75 years since the start of Gordonstoun, very many aspects of life at the school have changed, but its ethos remains its own, with clear emphases on Hahnian principles that have endured. Most schools, for example, discuss their curriculum primarily in terms of the academic programme, with all other activities viewed as extra-curricular. At Gordonstoun the curriculum has traditionally been viewed in broader terms, with academic achievements taking their place alongside mass involvement in seaman-ship, the Services and expeditions. This breadth of experience is what sets Gordonstoun apart, and its belief in this style of education was roundly vindicated in spring 2009 by an HMI inspection, which recorded as particular strengths of the school:

- young people's well-developed confidence and their readiness to take on challenges in a wide range of situations
- the quality of leadership and responsibility shown by young people in and beyond the classroom, and their wider achievements
- the contributions young people make to the local and wider community through their service activities

Mark Pyper, Headmaster of Gordonstoun 1990–2011, makes the current ethos plain in a recent interview: '[Gordonstoun] really is the one school, certainly in the UK, that actually has a philosophy which says, what really counts is personal development – how people grow up. They obviously need to have exam qualifications and develop certain skills but it's how they grow up as people, so they can lead rewarding lives for themselves and do a bit for their communities which is really unusual . . . If you have a highly academic school there are only certain people who can go there; if you have a school which majors in sport all the time you have to be good at sport or the arts or whatever it is. The thing about Gordonstoun is that it is a suitable school for everyone.'

From the beginning, the school attracted staff excited by Hahn's ambitious aims. Henry Brereton (Headmaster 1953–59; Warden 1959–68), writing in 1968, remembered an exchange he had had with Hahn the first time they met in 1935: 'Our conversation was concerned with the disadvantages of sharply marked divisions in modern life

and in schools; class divisions, national divisions, the unreal division between academic education in the classroom and what goes on outside, the sharp unreality of the divisions between subjects. There has been some continuous policy to erase as unreal these sharp lines of division and definition.' He then goes on to describe a marking system in which pupils kept tally of their own progress on individual charts 'instead of mark percentages, recorded with official finality, allow[ing] greater flexibility in the meting out of encouragement or disapproval than the more rigid systems of tradition.'

Brereton remarked that Gordonstoun was at that time 'something of a comprehensive school . . . it has never set out to be a school specialising in coaching for examination nor organised so that the clever get the most skilled attention. There are no school prizes in the ordinary way and no orthodox mark system or form order. Care is taken not to favour the clever boys particularly in the social life of the school . . . [this leaves us] the opportunity of providing a truly "liberal" education, one in which the superficial mental manipulations and memorisation are played down and the meaning of things given the chance to claim the mind's attention.'

Projects were one innovation that was gradually picked up by schools in both the public and the private sector to the extent that they are now commonplace. Described by Brereton as 'a halfway house between formal studies and outside activities', this was a Gordonstoun institution which, to begin with, had no parallel elsewhere in British schools. Projects covered an almost unlimited range, as a few listed by Brereton demonstrate: 'A biological survey of the Gordonstoun lake. Model of a theatre. A study of the fishing industry of a section of the French Atlantic coast. Reconstructed model of a model "T" Ford with a history of all the problems that had to be overcome. Survey of all the bridges on the Lossie from source to mouth. Study of the wine industry of the Moselle valley. Study of the monastic communities on Mount Athos', and so on. The account of one individual whose Project was making a collection of seaweeds from the Moray coast is a splendid evocation of the benefits to be had from this *grande passion*, so far from classroom study: 'It is the demand that you do something entirely on your own initiative, in your own time, at your own pace. It is no less than a test and training in creativity. My choice was collecting seaweeds and this activity was to influence my life. To wander each Saturday in all weathers on the beaches was not all sheer delight: at first I was often afraid of the loneliness and the elements. Slowly I learnt the satisfaction of solitude and private contemplation of nature.

Above: Metalwork in the Projects Workshops located in the Nissen huts, c. 1961, with Jim Rawlings (who had been at the school since the 1950s) at the anvil.

Above right: Repairing a motorbike in the Pocock Workshops with the Head of Technology, John Cleaver, who greatly expanded the range of technological expertise practised at the school in the early 1970s.

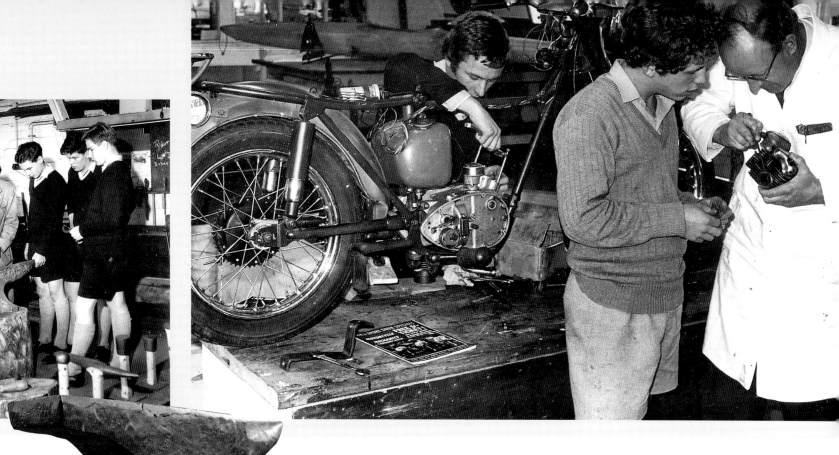

The anvil that still resides in the Design Technology workshops, a reminder of the days when all pupils were encouraged to try their hand at some form of manual craft or labour.

On looking back it now seems to me that through the lonely Project I was enabled to conquer the fear of loneliness within myself: never craving company for company's sake. Much later it was necessary to parachute frequently alone in the desert: fear frequently accompanied me but never the fear of solitude . . . Seaweeds taught me patient observation and the value of classification.'

Early on, Hahn managed to convince captains of industry and Oxford and Cambridge selection boards to accept a Project from Gordonstoun alongside traditional A-level qualifications as proof of a candidate's potential to be a good student. Projects continued to be allocated time in the school week through the 1980s and into the '90s, though by that time the focus had narrowed and they mainly involved art, pottery and working with wood or metal – activities to which the facilities in the Art School and Sunley Technology Workshops were well suited. Projects or course work are now commonly included in the syllabus of most examinable academic subjects, not least as a long-term result of the advocacy of Hahn, and this fact, which

inevitably put pressure both on staff time and on space within departments, meant that the traditional Gordonstoun Project was eventually squeezed out.

Not all Projects were solitary affairs, however, and Hahn's belief in the value of craft led to the development of the Project Workshops, which were established in some of the Nissen huts left by the army's wartime occupation of the school. Hahn adopted Plato's opinion that sculpture is best taught by a practising sculptor, painting by an artist and craft by a craftsman. He set great store by the character-forming effects of learning manual skills: 'There is a fine tradition of craftsmanship in our neighbourhood,' he reported to the Governors of the school in 1935, 'the boat builder, the smith, the carpenter, instruct our boys in their own workshops, and have proved as good educators as the artisans in the Salem valley.' After the war, building skills were encouraged on the estate with the help of estate staff (especially during the renovation of the Round Square) and a skilled carpenter taught carpentry.

John Kempe (Headmaster 1968–78), deciding that a department was needed 'to foster Design and Engineering and to relate to the new world of technology by encouraging boys to strip engines, design hovercraft, play with electronic equipment', arranged for the stripping out of the Nissen huts to accommodate the activity, where it functioned for eight years until the huts finally had to be abandoned and it moved to the Sunley Technology Workshops in 1979 with David Welton as Head of Department. Welton placed considerable emphasis on craftsmanship and creativity. He was ably assisted in his early years by Jim Rawlings, a trained craft teacher who was particularly skilled in metalwork and blacksmithing. Design swiftly became established as an A-level subject and the department focused chiefly on one-off artefacts which were finished by the students to a very high standard. The range of objects made and materials used was wide, and included millinery, a film, numerous pieces of furniture, including items of children's furniture for Duffus village hall, trailers of various sorts, a folding boat (produced by the daughter of a Cockleshell hero), a rescue cradle and covers for the school cricket square which are still in use today. In the lower part of the school all pupils passed through the department and made objects in wood and metal such as garden trowels and small wooden boxes. On Open Day there was always a magnificent display of artefacts produced both within and outside formal class time. When Rawlings retired in 1983, he was replaced by Andrew Thomas, a graduate in three-dimensional design. This opened up the possibility of offering Design at GCSE level, which eventually happened towards the end of Welton's tenure. Welton was succeeded as Head of Department in 1999 by Andy Cox. The combination of multi-media approaches to design, computer technology and the demands on designers in industry, among other issues, have all played their part in changing the nature of Design courses at the school, as has the shift in emphasis in the examination syllabus. Students now make prototypes that are suitable for batch or mass production, and must show that they have considered such things as cost effectiveness and the marketability of their designs. The department's enthusiasm for developing craft skills lives on, however. Cox himself, an able craftsman, is a maker of musical instruments.

Following the founding of the school, and for as long as numbers remained relatively small, the balance between academically able and less able pupils was not a major issue, and the school's ethos, and perhaps financial necessity, required a comprehensive intake.

By the late 1970s, when the school was of course much larger than in the early days, the considerable proportion of pupils with VRQs (verbal reasoning quotients) well below the level required for grammar school entry was reflected in the substantial number of entries for CSE rather than GCE, as well as the significant minority of pupils who repeated the fifth-form year.

Many staff identified a dilemma. In a small school, pupils with academic and other difficulties could be given substantial individual attention. In a larger school the reality was that it was the more able who coped best with the

One of a number of hovercraft designed and built in the Pocock Workshops in the 1970s.

FARQUHAR OGILVIE-LAING (Altyre, 1983–88) recalls the mixed feelings he had about his experience of school, which nevertheless gave him his first taste of a skill that was later to become the basis for a highly successful career.

'I was not the ideal student by any stretch of the imagination. This was due to the fact that my interests during my teenage years bore very little resemblance to the school's curriculum. And if I am honest, and to the annoyance of my parents, I was a typical teenager who did not have the faintest idea either how lucky I was or what I was going to do with my life. I scraped through O levels, and left school soon after. I played all the sports keenly (but not very well) and joined the Mountain Rescue Service. The high point of my school experience was a cruise on *Sea Spirit*. I did not involve myself academically and I hated History and English, in particular. In spite of this apparently unpromising beginning, I hope the following account will explain the gratitude I feel towards this unique school.

'What I am about to describe started in the Technology Department one term in about 1986. I was interested in moulding and casting. We were shown the moulding boxes, the "green" sand, the small furnace and some aluminium ingots. There were strange-looking tools for compacting the sand, and an irresistible atmosphere of creativity and adventure. Mr Welton showed me how to pack the sand on to a small wooden pattern placed in the bottom of the moulding box. Then the box was turned over and another box placed on top. Sand was once again packed. Then the two boxes were separated and the wooden pattern removed to reveal a negative shape of the school crest, complete with bireme, which was of course backwards in the sand. The mould was then reassembled and the furnace hummed to melt the aluminium alloy at 650°C. As the melting point approached, my excitement and anticipation reached boiling point. The furnace was silenced; it was time for action. Mr Welton slid the lid of the furnace over, revealing a red-hot 5 kg crucible

multi-faceted nature of the place, while the less able often found things difficult. Under Michael Mavor's leadership (1979–90), the commitment to catering for pupils with academic and other difficulties remained, but it was accepted that the school would work better for everyone if the more educationally challenged students formed a smaller proportion of the whole. In his first Open Day address he told the parents: 'I don't think that the boys and girls work hard enough here'. He then set about improving the academic culture.

Gordonstoun had the advantage of having become coeducational ahead of most of its Scottish competitors. Parents increasingly wanted to have all their children in the same school and in a competitive world were insistent on academic success. As girls' numbers increased, it became possible to be more selective with boys. It was made clear to pupils, parents and staff that pupils who were not prepared to work hard, or who prevented others from so doing, would not be tolerated. Study conditions in the houses were improved with new builds and refurbishments that substantially increased the number of single studies and

bedsits. Mavor strove to soften the school's image, particularly amongst prep school heads. He was himself a Scot, educated at schools in Scotland, and he served on the boards of several Scottish prep schools. There was a marked increase in the proportion of pupils who were Scots or who were domiciled in Scotland, and this meant that parents visited the school much more often and showed a more active interest in all aspects of their children's development. The tightening up on the academic front was paralleled in other areas. Mavor paid great attention to detail. It was perhaps inevitable that some of the longer serving members of staff would feel that he was turning Gordonstoun into a traditional independent school. By the time he left for Rugby, it was certainly in the academic mainstream.

A major innovation in the second half of the 1980s was the introduction of Information Technology to the curriculum. An IT centre was developed in wooden buildings in the Bank Block, which had originally come from RNAS Evanton and had at one time housed domestic staff quarters, the Linen Room and classrooms. The conversion of the accommodation and the development

containing the most beautiful, shimmering, silvery, molten aluminium. I was not allowed to handle molten metal, but watched intently from a safe distance. The crucible was clamped using the bell irons, and pulled from its little hell. It was then handled with concentration and care. It seemed like the most important and valuable object in the world. It was carefully tilted and a fine flow of metal poured into the mould. A moment later it was all over, and an acrid plume of smoke emanated from the small mould as the metal cooled inside for ever.

'The other day I dug out this casting from an old shoe box of school memories. It still gleams as if it had been made yesterday. But something happened that day that may just have changed my life.

'I now run Black Isle Bronze Foundry in Nairn, just along the coast from Gordonstoun. I have a staff of thirteen, in the only purpose-built foundry in the UK. The furnace does not hum, it roars, and the crucible will hold 250 kg of bronze at 1150°C. We have just completed the 27-foot-tall *Core Values* sculpture at Twickenham for the RFU, the monument of Harry Hotspur in Alnwick, Sir Alfred Gilbert's *Eros* (as in Piccadilly Circus) and the *Monument to the Rainbow Division of Alabama* for the battlefields of the Somme. The foundry champions creativity, heritage, fine art, architecture and manufacturing skills. Our order book is full as I write this, with orders from all over Europe.

'It took me years to realise how lucky I was to be introduced to so many things, so many experiences, leadership, interests, sports and people. It would not be true to say that Gordonstoun opened doors for me, but, far more importantly, it did show me where the doors were. And as the awkward, hesitant years of adolescence gave way to complete and utter focus I realised how lucky I had been. I am now even passionate about English and History.'

of the department owed a huge amount to Tim Schroder who was appointed Head of IT in 1992.

One of the key aspects of Kurt Hahn's philosophy of education has been the focus on positive expectations for every student in all aspects of their school life. In the late 1990s, in keeping with this aim, there was a change of emphasis in the culture of the school in order to build further on this ideal through a number of initiatives. The first step was to develop the School Charter in which the expectations of students' behaviour are set out in matching sets of rights and responsibilities. Each student is required to sign the Charter within the first weeks of his or her arrival. At the same time, in 1997, the Discipline Handbook was drawn up where the school's expectations were deliberately expressed positively as a code of conduct, rather than as a set of negative rules. This document also contains the school policies regarding alcohol, relationships, smoking, etc., with the scale of consequences for poor behaviour clearly set out.

1998 saw the introduction of Credit Slips as a system of recognition of success and positive contribution in all areas of school life. First paper and now electronic, these are read out in house meetings once a week; in addition the student receives a personal e-mail with the detail of the Credit Slip, and academic credits are also recorded on a student's report. In this way, generosity, acts of service and real effort both inside and outside the classroom can be recognised and rewarded. In 2008 Colour Bearer Credit Slips were

introduced so that Colour Bearers could reward other students for acts of generosity and care. This was, to some extent, to balance out the Colour Bearers' right to hand out Sunday Labour for minor infringements of school rules. At the end of each term, a cup is given to the person who has collected the largest number of Credit Slips.

A further development in rewarding positive achievement has been the end of term Prize Giving where endeavour just as much as achievement in all areas of school life are recognised through the award of Certificates of Merit and Distinction. The names of all students who are commended for their contracts are displayed, together with a photographic record of the highlights of the term. Trophies are awarded throughout the school year for team events, for example, in sport, rather than for individuals; thus there is no move towards a traditional speech and prize-giving day.

In 2001 the Student Development Scheme was introduced through which every student's achievements are recorded by their tutor on a weekly basis under the headings of Academic Work, Sport, Cultural Activities, Outdoor Education, Responsibility and Service. The weekly discussion with a tutor helps students to understand the aims of the citizenship training they are receiving and to balance their activities and contributions and thus make sure they participate in all areas of school life. This culminates at the end of Years 11 and 13 in the Founder's Award which each student gains in one of three categories – Pass, Merit and Distinction.

Year 9 students demonstrating sandboards made in their Design Technology classes on the beach at Lossiemouth, 2010.

DRAMA

Hahn was passionate about Shakespeare, being fascinated especially by the repeated failure of good and noble characters, which enabled him to make a lesson out of their misfortune, to point out how they might have saved themselves. A small number of plays were repeated many times: *King Lear*, *Hamlet*, *Macbeth*, *Julius Caesar* and *Henry IV*. John Pease remembers some of those early performances: 'July 1945 we did *Macbeth*. Kurt Hahn had 'phoned the C.O. at RNAS Lossiemouth to see if he would ground all aircraft while the performance was taking place, but the request was refused. There was a story that my brother told me of a pre-war performance of *Macbeth*, when a plane from Lossiemouth had appeared over the treetops just as Macbeth was saying his lines, "Hang out the banners on the outward walls; the cry is still 'they come'. . . What is that noise?" In July 1947 we did *Julius Caesar*. Godfrey Burchardt managed to get the school orchestra under the stage, which had been built at the bottom of the south lawn, and they provided suitable music for the performance.'

Although Drama always flourished at the school, it was based mainly on individual inspiration, enthusiastic teachers passing through, student initiatives and the like, and remained a largely extracurricular activity and a sporadic occurrence, despite some memorable productions. During the nine-year life of Altyre, Forres, a tradition of musicals quickly built up, largely as a result of what Tony White, one of the teachers there, referred to as 'the skilled enthusiasm of John Gillespie'. White describes being approached by a boy called Graham Neil within a few days of his arrival: ' "Sir, can you write tunes – I mean, if I sing you a tune, can you write it down?" "Yes." "Well, can you write this one down? It's for this term's pantomime." And what followed, in

December, was *The Babes in the Wood.* It was very home-made, full of in-jokes, and with music culled from all sorts of sources. But the genre developed, and two years later *Robin Hood* appeared, followed in succession by *Tottering Towers, Kleinemunschein* and *Beastie Beware!,* the last of which we were bold enough to present at the Edinburgh Festival Fringe. I still do not know how we managed to write, rehearse and perform each of these within a single autumn term, and on a tiny stage constructed for the occasion.'

Barry Cooper remembers Drama at the school in the '60s: 'My first encounter with Drama at Gordonstoun was an operetta. Not the usual Gilbert and Sullivan, however, but our very own Gillespie and White, two members of staff who had between them devised *The Curse of the Pomfrets*. All right, the plot was as far-fetched as Gilbert's, and the music no advance on Sullivan, but it was very cleverly put together and excellently produced. The main dramatic event at the school was the annual Shakespeare play in the Round Square. Well it was meant to be annual, but it didn't happen in 1964 – ironically the Shakespeare centenary year. In 1963 it was *Julius Caesar*. I was cast as Lucius, who has to sing a song at one point, accompanying himself on the lute. The school didn't have a lute, but they dug out a mandolin (with one string missing) from the Art department and I had to learn to play it. Someone commented afterwards that they were amazed at how the producers managed to get the "recording" to sound so realistic that it seemed to be actually coming from my mouth and the instrument I was holding!

'In 1965 it was *Henry V*, with "God for Harry, England and Saint George!" My most abiding memory is of the King hurling a tennis ball on to the roof of the Round Square, after being presented with a set as an insult from the French king. It was great to have a real French boy speaking

Above left: Performance of Ben Jonson's *The Alchemist*, 7 July 1970.

Above: *King Lear* being performed in 1938.

Below: Prince Edward in *Hay Fever*, 1982.

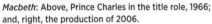
Macbeth: Above, Prince Charles in the title role, 1966; and, right, the production of 2006.

some of the French lines in the play, and a real Welsh boy playing Fluellen. The final performance was threatened with continuous rain, so it was hastily moved to the Services Centre, where the King had to throw his tennis ball at a curtain, to prevent it bouncing all round the auditorium.

'The next term we did *Macbeth*, again in the Services Centre. This required making a model of Macbeth's head, for the line "Behold where stands the usurper's cursed head", and producer Eric Anderson decided against this (it would have caused practical problems and probably produced titters from the audience). Instead he bowdlerised the line to: "Behold where lies the curs'd usurper, dead", which we could cope with. I played King Duncan, so my opening lines were: "What bloody man is that?" Not the sort of language one would normally use in front of royalty (who were in the audience on the last night).

'Other plays were performed occasionally, but one I particularly loved was a nativity play; no ordinary nativity play but an ancient German one, filled with beautiful chorales sung between scenes. I was told it used to be performed every year but was now done only once every four years; this production was actually one of the last, if not the last. The cast was hand-picked by Godfrey Burchardt,

and for some boys it was their first experience of acting, but the casting was brilliant. And each of the three boys playing the learned scribes later won places at Oxford or Cambridge. The event has been little mentioned or reported, but for me it was one of the highlights of my time at Gordonstoun.'

House drama had always happened, and the 1980s saw every house involved in something somewhere, sometimes combining resources (*Guys and Dolls* – Hopeman/Round Square; *Trial by Jury* – Plewlands/Bruce), sometimes winging it alone (*Up 'n' Under* – Duffus). Student revues became a popular end-of-year feature. Staff were encouraged to have a go at productions, and staff shows became an annual event culminating, after a series of staff revues, in riotous productions of *Joseph and His Amazing Technicolor Dreamcoat*, *Grease* and *Bugsy Malone*. These were notable for involving the whole staff (not just teachers) and often spouses or partners too. One can see the importance of musicals in this list, and the period was notable for the joint Drama/Music department productions which became annual highlights of the school year, often on Open Day. From opera (*Gianni Schicchi, Carmen*) to musicals (*Guys and Dolls, Street Scene, Kiss me Kate, West Side Story*), successive batches of students trod the boards, somehow finding time to commit to these productions amongst the Gordonstoun maze of Projects, cruises, expeditions and examinations. Almost all of the productions were inspired or organised by the indefatigable John Lofthouse, who had arrived at the school in 1980.

A feature which would surely have gladdened Hahn's heart was the extraordinary range of sites on which productions occurred and the creative improvisation and imagination needed to carry them through, especially on the technical and backstage side. *A Midsummer Night's Dream* was staged on the lake, *The Visit* on Gordonstoun House steps, *Hotel Paradiso* outside St Christopher's, the *15-minute Hamlet* on a wagon touring the compound at night by torch-light, *The Duchess of Malfi* and *The Merry Wives of Windsor* in the Round Square, *Bedroom Farce, The Boyfriend, The Sea* and *Ghost Train* in the Services Centre, *Top Girls* in Plewlands Common Room, improvisations in Cumming House, *The Master and the Maid* in the South Room and all the operas and many musicals in St Christopher's. In all this the Drama department was indebted to the uncomplaining efforts and thoroughgoing support of the estate staff, most spectacularly in the building of vast stage sets when productions were put on in the chapel. Alison Montgomery, wife of the Chaplain, was for many years responsible for the design of numerous impressive sets.

In 1990, when old Bruce House was abandoned as a boarding house, it was turned into drama studios and renamed the Ogstoun Studios. At last there was a dedicated space for Drama at the school, albeit with relatively few facilities. More significant changes were imminent, however, when innovative developments in the National Curriculum, a greater awareness of the value of Drama as a core element in an all-round education, and the arrival of a new Headmaster (Mark Pyper) all led to an upsurge in thespian activity at the school. By now two things had become obvious: the need for a performing arts centre and the establishment of a central organisation to formalise all this essentially extra-curricular activity. In 1991 the new post of Director of Drama was filled by John Lofthouse. Soon Drama was established as a core element in the Gordonstoun curriculum and treated on a level with all other academic departments in terms of budget, resources, professional training and examination responsibilities. Productions continued apace, but Drama now developed in other ways: as a component of PSE (personal and social education), a support for other departments, and as a useful element in the school's public relations and admission initiatives (the Prep Schools' Challenge, for example). Tours were undertaken (the Edinburgh Festival Fringe, school tours). At the same time, students were

entered for public examinations for the first time (GCSE Drama and A-level Theatre Studies), and Drama became an obligatory subject in certain curricular areas such as the third-year Arts Carousel.

In 1996, when Lofthouse left the school, Nigel Williams took on the mantle of Director of Drama, inheriting an impressive performance programme and the beginnings of Drama taking off as an academic subject. Harking back to the earliest dramatic productions at the school, Mark Pyper had reintroduced outdoor productions of Shakespeare in the summer term, and these have continued: a memorable 'tribal' rendering of *Macbeth* on the South Lawn one year, a performance of *The Tempest* around a huge ship built in the Round Square in another; touring productions of *Romeo and Juliet* and productions of *A Midsummer Night's Dream* and *Hamlet* in Edinburgh have earned the school a high reputation (and gratifying reviews in the press) for quirky, inventive and refreshing interpretations.

Over the sixteen years that Williams has been in post, the achievements of the school's Drama department have been nothing short of impressive. His clear objectives for this aspect of life at Gordonstoun were (and remain) multi-faceted: to consolidate and push curricular Drama as an important academic subject that is accessible and available to all students in younger years and genuinely challenges more senior students as an academic study of choice; to create a programme of performances that is diverse, relevant and challenging to the school community whether they be performers or spectators; to take the work created into the local community, and further afield, both to share it

Below: Oberon in *A Midsummer Night's Dream*, which was staged outside in the Round Square, 2009.

Bottom: *Cabaret*, 2003, performed in the Services Centre, before the Ogstoun Theatre was built.

and to showcase the school's achievements; to manage a dedicated performing arts building in such a way that the whole school community has a sense of ownership of it, as well as providing a window onto the impressive quality of Gordonstoun's performing arts.

Drama as an academic subject is now a popular choice at both GCSE and A level, as well as a compulsory part of the curriculum for all junior students. The healthy numbers of students opting to take Drama in Years 10 and 11 speak for themselves, and results have been excellent: two Gordonstoun students were among the top ten GCSE Drama achievers in 2008 out of 62,000 entries nationwide. Edexcel, the school's examination board, has used units of Gordonstoun's work as exemplar material for the current curriculum, and recordings of exam performances as material for training examiners.

Williams has worked hard to balance a policy of 'theatre for all' – whereby there is an opportunity for all students of all standards to get involved in school productions – with providing the chances to shine for the most skilled performers in the school: 'In the same way that while all students can enjoy sport, it is still important to have a first team to set standards for others to aspire to, and to carry the school flag in fixtures and tournaments, so it should be in theatre.' Among multiple achievements, Williams picks out a number of highlights over the last decade and a half: 'In 1997, Gordonstoun was asked to peform a new play called *Asleep Under the Dark Earth* at the Eden Court Theatre in Inverness as part of the nationwide National Theatre Connections new writing project – the first of many produced by the school as part of this scheme. This has involved trips to the Royal Lyceum in Edinburgh over a number of years. In 1999 the school was paid the considerable compliment of being asked to represent Scotland at a European Youth Theatre Festival in Grenoble with a dyamic reinvention of Shakespeare's *A Comedy of Errors*; in 2000 a new musical, *That Was Then*, was taken, along with a full programme of street theatre and dance, to America's East Coast, marking the beginning of the international touring projects that are now an integral and important part of the department's work. In 2001 Gordonstoun was invited to perform a new play called *Happy Endings* at the Royal National Theatre in London as one of the best youth theatre groups in Britain.

'In 2005, in what must have felt like the most fitting reward for the efforts of all those who have made the Drama department such a success, the Ogstoun Theatre complex was opened – the fruit of the consistent and persistent support for this project of Mark Pyper and the

Board of Governors led by Bryan Williams. Nigel Williams's enthusiasm for this new dedicated facility is palpable: 'We now had a beautiful purpose-built space that could be both three working studios during the teaching day and, in a quick transition with the removal of a clever acoustic screen, transformed into a 200-seat raked auditorium with a huge floor space and back stage area . . . The building has worked hard in its brief lifetime. There is not a moment in the school week when it is not in use for lessons, rehearsals, workshops, activities, productions, dances, visiting groups, concerts and even the staff show. It has served us well to date and continues to smile back at us through its fantastic atrium foyer with its huge photographs of previous shows and past students . . . The numbers of theatre alumni grow each year . . . We now have students working on mainstream television as performers, directors, theatre actors, film actors, drama lecturers and film producers.'

DANCE

Before 1994, if you had mentioned Dance to an OG they would probably have spoken about their experiences learning traditional Scottish dancing and described taking part in reels sessions in the South Room of Gordonstoun House. Sixteen years on, things are very different. Scottish

Top: *Columbinus*, 2009 – a play created by the United States Theatre Project and provoked by the April 1999 massacre at Columbine High School in Jefferson County, Colorado.

Above: HRH The Princess Royal at the opening of the Ogstoun Theatre in 2005. Princess Anne served as a Governor when her children were at the school and since 2001 she has been Warden, sharing the role since 2003 with Sir James Weatherall.

reels are still danced in the South Room, but now students can take GCSE Dance, AS Dance and even become members of Gordonstoun Youth Dance Company. There are already three ex-Gordonstoun dance students studying Dance in higher education, including one who is completing a degree in Choreography.

In 1994 Sarah DaBell, a newly appointed dance specialist in education and community dance, was asked by Mark Pyper to introduce Dance into the Year 9 Performing Arts Curriculum. Dance is compulsory for all students in Year 7 to Year 9, removing any lingering misconception that dance is just for girls. As Sarah DaBell explains, 'what [the boys] discover is that to dance you need strength, stamina and of course a degree of flexibility . . . they soon realise how physically challenging Dance can be. The athletic and gymnastic styles of movement that you find in break dance really appeal.' DaBell also set up a number of recreational dance activities, and since 1995, when the first dance showcase was greeted with a standing ovation, there have been numerous dance performances at the school both by Gordonstoun students and by visiting amateur and professional companies.

In 1996 GCSE Dance was introduced, and included in the syllabus were contemporary dance, technical dance skills, dance composition and appreciation. AS Dance followed soon after, an option that allows students to study to a level that will prepare them for Dance courses in higher education.

Laura Paterson (née Stockley) was one of the first students to benefit from the introduction of Dance into the curriculum, first arriving in the Dance department as a sixth-form student in 1997. She went on to take a BA in Contemporary Dance Studies at the Laban Centre in London and a PGCE at the Royal Academy of Dance. She remembers being struck by the keenness of 'strong rugby-playing boys' to participate and has clear memories of the first opportunity the students had to show off their dance skills outside the school, which came with their participation in the BT Dance Connections festival at Eden Court Theatre in Inverness in the summer of 1998. There, Gordonstoun dancers were selected to represent the Highlands at the Scottish final, performing their own version of *Romeo and Juliet* in Edinburgh.

Having returned to Gordonstoun in a teaching capacity, Paterson remarks that the wide variety of backgrounds and countries from which Gordonstoun students are drawn is reflected by the rich selection of dance styles they bring with them, so that ballet, tap, jazz, hip hop, salsa, ballroom, flamenco and break dance have all featured in performances over the years.

In 2005 Gordonstoun Youth Dance Company was set up by Sarah DaBell and Laura Paterson. The company is open to sixth-form students, entry is by audition only, and there are currently eighteen members, both male and female, who benefit from more performance opportunities and occasionally tour. They have so far performed at Dance City in Newcastle, the Gala Theatre, Durham, and Eden Court. 'The founding of the school's Dance Company has been a significant development,' says Paterson, 'and all the participating students I have known have been a delight to work with, often on pieces which are technically very challenging.' Paterson was responsible for the first dance choreographed specifically for the Dance Company in 2005: *Fin* has been performed numerous times both in shows at the school and on tour as part of a rapidly growing, always challenging repertoire.

One of the first performances by the Gordonstoun Youth Dance Company in 2005.

Left: The Pipe Band, early 1960s.

Above: Susie Lachmann, who taught music at Gordonstoun from 1936 to 1967.

Opposite: Music in the South Room, originally known as the Long Room, c. 1938.

MUSIC

There was an air of vibrant anticipation when Hahn announced that a wonderful violin teacher and musician was about to arrive to join the staff at Gordonstoun. A small woman joined other guests at Gordonstoun House, and, like everyone else, was at once informed of the news that a marvellous musician was expected imminently. Susie Lachmann was somewhat put out, assuming that she was about to meet a contender for the position she had thought she was coming to fill. Although small of stature, Lachmann was a strong personality and had been leader of a chamber orchestra in Hamburg and a member of a well-known string quartet; personally acquainted with Hindemith, she had given several first performances of his works. Her career was utterly disrupted by the need to flee Hitler's Germany – Bob Waddell, who taught at Gordonstoun from 1959 to 1989, remembers that she had escaped with only her violin, setting off from home on the pretext that she was going to a rehearsal. All those who knew her testify to her single-minded determination to create an orchestra and chamber music at Gordonstoun, showing herself more than willing to conduct and to teach violin and indeed any other instrument for which a teacher was not available. Lachmann's sister, a 'cellist, soon came to join her and both women lived at West Lodge. Hilary Tunstall-Behrens recounts a story told by his father, who had been recruited to buy horses for the school and start the riding department. Henry Brereton had designs on the West Lodge for a newly appointed member of his staff, and put pressure on Hahn to oust the Lachmanns. Brereton, Hahn and Tunstall-Behrens walked down the drive to the Lodge

to settle the matter. Arriving unannounced, they looked over the hedge and there was Susie Lachman, in her tweed skirt, her back towards them, bending over dealing with the plants in her flourishing vegetable garden. Hahn apparently rubbed his hands together and in a tone of reverence and respect said, 'But my dear Brereton, look, she's cultivated the land!' And that settled it. No-one dared to interfere. Music at Gordonstoun continued to flourish.

Over at Altyre, Forres, in the 1950s boys agitated to begin a pipe band, and Tony White, on his arrival there as a newly recruited member of staff, was approached by Alistair Paterson who had overseen the weekly piping classes taught by the veteran Pipe-Major Logie. White describes his instructions: 'He said, "You're the music man – you'd better take charge of this". It was a world unfamiliar to me. The boys, Graham Neil prominent among them, pressed me to beg or borrow more sets of pipes, and later, with pressure from Donald Fairgrieve, to arrange drumming classes with a dream of forming a pipe band. Such was their enthusiasm that before either of them had left school this was achieved, which stunned the main campus when suddenly the band, whose existence was as yet unknown there, won the first prize at the Projects Exhibition. The pipe band jealously guarded its civilian status when, in subsequent years, it played at the annual ceremonial parade of the Combined Cadet Force – no caps or saluting for us! It also received increasing invitations to play when local gardens were opened to the public. I gather that, after my time, this extended even as far as Eilean Donan Castle. Although, later, there was a gap in piping activity, I am delighted to know that a pipe band is now flourishing once again.'

Bagpipe playing at the Tsunami Charity Concert in 2005.

John and Mary Nicholson arrived at Gordonstoun in September 1972, having spent the previous four years working at the Royal Opera House Covent Garden: Mary as a singer, and John as a member of the production staff. Nicholson describes the background to music at the school at that point: 'The staff room, back then, included several other unconventional amateur musicians. Godfrey Burchardt, a Hahn original, ran a madrigal choir for students and staff, and Angus MacKnight, the school doctor, had produced a string of Gilbert and Sullivan operas at the school, using girls borrowed from Elgin Academy. There was only one other full-time music teacher, with whom I shared the daily chapel organ playing, but several local musicians were teaching part time: the most formidable being the indomitable Kim Murray, violin teacher and Elgin musical entrepreneur, who

had introduced Prince Charles to playing the 'cello, and had recruited him into her private Elgin orchestra. She had been teaching violin and 'cello at Gordonstoun ever since the retirement of Susie Lachmann.'

The Music department had just one classroom and three small practice rooms around St Christopher's; accommodation was so scarce that for several years two wedge-shaped store rooms either side of the chapel were in constant use for instrumental teaching. After about eight years, two glass-walled rooms were added in the ambulatory, and then, a few years later, the first part of the new wing of music studios was added to the north side of the chapel.

Nicholson had done some school opera productions in Lancashire before going to Covent Garden, and it was not long before he and his wife started producing operas on a

THE FIRST MUSIC SCHOLAR AT GORDONSTOUN

Resources for music at the school were for many years meagre, and arrangements were often fairly *ad hoc*, as Barry Cooper (now Professor of Music at Manchester University) testifies: 'I was the first ever music scholar at Gordonstoun, when the school set up a music scholarship in 1962. Thus my most enduring memories of the school are not of the rugby pitch or the cutters at Hopeman harbour but of Godfrey Burchardt's madrigal group, a trip to Edinburgh with choir and orchestra on leap-year day 1964, singing in Handel's *Messiah* in Elgin Town Hall, piano lessons with Michael Holloway, and organ lessons with Patrick Criswell.

'Those organ lessons! The first problem was that, when I arrived with two years' experience on the organ, the school had no organ for me to learn on. The school's embarrassment was compounded by the fact that I had come from a state school (Southend High) which did have an organ. What could be done? There was an instrument in the Michael Kirk, but it required someone to operate the bellows by hand. Moreover, it had no pedal board – a *sine qua non* for anyone learning the organ. And after I'd been at the school for only two or three weeks a boy managed to break the bellows irreparably with some over-enthusiastic pumping, so I never

even got to see the instrument. The nearest church with an organ was in Hopeman. It took about six weeks to set up the arrangements. Once a week I cycled to Hopeman almost entirely uphill and always against a strong wind. Reaching Harbour Street, I had to go to the baker's shop and collect the key to the church from the baker's wife, Mrs Main (nearly everyone in Hopeman seemed to be called Main). Then it was back up the hill to a freezing cold church, for you couldn't expect them to heat such a large building just for me. A short lesson and practice followed, my fingers becoming increasingly numbed with cold, then a welcome lift back to school in Mr Criswell's van. Not the best way to learn a difficult instrument.

'Later I had lessons on an electronic organ in Mr Criswell's house at the edge of Hopeman. The organ stops had an impressive variety of names, but each stop actually sounded more or less the same, with just a slightly different form of electrical buzz. It must have been one of the first electronic organs ever made. Eventually I was able to practise a little more often, when a small one-manual pipe organ was placed in the Michael Kirk. The trouble was that I was learning a piece that needed three manuals (rows of keys), so at the appropriate points in the piece I

just had to imagine that I was changing manuals. At least there was a pedal board.

'On such limited facilities I was attempting to become an Associate of the Royal College of Organists (ARCO). That I eventually succeeded is a tribute to Mr Criswell's excellent teaching, and it was such a rare event for a Gordonstoun boy that I was allowed to go down to London during term to collect my diploma. At the ceremony I met Edward Heath, the new leader of the Conservatives (he had once been an organ scholar at Oxford). When he was told that I was from Gordonstoun, his response was, "Oh, I didn't know they went in for that sort of thing up there." At the time any mention of Gordonstoun in the press referred to it as a strikingly Spartan place, and even a leading politician didn't know any different. But things were changing, and the music scholarship was symptomatic of the school gradually paying more attention to the arts, and a softer, more cultured way of living . . . I watched St Christopher's being built, and took part in the opening ceremony two days before I left. Two years later I was invited back to give a recital on the newly installed organ. Things had come a long way since those freezing afternoons in Hopeman church.'

Top: Brass ensemble
rehearsal, early 1970s.

Above: School orchestra
and choir, 2009.

to create massive stages which allowed the orchestra to play out of sight, below the stage, Bayreuth-style. On alternate years, we would take the senior orchestra on a foreign tour, playing the same programme at seven or eight venues over a ten-day period.'

By the early 1980s there were five or six full-time Music teachers, and Nicholson pays tribute especially to Kenneth Bews, 'who for the rest of my time at the school would be my most supportive colleague, choral director, and voice of common sense and integrity when confronted with some of my more hare-brained schemes.' By this time, there were resident specialists for most of the orchestral instruments, and soon there was a 'reasonable-sounding' youth orchestra of 45 or 50 players with equal numbers of boys and girls in the orchestral ranks. As the required entry standard for senior orchestra members crept up to Grade 6 plus, the repertoire became more and more ambitious. Ruth Wall, who now performs new and ancient music on medieval, renaissance and modern harps all over the world, is in no doubt as to the value of Kenneth Bews' quiet encouragement for her: 'I arrived as a music scholar to Gordonstoun in 1985 from a big, noisy family on the outskirts of the mini village of Bonar Bridge, an hour north of Inverness. This was a traumatic move. Most of the pupils were English and couldn't understand my Highland accent (which I adapted to make for an easier social life) and had shared backgrounds with other pupils which I felt I had no part of. Luckily music encouraged me into meeting others – however different – and building my confidence. For five years I pretty much lived in the chapel, mostly bashing away on a piano in one of the little glass practice rooms. I studied with Kenneth Bews who is a wonderful teacher and human being – patient, inspiring and keen to feed my playing with as much historical and stylistic background as I could take. He encouraged me to make decisions based on my own informed judgement and I think of these lessons almost every time I practise and play on the harp or piano nowadays. The inspirational John Nicholson put his life into the musicals, operas and orchestra he led, and to have the chance to be involved in these productions was thrilling. I played a wobbly flute in *Figaro*, pranced around in *Kiss me Kate,* sang in *The Magic Flute*, became an old cigar-smoking man in *Albert Herring* and saw the world from behind the timps on orchestra tours. I loved singing in Kenneth Bews' choir, and began to lose my nerves by performing in lunchtime concerts, wind bands and accompanying gifted older pupils. As a homesick thirteen-year-old, I was propelled by these amazing experiences, the kindness and constant encouragement of all the music staff and the close friendships I made through music propelled me through my adolesence and set me on my current musical path.'

regular basis at Gordonstoun. An *Iolanthe* and a *Ruddigore* were staged in the Services Centre, then a *Noye's Fludde* and what he describes as 'a rather dodgy *Magic Flute*' were performed on specially built stages in the chapel. 'At least *The Magic Flute* looked good,' remarks Nicholson, 'because I had used my old Covent Garden contacts to borrow the complete Glyndebourne production, designed by Oliver Messel, which had the most magnificent costumes. We got into the routine of doing a big school opera every other year, using the skills and ingenuity of the estate carpenters

The first overseas tour took place in 1978 to Gordonstoun's sister school, Salem, and a couple of other venues in southern Germany, and in 1981, during the first year of Michael Mavor's headmastership, a substantial tour of the eastern states of the USA was organised, playing a programme which began with Wagner's *Meistersinger* overture and included two modern works specially written for the orchestra by David Bedford, who joined the tour to conduct his pieces. 'Michael Mavor,' remembers Nicholson, 'visiting his old haunts in New England, was drafted into the orchestra ranks as an extra percussion player, and almost got it right at least once.' Salem was visited again in 1983, and in 1988 70 members of the choir and orchestra played at concerts in Italy, including a memorable performance in Venice at the Chiesa di Vivaldi.

The association with the composer David Bedford also bore fruit operatically, with three massive school operas based on Norse legends – *The Death of Baldur*, and two sequels, *Ragnarok* and *Fridiof's Saga*. Each of these involved a cast of over 80 singers, plus a full orchestra of 45, so that

about a third of the school were involved in some way, musically or backstage. As an antidote to the Bedford operas, the 50th anniversary in 1984 of the school's foundation was celebrated with a production of Puccini's comic one-act masterpiece *Gianni Schicchi*.

In the early 1980s Nicholson had done a complete re-orchestration of Bizet's *Carmen* for a joint production with John Lofthouse in St Christopher's. Some of the pupils who took part in it decided they would like to do 'something more professional', and over a twelve-month period a group

of about ten singers, plus chorus and orchestra, worked with the Nicholsons on a production of Mozart's *The Marriage of Figaro*. 'The results surpassed every expectation', recalls Nicholson. 'The cast were rock-solid, musically and dramatically, and it was a production which I remember with great affection . . . the students . . . were the motivating force, and it was their dogged attention to detail which paid off so well.'

Meanwhile, other initiatives were taking root. Nicholson started the Gordonstoun Concerts Society, which enabled him to tap into Arts Council funding and promote concerts at the school by internationally famous musicians, including John Ogdon and Nigel Kennedy. On a more modest scale, weekly lunchtime recitals took place in the South Room, where pupils could develop their performance skills by playing before an audience of their contemporaries.

As the 1980s went on, a growing number of singers decided to study music professionally after leaving Gordonstoun. 'Mary and I are still in touch with many of the outstanding musicians who passed through Gordonstoun during our time there, and it's very satisfying to watch them developing in their musical careers . . . We remember our former pupils with great affection, and have a great appreciation of the massive support (both practical and financial) which the Music department received from Michael Mavor and the Board of Governors during the 1980s.' The Nicholsons' warm recollections are roundly reciprocated. Alycia Fashae (1985–90), now a professional

Above: The string orchestra at the Spring Concert, 2007.

Left: Chamber choir at the Christmas Concert, 2010.

The Ghana Music Tour, 2006.

Performance at the school Rock Concert in 2010 (above), and (above right) the 2004 Jazz Rock Concert at Gordonstoun.

Inset right: Pop concert at the school, c. 1970.

Aberlour House orchestra rehearsal, 2010.

opera singer, has no doubts about the effects of the couple's skilled nurturing of talent in her case: 'In your life, you may encounter a few people who have influenced the decisions you have made, but rarely can you say without hyperbole that you owe the entire course of your adult life to the influence of two specific people. Yet that is exactly the effect that John and Mary Nicholson had on my life. I owe to these wonderful people, my career, my friends, my husband and therefore my daughter. Most of my joys and a few of my sorrows flow from the gift they recognised and developed in me when I was at Gordonstoun. They not only gave me a mode of self-expression, but instilled in me sufficient passion and skill for it to take me around the world. I was blessed that my years at Gordonstoun coincided with the time when the Nicholsons were there. It was a shining period in Gordonstoun's musical history.' Richard Rowe discovered just after his arrival at the school in 1988 that his mother had arranged for him to have singing lessons: 'I had already been involved in amateur opera choruses in the north-east of England where I had been living previously, but was intimidated by the thought of being at this new school and having these lessons. My somewhat feeble protestations that I could already sing

were pushed aside and my first lesson approached swiftly. It was probably the most defining moment of my life at Gordonstoun. It was a bright day and the light was streaming into the chapel. The piano was in the centre of the chapel in front of the altar and, quite intimidated, I got underway. What a glorious building to sing in – the wonderful resonant acoustic made you sound fabulous, and gave you the self-belief to try for more and more. It was quickly established that I was a tenor (not a baritone as I had previously thought!) and I was promptly signed up to play Tamino in the school's production of *The Magic Flute*. Looking back it is astonishing that the Music department had such ambition and confidence in its abilities.

'That ambition was well founded. With a powerful orchestra consisting of both pupils and professionals, a huge set and stage, the opera was a great success. All of it was founded, however, on the brilliance, professional approach and ambitious belief in us, the pupils, of the then Music master, John Nicholson and his singing teacher wife, Mary Nicholson. In my second year at Gordonstoun I played the title role in Benjamin Britten's opera *Albert Herring*. A truly jaw-dropping experience for all concerned.

'After a career in business working – amongst other places – at the head office of Marks & Spencer, I decided that I wanted to change not only job, but career. The love of singing instilled in me at Gordonstoun had stayed with me and I had started singing seriously again in my mid-twenties. So I auditioned for the Royal Academy, got a place, and did the Opera Course, graduating with a DipRAM, and various prizes under my belt, gained an agent and went off to work as a professional singer. Thus far I have worked all over the UK and Europe, including for Scottish Opera and Opera North, and sung in some spectacular venues. All in all, Gordonstoun changed my life, gave me the career I have today, friends that I still hold dear, and the belief that I can do whatever it is I want to do – *plus est en vous* indeed.'

Nicholson left the school in 1991 after nineteen years in the post of Director of Music, and it was obvious that his would be a hard act to follow. After him there was a series of Directors of Music, none of whom stayed for long, and it is a credit to Kenneth Bews that he stepped in on several occasions to fill the breach. Bews also continued to take charge of the weekly school hymn practice until he finally retired in 2010. Peter Sunman, an able clarinettist, was one of the Directors in the early 1990s until he left to return to Australia, and it was he who successfully organised and directed a Gordonstoun Arts Festival in 1992. He also started a swing band consisting mainly of saxophones and

Members of the brass ensemble in 2008.

brass (which was later to become the school jazz band under Nigel Gaston's leadership). Michael Appleford, a long-established member of the Music department, took over as Director in 1994, and under his leadership stability began to be restored. The orchestra embarked on tours to New York and Boston in 1995 and St Petersburg two years later. In 1999 a chamber orchestra toured New Zealand. During this period there were to be numerous memorable performances from the orchestra including a Shostakovich piano concerto played by Young Ju Ha. The orchestra also accompanied the choir in performances of Handel's *Messiah*, Vivaldi's *Gloria* and Carl Orff's *Carmina Burana*. Chamber music flourished: music for wind ensemble and for string quartet featured regularly in concert programmes.

As the Drama department developed so the nature of combined productions changed: the challenge of opera gave way to no less difficult but more approachable musicals following the 1996 production of Leonard Bernstein's *Mass*. Due to its difficulty and the numbers required for it, this major work is rarely performed, and the department's triumphant presentation of it was a remarkable achievement. Academic music also began to change in the late 1990s. With the new emphasis on Drama and Dance, class Music gave way to a Performing Arts course. This format was to continue until Nigel Gaston took over as Director of Music in 2001. Numbers of pupils studying Music at GCSE and A level remained small, but a consistently high standard was achieved and concerts regularly featured pupil compositions.

Hobart Earle, now Principal Conductor of the Odessa Philharmonic, reflects on what music at Gordonstoun gave to him: 'Throughout the 1970s, the performing arts in Gordonstoun were a regular part of school life . . . During my second year, I was given the role of "Marius" in the play of the same name by Marcel Pagnol, which we performed in the original French . . . I also have vivid memories of *Noye's Fludde* (by Benjamin Britten) and *Salad Days* (by Julian Slade). Music had been with me since childhood; my mother was a choral conductor and my aunt a composer, and I was actively involved in all sorts of music-making during my years at Gordonstoun. My early years in Odessa, right at the time of the break-up of the USSR, were probably the big Gordonstoun moment in my life; that "*plus est en vous*, now-is-the-time-to rise-to-the-challenge" moment. I am often asked how I managed to adapt to my new surroundings during those difficult years. Usually at a loss for words, my best answer seems to be to mention the philosophy behind Gordonstoun. After leaving school in 1979, it took me twelve years to return to Scotland. When I was invited back to take part in John Nicholson's 1991 farewell concert, I remember being struck by the awesome natural beauty of the region, something I had obviously become accustomed to during school years, but somehow failed to digest fully. More recently, my son spent five happy years in Duffus House, providing a welcome opportunity for me to visit the school on occasion. The total transformation Gordonstoun has undergone since the 1970s is immediately apparent, but at the end of the day, the place still feels the same.'

Since 2001 the range of opportunities to make and enjoy music has broadened considerably. Nigel Gaston actively developed a pipe band and vocal groups of various sorts as well as the jazz band. His music tours abroad to Norway (2002), Greece (2004) and Ghana (2006) involved several different groups, mostly vocal, and for the tour to Ghana the pipe band went too.

Touring has continued under Simon Burbury who became Director of Music in 2008. A tour to Egypt in 2009 included a chamber choir, chamber orchestra and pipers. Highlights were a performance at the British Embassy and a day spent at a home for Cairo street children. Other recent highlights include Vivaldi's *Gloria*, performed in St Giles' Church, Elgin (2009), *Zadok the Priest* at the Universal Hall, Findhorn (2010), and an outstanding production of *Les Misérables*, a joint project with the Drama and Dance departments (2009). There is a new purpose-built digital recording studio, and Music Technology has been introduced as an A-level subject.

Perhaps Burbury's most impressive achievement is the chamber choir he has set up. He writes: 'Whilst singing was popular and the main Gordonstoun choir was certainly very healthy (on my arrival), I introduced a smaller, more dedicated, chamber choir – a smaller group of "auditioned" students, which has since had considerable success with tours, concerts and competitions.' The choir recently reached the semi-final of the BBC Schools' Choir of the Year competition (2011).

Burbury's aim is to ensure the availability of a broad, balanced and varied diet of musical styles and tastes. There is a healthy array of rock bands, a symphonic choir and chamber choir, a symphony orchestra and chamber orchestra, a number of chamber ensembles, folk groups and smaller vocal ensembles and a pipe band which, following two years of fund-raising, has just acquired a uniform. There are eighteen visiting instrumental teachers, growing numbers taking Music as an examination subject, and more collaboration between the Dance and Drama departments. When major concerts take place, St Christopher's can scarcely accommodate the enthusiastic audiences for them.

Top: An art class, 1950s, led by Roy McComish.

Above: Display of ceramics, c. 1967.

ART

'Art was important to Kurt Hahn', writes Michael Evans, who arrived in the Art department at Gordonstoun in 1980. 'Contemporaries fleeing Germany in the 1930s numbered among them famous academics and art historians such as Aby Warburg and Ernst Gombrich, and Hahn's ideas had much in common with those of Walter Gropius in his founding of the Bauhaus at Weimar. Intellectual problem-solving and hands-on craftsmanship were to complement each other and accordingly both practising artist/craftsmen and artist theorists/historians should work together. Being led in a studio system while being surrounded by original works of art and craftsmanship in the boarding houses, students would thus be "impelled into experience", as Hahn put it.'

The first art master at Gordonstoun, Dr Erich Meissner, himself a painter, had taught at Salem and soon had to follow Hahn in leaving Germany. His paintings can still be seen in the school, some of them depicting quasi-allegorical scenes from the life and times of the Founder. He was followed by Roy McComish (until 1958), whose pen and ink drawings and cartoons regularly appeared in *The Gordonstoun Record*. Alistair Paterson was Head of Art at Altyre, Forres 1951–59, and then headed the department at Gordonstoun until his retirement in 1980. Bob Waddell arrived at Altyre in 1959, and, after an initial year there, taught at Gordonstun for nearly 30 years, succeeding Paterson as Head of Department. 'The Altyre art room was primitive,' he remembers, 'housed above the stables in the estate square: buckets of water were carried up from below and the palettes were old, cracked, dinner plates. Miraculously, and in spite of the lack of materials, there was an immense amount of creative talent of an exceptional standard.' At Gordonstoun, Waddell shared the Art teaching with Alistair Paterson 'in a rusty, leaking Nissen hut', where they taught History of Art and Architecture, and some of the pupils learned to paint. There was a pottery with one wheel and a small kiln. 'After a few years,' recalls Waddell, 'the pottery became extremely popular (free Christmas presents for entire families and a must for grannies!).' More wheels were bought, and a benefactor donated a large, gas-fired kiln, which meant that objects of up to three feet high – both pots and modelled figures – could now be fired. 'The end results', remembers Waddell, 'were often of a professional standard.' After a while, the Nissen hut became unusable, and a new Art department was built. Paterson and Waddell had some part in its design, rejecting the initial plan which used much valuable space on corridors, and arranging instead for the creation of two large art rooms, a spacious pottery and a small lecture room for those taking History of Art or Architecture at A level. Weekly lantern lectures were instituted to foster an interest in art, architecture and antiques among pupils who were not taking Art A levels. 'These were a great success,' relates Waddell, 'and, even now, I receive postcards from art "philistines" saying, "you won't believe it – I am in the Prado; all *your* fault!" '

For many years, Waddell and Paterson took it in turns to help with Art teaching at Aberlour once a week. Exposure to younger pupils was something both of them enjoyed: 'Such a relief to find that seven- to ten-year-olds will, happily, paint a portrait with a purple face and lime-green eyes; post ten the need to conform to realism is all-consuming – it takes another ten years to make them accept that a purple face is not only acceptable, it is practically *de rigueur*.'

In 1983 a post was advertised at the school for 'a practising artist who can also teach the history of art'. Michael Evans filled the position (becoming Head of Department when Waddell retired), and made conscious

efforts to hold these two aspects of the subject in balance: 'With A-level courses in both Art and the History of Art running in parallel and under the same roof, we did bemoan the distance to the Design Technology workshops. But Art, History of Art and Design Technology was a popular A-level combination and our courses could and did supplant the Bauhaus-based Foundation Studies of the first year at art colleges, our students being admitted directly to final degree studies.' He continues, 'We were keen also to work in combination with Drama and Music on the good Wagnerian concept of the *Gesamtkunstwerk* (total work of art), in producing operas such as *Gianni Schicchi*, *Carmen*, *The Magic Flute*, *The Marriage of Figaro*, etc. We felt Hahn would strongly approve. Regular involvement in such productions was a major part of the all-round education we provided and accordingly we were careful to amass huge casts both on stage and in supporting roles drawn from across the school.

'Some measure of our success in this can be gauged by the enormous range of fields in which I encounter those I taught. I find at airports I sit on furnishings designed by a former student. I notice from an attribution on an advert that a fiercely opinionated individual is now in a senior position with Saatchi. Absentmindedly viewing film credits, my eye is caught by the name of the chief cameraman whose "grand passion" for photography to the exclusion of all else was of serious concern to us at school. Wandering through the British Museum, I am accosted by their publicity officer who invites me to an exhibition preview: we studied Renaissance drawings in class together what seems such a short time ago. Idly perusing academic journals I find that one of my most brilliant art historians is now a professor at

A Year 9 Art lesson, 2008.

Above: Hugh Ebdy, *Self-portrait*, 2010.

Right: Nicholas Curnow, *Prometheus Bound*, 2010.

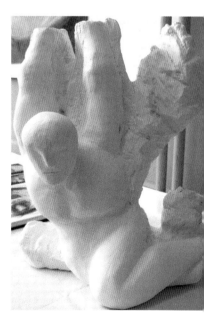

Heavenly Creations, the art exhibition for Open Day, 2010. Left: *OCD* by Maddie Grille, an interactive soft sculpture of a toothbrush evoking, through the five senses, the experience of cleaning teeth. Above: Minty Sainsbury's representation of Gordonstoun House, in oil on board; the central section is drawn from plans of the original interior in the school archive.

a red-brick university, another is a senior tutor at an Oxbridge college and a third is writing the most penetrating architectural criticism. And, of course, Peter Doig was short listed for the Turner Prize a few years ago.'

In 2004 Caroline McCallum was appointed Head of Department. In line with developments in art education elsewhere, courses were expanded to encompass a diverse range of media specialisms, from fine art and ceramics to printmaking, film and video, textiles and digital photography. Junior pupils from Aberlour use the facilities alongside students from the main school, so that it is not uncommon for broad mixtures of year groups to be working together.

The Art Scholars programme has been enhanced, with those holding scholarships being given the opportunity to develop their own work for national and international competitions and involvement in art for the community. 'The Big Draw' is now an established biennial event in the school in which the whole school takes part, students and staff alike, including domestic and administrative staff. 2008 saw a huge reproduction of Meissner's *The Wizard of Gordonstoun* painting in the form of a patchwork put together from over 100 individual contributions. Outside

formal class time, the art activities programme has also expanded for students at both junior and senior level, with a large variety of options, from animation and digital art to watercolour sessions.

Under the umbrella of Community Service, an Art Service was piloted in 2009, enabling students to take art into the wider community by teaching art for a term at local primary schools. So far the Medical Centre has benefited from an aesthetic makeover with murals, and the Art Service has its sights set firmly on various other locations around the school. Every year sixth-form artists produce large pieces for the Sixth Form Centre, which, at the end of the year are moved to be hung in boarding houses to make way for new work.

The biggest event of the year for the Art department is its exhibition. All art students, from Years 4 to 13, have at least one piece of work on display for their peers and parents to view during the week of Open Day in the summer term. There is a private view, complete with drinks, nibbles and guests invited from the local community, in keeping with the school's belief that everyone at the school should be able to experience all aspects of the creation of art, including showing their efforts in an exhibition.

GISS student (who subsequently became a full-time student at Gordonstoun) enjoying an outdoor activity on the west coast of Scotland, 2009.

GORDONSTOUN INTERNATIONAL SUMMER SCHOOL

A forerunner of the Gordonstoun International Summer School (GISS) was held in 1972, when a group of Americans visited Gordonstoun during the summer holidays, hosted by John Ruscoe, the then financial controller of the school. Two years later, a summer course designed for young people whose native language was not English was launched at the Dorchester Hotel in London, and in 1976 the first Gordonstoun Summer Course, as it was then called, took place, attended by 23 boys, mainly from the Middle East, and run by James FitzGibbon. The following year it was convened again and almost double the number of boys attended, this time hailing mainly from continental Europe. By this time James Thomas had been appointed Director of the course. It was not long before the Summer School mirrored the main school's co-educational intake, and drew its boys and girls from an ever-increasing number of countries. Jenny Needham, who had worked for the Summer School since 1985, became Director when James Thomas retired in 2000.

John Kempe described Gordonstoun's aims in instigating the Summer School thus: 'to extend our facilities to overseas pupils and by doing so perhaps to encourage some schools overseas to examine the value of this kind of education; to put our capital resources to more intensive use throughout the year and so to spread the cost of overheads; and if possible to make a profit for scholarship funds.' He added that participants were to learn English through 'a few well-structured formal classes and by involvement in as broad and varied a range of activities as possible.' These intentions remain at the heart of the enterprise, though the Summer School has also become a good way for children whose parents are considering where they should be educated to experience a taster of a Gordonstoun education.

When they attend the Summer School, students are challenged in the classroom, on the sports field, in the creative and performing arts, in the mountains and at sea, in a micro version of the experience of full-time students at Gordonstoun. Students select from English as an Additional Language (EAL), French, IT and Literature with English Skills as academic courses, and take part in a range of sport without specialisation – squash, badminton, hockey, soccer, athletics, lacrosse, basketball, tennis, volleyball, swimming, canoeing as well as initiative tests and sessions on the climbing wall and obstacle course. They spend time in the technology workshops, the art room, and in music and drama sessions. Recreational activities are popular too – quad biking, clay-pigeon shooting, horse riding, go-karting, laser tag, cooking, golf, ice skating, and, of course, shopping!

The highlight of the course for many is the week spent on the west coast of Scotland when students spend three days based at an adventure centre where they go gorge walking, rock climbing and abseiling, mountain biking, coasteering and canoeing; they then spend a further three days sailing on one of the GISS fleet of 40-foot ocean-going yachts chartered for the occasion. At the height of the summer the GISS fleet rises to ten yachts.

Over the years, there have been regular marketing tours and functions across the world organised by GISS staff to encourage families to send their children to the Summer School. The OG network, in particular The Gordonstoun American Foundation, has provided invaluable support, including the award of GISS scholarships for deserving students from the USA each summer. Other annual scholarships are endowed by the Boys and Girls Clubs of America in Annapolis, Maryland, and the Ueno Gakuen College and University in Tokyo. Numbers have risen to over 300 boys and girls, aged eight to sixteen, with a high returnee rate and many students attending for several consecutive summers.

The GISS courses come to a climax during the final weekend when a series of inter-clan competitions are held. These include a swimming gala, obstacle-course race and athletics competition, and, on one evening, 'Showtime' – a popular event when student groups stage a short piece which they have prepared during the drama courses. All take part!

On the final evening, the course ends with a formal dinner attended by all staff and students, and many parents too. The haggis is piped in, prizes are presented and trophies awarded: a fitting finale to celebrate skills learned, challenges overcome and new friendships made.

SEAMANSHIP
AND SAILING

'The Moray Firth is my sternest schoolmaster' KURT HAHN

Gordonstoun's first boat, *Gairloch*, in the 1930s.

'IN 1934,' WROTE Chrystall Nohl-Oser, one of the boys who had followed Hahn from Salem, 'we were living in a barely furnished large mansion. One day Kurt Hahn took me to the rocky coast of the Moray Firth nearby, and looking across the sea he said: "My boy, we shall have a school boat and it will sail across the North Sea manned by boys." I was incredulous. Three years later that vision materialised.'

The very first seamanship log book (an orange copy-book) was begun in 1934 by Jocelin Winthrop Young, who was to become first Captain of Boats on 3 June that year, though the term 'boats' reflected a certain amount of wishful thinking, as the school had only one craft at that time: a hired, 15-foot clinker-built, four-oared rowing boat *Gairloch*, used for rowing on the lake. The log gives some interesting details of early seamanship at Gordonstoun which must have begun as soon as the school had moved to Duffus from Rothiemurchus. The boys first went to sea on 6 June 1934. A small sailing boat was hired for two days from George Young of Hopeman and sailed each day to Burghead. The crew of four, three boys and George Young

Top: Prince Philip engaged in boat maintenance at Hopeman harbour, mid-1930s.

Above: Kurt Hahn with one of the Moray fishermen he held in such high esteem, 1934.

Opposite: *Ocean Spirit* in the Solent, 2000.

himself, had to row back against the wind, baling all the way. Further outings with George Young followed until later in June, when a small leaky yacht owned by a Mr Noble of Burghead was tried out and then bought for £10 by a syndicate of masters (Kurt Hahn contributed £5, John Lewty and another master £2 10s each).

Boys started work with the Hopeman boat builder, Alexander Findlay, in the spring of 1934. They travelled to and from Hopeman by bus and helped to build two fishing boats, first the *Braemou* and then the *Energy*. In his report on the school in July 1935, Hahn reports that 'All boys do seamanship but seven boys have voluntarily joined the Seaman's Guild. Last weekend with Commander John Lewty and Mr Chew in the cutter which has been given us, and in our yacht, they sailed over the Moray Firth in windy weather. They are clamouring for a bigger boat to go on longer voyages.' In September 1934 Findlay started working with boys on two dipping-lug cutters; the first, the *Mansfield Cumming*, was launched in October 1935, and the second, the *May Cumming*, in June 1936.

The first issue of *The Gordonstoun School News* reported in March 1936 that at Hopeman 'work has begun on a new yacht for sailing in the Findhorn Bay [again under the guidance of Alec Findlay]. Her length is to be eighteen foot, and she is to have a centre-board. It is hoped that she will be ready for the next season.' When completed, the yacht was used in Findhorn Bay, along with a small rowing boat, the *Salem*.

The main use of the two cutters was for weekday seamanship, and each house sent a team to Hopeman harbour for one afternoon a week. Joseph Pease gives an indication of the work involved: 'Seamanship began with

scraping oars for re-varnishing. Later, as the weather improved, we ventured out in one or other of the two cutters, *May* and *Mansfield*, in seas that were anything from calm to comparatively rough. One afternoon, when we were returning to the harbour in a heavy sea, something went wrong and we were being carried fast towards the harbour wall. A line thrown down by a fisherman swung the cutter into the entrance.'

When Gordonstoun was evacuated to Wales it was decided that the cutters should follow by rail (in 1940); *en route*, the *Mansfield* caught fire, presumably set alight by a spark from the train's engine, and her gear was destroyed though her hull remained intact. The *May* was dragged to a small lake halfway up a mountain near Llandinam, but the lake was too small and too shallow for meaningful seamanship. A home was found for the cutters some 25 miles away in the tidal estuary at Aberdovey. Boys went from their new abode at Llandinam to Aberdovey by rail at weekends to be instructed in cutter sailing by a local ferryman, Ellis Williams, and in general seamanship by Captain Roberts, Master Mariner.

Early on in the life of the school, boys with a particular interest in seamanship joined the Sea Scouts and had the opportunity of sailing on summer holiday cruises in a larger boat than the cutters. First the school owned a Cornish training ketch, *Diligent*, purchased in Plymouth by Colonel Edward Varvill, a parent whose three boys would all eventually pass through the school. In 1936 *Diligent* sailed to Orkney and Shetland, skippered by Captain Geoffrey Wicksteed, a member of staff with a passion for sail training. Next the school owned a large ketch named *Henrietta*, presented by a Mr Ward. She had previously moved coal and, once refitted by Alec Findlay in Hopeman, was available in 1937 for a summer cruise to Norway, again under the command of Captain Wicksteed. On the voyage were six adults and 23 boys, one of whom was Prince Philip of Greece.

In June 1938 the school acquired a 73-foot schooner, the *Maisie Graham*. Built in 1878 as a Baltic Pilot ship, the *Bremen*, she had been sold in 1922 to the Royal Mission to Deep Sea Fishermen and renamed *Lead Kindly Light*; after this she was used for fifteen years as a sail-training ship

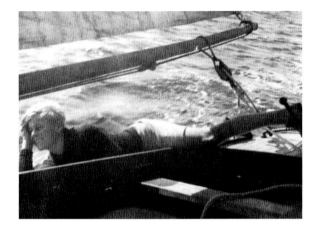

Right: Prince Philip on one of the school's first boats.

(owned by the Scarborough Education Authority) as the *Maisie Graham*. No refit was needed when Gordonstoun acquired her, and she was pressed into service straight away for the summer cruise to the west coast of Scotland, skippered by Commander Lewty. In February 1939 she was re-named *Prince Louis*, after Prince Louis of Battenburg, the father of Lord Louis Mountbatten.

At the start of the war the *Prince Louis* lay idle in Hopeman harbour until the boys managed to convince Kurt Hahn that she should be moved down to Wales. In 1941, piloted by the Admiralty, she set sail for Aberdovey via the Caledonian Canal, Oban and the Menai Straits. The Blue Funnel Line (Alfred Holt & Co.) funded the voyage and provided a sail-trained master and rigger, a bosun and an engineer. The rest of the crew consisted of eight Gordonstoun boys, including James Main of Burghead. Emerging from the canal, *Prince Louis* was 'lost' for four days during which she found herself in the middle of a blacked-out convoy and narrowly missed a ramming. When she finally arrived in Wales, after three weeks' voyage, she anchored at Bangor, close to the training ship HMS *Conway*, a nineteenth-century wooden battleship used as a nautical school for training officers for the Merchant Navy, and was

Left: G.R. Guthrie carrying out maintenance on the *Henrietta*.

Below: The *Henrietta* under full sail.

met by Kurt Hahn and Lawrence Holt, owner of the Blue Funnel Line and Chairman of the Conway Committee. Holt is said to have turned to Hahn and the captain of *Conway* and declared: 'You must pool what you have in experience and good sense and, with your joint support, we can start a sea school at Aberdovey.' During the summer of 1941 the *Prince Louis* was repaired by Blue Funnel staff, and in October of that year the Aberdovey Sea School began; early in 1942 it became the first Outward Bound Sea School.

There were, in fact, already connections between Alfred Holt's Blue Funnel Line and Gordonstoun. Lawrence Holt had sent two sons to the school, and by 1938 the company was financing two scholarships offered to local boys whose parents were engaged in the fishing industry; a third was funded by sponsors referred to as Friends of Gordonstoun. Interviews were held in July at Wester Elchies, and two boys from Hopeman, and one from Burghead were successful. James Main (at twelve, the youngest) describes the routine: 'We had to be at the school for breakfast at 8 am each day and follow the normal routine, returning home about 8.30 pm after dinner at the school.' After spending time with the school in Wales, Main became Guardian and then went to sea in 1943 as a midshipman for Alfred Holt, as did the other two boys who had joined the school with him.

Henry Brereton describes the beginnings of the Nautical department: '[During the war] many boys were volunteering and HMS *Conway* was filled to capacity so that her captain had to refuse much promising material. We were therefore asked whether we would open a small nautical department to assist in the vocational training of some of these boys. We agreed and so began, for the first time, to train boys *for* as well as *through* the sea.' Captain Jack MacGregor was Housemaster (in Wales) to the Conway boys. He had lost a leg through enemy action whilst in the Merchant Navy aboard one of Alfred Holt's Blue Funnel ships and was, as Ralph Tattersall puts it, 'invited to take on the daunting task of teaching us Conway Class boys enough Navigation and Seamanship to enable us to slot in after a year, aboard the ship, halfway through their curriculum.'

Anthony Spivey, another Conway boy, spent his first term in Wales and then moved with the school back to Moray. 'The Conway cadets were very different from the Gordonstoun full-time pupils. They came as a distinct group, and were tutored as such, each term's intake being a class size, and although Navigation and Seamanship were specialist subjects, they were taught the other academic subjects as the same separate class. The majority, if not all, had come from grammar schools . . . and they had the motivation that if you didn't work, you didn't go to sea. A

disadvantage of the Conway intake was their normal stay of one year, after which they moved on for their second year on HMS *Conway*. This precluded any promotion to prefectorial rank, and had the added disadvantage that we had to purchase full Gordonstoun kit using my clothing coupons, then full Conway kit with my parents' and sister's coupons. My father, realising that in the real world a widely recognised piece of paper was essential, insisted I stay a fourth term to take and pass the old School Certificate, a wise move. Apart from the academic side, the pupils were totally integrated in activities, sports, dormitories, meals, etc., and a lot was learned by all parties . . . The regulars learned to cope with our North Country and Midland accents, and we learned to cope with theirs.' Tattersall echoes this satisfaction at the way everyone got on: 'As for bullying, I can't remember a single instance, and in a school with pupils from such a diverse mixture of social backgrounds and cultures as dukes' and fishermen's sons, quite remarkable. I had been very unhappy at my conventional preparatory school as a nine year old, but here I found nothing but understanding and compassion from the staff, and good companionship from fellow pupils, although individually some of the "better off" took a little time to accept the experimental Conway intake, until they

This page and opposite: The *Prince Louis*, sailing off Northern Ireland, 1946, and setting the sails.

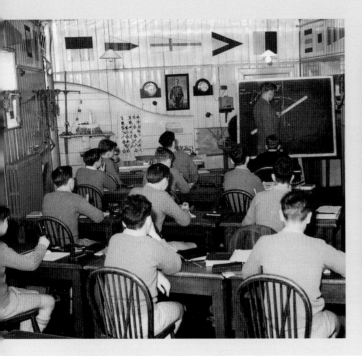

Above: Nautical Course lesson taking place in the Navigation Room, the Round Square, 1950s.

Above right: Morning Prayers aboard the *Prince Louis*, Sound of Mull, c. 1947.

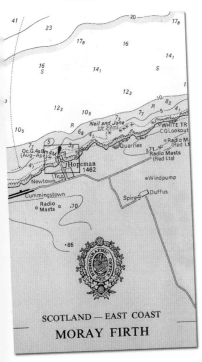

SCOTLAND — EAST COAST
MORAY FIRTH

found, with a few exceptions, we were not as riff-raffish as they had expected.'

Brereton was clear about the mutually beneficial nature of the decision to continue with the Nautical Course at Gordonstoun: 'The vocational nautical department had a number of advantages for the school. The whole seamanship activity gained by the organised technical instruction in navigation and the special nautical equipment which we had to introduce . . . Much more important was the new recruiting ground which was opened up to us. We were able to take into the school a larger proportion of boys from the splendid stock of the Scottish fishing communities which so attracted Dr Hahn nearly forty years ago . . . Through this department boys under vocational training got an opportunity of a non-vocational education at the same time. This was something new in English (or Scottish) education . . . Vocational training suffers from an isolation of its own. The young Merchant Service apprentice gained a wider horizon when he spent two of his most formative years in the companionship of boys preparing for the universities or business or farming or the army; and the bargain was not one-sided.'

Although the Conway–Gordonstoun connection continued only until 1947, the school's Nautical department ran for 25 years, until 1967. The Nautical department prepared boys to become officers in the Merchant Navy and the two-year course was recognised by the Board of Trade as equal to a year's training at sea – 'one year off a five-year cadetship', remembers Charles Legge (Duffus, 1955–57),

'valuable to say the least!' Many of the boys were provided with bursaries by merchant shipping companies and other sea-going related organisations: The Blue Funnel Line of Alfred Holt & Co, the Clan Line, the Blue Star Line, the Pacific Steam Navigation Company, Shell Tankers Ltd, the Hon. Company of Master Mariners and the Marine Society all contributed, with further assistance from Scottish local authorities. Legge recalls that he was awarded a Shell scholarship, but not directly by the company; it was his local education authority in Banffshire that selected boys to go to interview at Gordonstoun: 'I was lucky enough to receive a place . . . In addition to this, because of my parents' income, I was awarded a bursary from the same authority with my parents paying the remainder . . . Hahn was most keen to promote a broad cross-section of pupils at his school, believing that we could all learn from each other. Gordonstoun was never just for the privileged few. Another manifestation of this principle was that there was always a local boy present at the school, usually in the Navigation department because of their sea-going heritage, but not necessarily so. Funding would be negotiated in a sympathetic manner with or without shipping company sponsorship. I believe that "local" meant anywhere between Burghead, Hopeman and Lossiemouth . . . The classroom was at the west side of Round Square, opposite the bike shed. We would only be together as a class for Navigation, for other subjects we would be divided as deemed suitable by the school according to our abilities.'

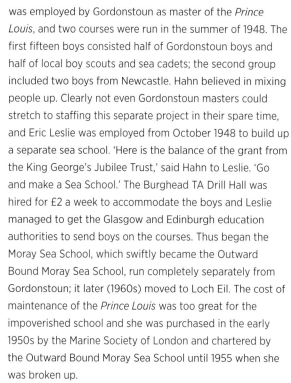

Right: Adam Brown and Jocelin Winthrop Young aboard the *Henrietta*, 1937. From the beginning the boys sailed in all weathers (below).

On the school's return to Moray in 1945, the two pre-war cutters stayed in Wales at the Outward Bound School. They were immediately replaced in Scotland by two more of Alec Findlay's boats: a 24-foot dipping lug cutter (built as a fishing boat with space for an engine), and a 14-foot skiff with a single lug sail. By the summer of 1947 a new cutter had been built, and in 1949 a second was completed, though neither was ever named; they were just known as 'the old cutter' and 'the new cutter'. Each took eight boys, and with four boats in use (two more belonging to the Sea Cadets), it was not unusual for 30 boys (out of a total of 150 at the school) to go down to the harbour at a time. At the end of 1946 an old 24-foot lobster boat named *Charm* was purchased and used as a safety boat, but she was seldom in working order. Eventually she broke her back on the rocks in the outer harbour when her mooring lines chafed through in a gale. Pat Whitworth remembers the somewhat risky business of priming her with petrol through a small tap funnel: 'You turned the tap off, turned the engine with the handle to start it, and then opened the tap to see the flames inside, taking care not to lose your eyebrows.'

In June 1946 the *Prince Louis* was sailed back to Moray, with Commander Godwin as skipper and Danny Main from Hopeman as bosun and engineer. The voyage was not without incident, and the *Prince Louis* was hit by a fierce gale in the Sound of Jura: 'We passed through the Corran Narrows into the teeth of the gale and found that the two engines were scarcely powerful enough to make way against it,' recalls David Astall. 'Godwin later said it was a salutary lesson for the boys; that engines don't always get you out of trouble. A service of thanksgiving was held on deck after the storm.'

Back in Moray, the *Prince Louis* lay in Hopeman harbour while boys refitted her; she was then moved to Burghead from where she could set sail more easily. Ever keen to spread opportunities beyond the school, Hahn conceived the idea of running short courses on the boat for outsiders, similar to those that had taken place at Aberdovey. He approached the King George's Jubilee Trust, which gave him £1,000 in 1947 and a further £3,000 over the next three years. Lt Michael Wallrock RN, who had a Master's Ticket,

Danny Main, a local skipper, who frequently assisted in the Seamanship department between 1936 and 1964.

was employed by Gordonstoun as master of the *Prince Louis*, and two courses were run in the summer of 1948. The first fifteen boys consisted half of Gordonstoun boys and half of local boy scouts and sea cadets; the second group included two boys from Newcastle. Hahn believed in mixing people up. Clearly not even Gordonstoun masters could stretch to staffing this separate project in their spare time, and Eric Leslie was employed from October 1948 to build up a separate sea school. 'Here is the balance of the grant from the King George's Jubilee Trust,' said Hahn to Leslie. 'Go and make a Sea School.' The Burghead TA Drill Hall was hired for £2 a week to accommodate the boys and Leslie managed to get the Glasgow and Edinburgh education authorities to send boys on the courses. Thus began the Moray Sea School, which swiftly became the Outward Bound Moray Sea School, run completely separately from Gordonstoun; it later (1960s) moved to Loch Eil. The cost of maintenance of the *Prince Louis* was too great for the impoverished school and she was purchased in the early 1950s by the Marine Society of London and chartered by the Outward Bound Moray Sea School until 1955 when she was broken up.

As in Wales, the Nautical department, and now general seamanship, were headed by Captain MacGregor. Lt Cdr Peter Godwin RN assisted him and was responsible for sailing and cruises. Hahn delighted in the competitive relationship between the two. Either one or the other usually staffed the cutters accompanied by Danny Main, a Hopeman fishing boat skipper, who had done wartime service in the Merchant Navy. There was no safety boat and the boys wore simple kapok-filled life jackets. Once they had passed certain tests, they were encouraged to take charge of the cutters and to sail them on their own. Facing the elements taught them more about discipline than could any schoolmaster. 'Seamanship,' remarked Kurt Hahn, 'gives greater exercise to the thinking facility . . . The Moray Firth is intolerant of mistakes.'

By the late 1940s two large boats belonging to Gordonstoun masters were being used for practising boat-maintenance skills during Saturday Projects. One was a gaff ketch known as *Salt Horse*, owned by Godwin, the other a Mevagissey lugger called the *Ellen Louise*, owned by Harry Leney, a Physics master. 'The *Ellen Louise*,' remembers David Byatt, 'had an old Bollinder engine with a faulty air compressor in the starter. The only way to start it was to wind a rope round and round the fly wheel, pass it up through a hatch to a line of boys who would pull as instructed. If pulled at the wrong moment, the engine might fire and go backwards pulling the boys down the hatch.'

No risk assessments in those days!' *Salt Horse* was used for summer cruises from 1946 until 1954, visiting both the south coast and the Baltic, until she was replaced in 1955 by *Soldian,* a 43-foot gaff ketch built in Lerwick and purchased with money from the school's 21st birthday appeal.

By 1951 the school had increased in size to 250, and sailing in the cutters continued to take place on most mornings and afternoons throughout the year. Morning seamanship training involved one form at a time and took place for a whole week. Afternoon seamanship, on the other hand, was just one of many activities happening alongside games, although each boy was obliged to do two terms of afternoon seamanship during his time at the school, once as a junior and once as a senior. As in pre-war days, there were occasional long weekend expeditions in the cutters across the Moray Firth. In time, when the two Hopeman-built cutters were given to the Moray Sea School, they were replaced in 1967 by two 'Shetland' cutters, *Fortitude* and *Tenacity,* which remained in use until 2007. Boys still cycled out to Hopeman for seamanship right up until the late 1970s when transport had to be provided to save time. Alasdair Gordon-Gibson (1973–78) has extremely clear recollections of those cycle trips: 'Running the gauntlet through the village past the local boys was perhaps the most challenging part, since we all felt rather conspicuous as we cycled by, dressed in heavy woollen jumpers and baggy, blue-serge bell-bottoms. I am aware that certain pupils even resorted to hiring a taxi from Jimmy Sutherland in Hopeman for the daily trip – quite against the rules, of course – I believe the reason was not so much fear or embarrassment . . . but rather a means to avoid cycling against the head winds and driving rain that were a regular feature of the climate on the road to the harbour from school.'

Above left: *Salt Horse,* owned by Lieutenant Commander Godwin, was wrecked off the Island of Lolland in July 1954.

Above: *Soldian* in the harbour at Hopeman.

Above: *Pinta*, 1950s.

Below: *Sea Spirit*, 1984; below right: *Sea Spirit's* first crew, October 1969.

In 1958 the school borrowed a larger boat – a 60- foot yawl, *Pinta* – for the Sail Training Race from Brest to Corunna. The boys did so well in her that in 1960 she was given to the school by her owner, George Christie, and was used by the school alongside *Soldian* for west coast cruising until *Soldian* was sold in 1965. *Pinta*'s last season was 1968; in 1969 she was replaced by a new school yacht, *Sea Spirit,* built in Holland to an Ocean Youth Club design with money from the Bernard Sunley Trust. Hobart Earle (1974–79), recalls the abrupt realisation that sailing from Gordonstoun was not going to be quite what he was used to: 'Having spent the first twelve years of my life in the tropics, the north of Scotland was quite a shock for me. I had never seen snow before, let alone worn winter clothing. As a child, I learned to sail in the Caribbean and loved spending time on the (warm!) water. This, however, was of little use in preparing me for an unforgettable force 10 gale in the summer of 1975 near Oban, which was a crude version of

mid-winter in its barest form. Those of us onboard the *Sea Spirit* felt as if we were freezing to death, never mind being thrown around all night long. We awoke to find our anchor had dragged several hundred yards during the night, and thanked our lucky stars we were relatively sheltered, and not out in the open sea! That was a night all of us, including Trevor Jones and HRH The Duke of York, are certain to remember.'

Sea Spirit did valiant service for the school, cruising on the west coast for nearly 30 years and entering the Tall Ships Race several times. Designed for sail training, she had, at first, no mechanical winches, and the crew all had to work seriously hard. Accommodation was all in one large central compartment, with curtains later added to shield the girls' bunks. *Sea Spirit* sailed west at the end of April and did not return to Moray until October each year. Crew changes took place at various locations along the west coast. Week-long sail-training voyages (somewhat

misleadingly referred to as cruises until recently) were now an established part of the curriculum. The Seamanship department was now responsible both for the routine training based at Hopeman harbour and for the west coast voyages. In preparation for these voyages, pupils experienced during the winter and spring months a week of Hopeman seamanship, sailing traditional dipping lug cutters out of Hopeman harbour and doing other basic training in the seamanship 'shed' there. In 1991 *Sea Spirit* was sailed by Gordonstoun students in the holidays, when Second Master David Byatt organised and skippered her entry in the Tall Ships Race from Aberdeen to Delfzijl, on the Dutch coast. She came first in her class. *Sea Spirit* was to cross the North Sea three more times in the decade, twice taking students on mountaineering expeditions in Norway, and again competing in the Tall Ships Race, this time to Trondheim.

CHIEF PETTY OFFICER 'Barney' Robinson, the mate on *Sea Spirit* and second-in-command in the Seamanship department for many years, will be remembered by generations of Gordonstoun sailors for 'Barney's stew', a concoction made from every tin of food remaining at the end of a cruise. Matthew Tawse (formerly Gibbs, Round Square, 1980–85) remembers being caught in a storm off the west coast on *Sea Spirit* along with Barney: 'I was one of only two pupils not suffering from sea sickness, which meant Barney gave me rather a lot of work to do! I was ordered to let down the staysail at the bow of the boat; this involved me clambering up to the front being soaked by huge waves, slipping all over the place, without a harness. I'm not sure that would be allowed today!'

During the 1990s, when there were many changes taking place in the way the rest of the school worked and applied the Hahnian ethos, the Seamanship department continued to function much as it always had. This was to change following the purchase of *Team Spirit of Wight* from the Ocean Youth Club in 1998. This was a nearly new Oyster-80 ketch, soon to be renamed *Ocean Spirit of Moray*. The replacement of *Sea Spirit* roughly coincided with John Tanner's retirement as Head of Seamanship and the tragic death in a fire at his home of Ian MacMillan, the bosun. The staffing of the department was restructured with two major objectives in view. The first was that the culture of the Seamanship department should develop in step with the rest of the school. The second was that the new vessel should be used for the benefit of Gordonstoun students throughout the sailing season, rather than sitting on a mooring for most of the long summer holidays. To achieve these, the skippering of *Ocean Spirit* and the teaching of seamanship in the dipping lug cutters at Hopeman were shared between John Trythall,

Above: Barney Robinson aboard a cutter, early 1970s. Behind him is the school's 'shed', which is still used for Seamanship classes.

Putting their backs into it: in 1938 (right); in 1978 with Graham Broad and Derek Edlestyn, the skipper of *Sea Spirit* (below); and in Hopeman harbour in 2004 (below right).

Cutters over the years.
Boys launching one of the
cutters, late 1930s (above);
cutter leaving Hopeman in the
late 1940s (centre); *Pole Star* in
2007 (right); *Fortitude* (below),
one of two identical cutters (the
other was *Tenacity*) which were
in service for some 40 years
until 2007.

the Outdoor Education Co-ordinator, and the newly
appointed, and vastly experienced, sail trainer Ian Lerner.
This increased staffing also enabled the voyages to be more
challenging for the students, without driving the staff into the
ground. The staff mates on *Ocean Spirit* were younger
trainee sail training professionals, who came to *Ocean Spirit*
with great enthusiasm for both working with the students
and developing their sail training skills before moving on in

a year or two, often to positions of command on other sail
training vessels.

After a first season of curricular cruises on the west
coast of Scotland and participation in the Tall Ships Race to
Britanny, *Ocean Spirit* had a major refit on the south coast
of England, and then embarked directly on Tall Ships 2000,
an ambitious race circuit to Cadiz, Bermuda, New York,
Halifax and Amsterdam that ran from April to August. She
was crewed by Gordonstoun students on the legs that fell
during the holidays, and mainly by old boys and girls on the
term-time legs. *Ocean Spirit* has undertaken long voyages in
every summer holiday since, either competing in the Tall
Ships Races to ports all over Europe or making voyages as
far west as the Azores, and as far north as Spitsbergen, only
600 miles short of the North Pole.

Despite the number of student berths increasing from
the twelve on *Sea Spirit* to sixteen, the size of the current
sixth form has again meant that the school has had to find

berths for some students on another vessel. Fortunately, an excellent relationship has developed between the school and Ocean Youth Trust Scotland, one of the UK's leading sail training organisations. *Ocean Spirit* and *Alba Venturer*, a near sister ship of *Ocean Spirit*, have undertaken many voyages in company, with Gordonstoun crews on both vessels.

How has the sail-training experience changed for a Gordonstoun student over the last ten or twenty years? The sea remains unchanged. Richard Rowe's delight at discovering the joys of sailing in the late 1980s will find echoes in the experiences of many others: 'The feeling of the sails filling for the first time and the boat ploughing through the waves silently powered only by the wind is something that I will never forget. Memories of lazy days in summer sailing up the Moray coast watching the dolphins and porpoises are indelibly engraved in my brain.' *Ocean Spirit* is a magnificent vessel, but so was *Sea Spirit*. The curricular voyages have become more ambitious in range – visiting North Rona (the northernmost of the Orkney Islands), St Kilda and the Irish Republic, with more time spent on passage than before. This has naturally increased the demands on the students, and has perhaps replaced a quasi-naval style of discipline with that more naturally imposed by the challenges of the extended voyages. The students have increased their contact with young people of other nationalities and backgrounds, through participation in Tall Ships Races, and the greater involvement of Gordonstoun in the sail-training community, as a result of the school's membership of the UK's Association of Sail Training Organisations.

Perhaps the area where the student's experience is least changed is that of Hopeman seamanship. Given that the operational design of the cutters remains the same, and the Moray Firth presents the same challenges, the crews still need to operate as a trained team before they can safely sail out of Hopeman harbour. There is little latitude for experimentation. When the time came, in 2007, to replace the cutters, Nigel Irens, an expert in traditional designs as well as racing catamarans, produced a design with an almost identical rig to that on the original cutters, but on a timber and epoxy hull, meeting the demanding stability and buoyancy requirements for today's sail training work. Two cutters, *Pole Star* and *Northern Light,* were beautifully built by Martin Cruden, a local traditional boatbuilder. They continue to give the students the same experience of working together as a team, where the safety of the vessel and crew depend on every crew member doing their job, despite being probably cold, perhaps seasick, and maybe a little apprehensive.

Yawl sailing with Hopeman village in the background, 2007.

DINGHY SAILING

When David Byatt returned as Second Master in 1971, he used a legacy to the Seamanship department to buy a suitable low-maintenance boat for summer use and chose a modern glass-fibre boat with Bermudan rig, known as a Devon Yawl, perfect for the exposed conditions of the Moray Firth. It was a 16-footer, had two masts and could take a crew of five. In time the fleet increased to five. A motor safety boat was also purchased and pupils could be allowed once again to take charge of their craft themselves. For a few years, sailing had not happened at Hopeman between April and September, but now every summer term, twice a week following lessons until supper, a group of dedicated students would sail the yawls in the Firth as a senior activity. Frequent sightings of bottlenose dolphins added greatly to the pleasure of the experience. During the winter a smaller group of students would do the necessary maintenance to keep the boats afloat the following summer. Again, in the early 1980s, the school was gifted some laser dinghies and two Dory power boats, and dinghy sailing at Findhorn emerged under the enthusiastic guidance of Ben Goss.

It was not long before the benefits of the Devon Yawl were recognised by the Gordonstoun International Summer School as an opportunity for their students to have a taste of seamanship training. This extended the use of the yawls into the summer holidays and allowed the Gordonstoun students who skippered them to pass on their knowledge to the international students.

In 1986 David Bell arrived at the school as the new Head of Biology; he was also a Royal Yachting Association (RYA) Senior Instructor. Under him, the structure of Gordonstoun's dinghy sailing at Findhorn became more formalised. A junior sailing activity was introduced with senior sailors and members of the SBS helping with instruction and safety boat duties. Weekend sailing also became a regular occurrence with race training as one aspect. This meant that the laser dinghies were now being used five or more days a week. In addition Bell obtained two 420 dinghies.

On the retirement of David Byatt in 1993, yawl sailing was amalgamated with laser sailing. This had the beneficial effect that when there was, for example, a strong ebbing tide at Findhorn that in the past would have led to the activity being cancelled, it could now be transferred safely to Hopeman; conversely, a rough sea at Hopeman might mean that the activity could be taken to the more sheltered waters of Findhorn Bay. Soon, Gordonstoun became a recognised RYA teaching centre, with annual inspections to monitor equipment and safety; it also benefited from a boat replacement policy through which the school obtained four Laser Vago dinghies, a high-performance modern dinghy with a trapeze and genakker. Bell was now able to run sailing and powerboat courses for many of the students. Since the retirement of David Bell from dinghy sailing in 2008, the activity has taken place at the Findhorn Marina Sailing School.

Above right: Laser sailing at Findhorn at the bay entrance with Culbin Forest in the background, 2007.

Right: Aberlour House pupils in yawls at Hopeman harbour under instruction from Gordonstoun students, 2007.

THE SERVICES

'A boarding school can contribute something essential to the health of the community immediately beyond it, and the community contributes something essential to the school' KURT HAHN

OF ALL KURT HAHN'S achievements at Gordonstoun, the establishment of the Services is the most unusual. For a school to support several groups trained to professional standards and dedicated to helping others, *in extremis* saving lives, is unique. That the principle has been followed, developed and remains so fundamental to the school ethos after 75 years is truly impressive. Hahn himself regarded what he called 'the Samaritan service' as 'the school's greatest contribution to the training of the young'. Ever keen to expound upon the moral power of these activities, Hahn explained their purpose: 'The experience of helping a fellow man in danger, or even of training in a realistic manner to be ready to give this help, tends to change the balance of power in a youth's inner life with the result that compassion can become the master motive' and 'True integrity, wholeness of purpose can never be achieved until a boy is able to shift the focus of his energies and interests from himself on to an aim outside himself.' 'The passion of rescue,' he remarked, 'reveals the highest dynamic of the human soul.' Participation in these activities also

Top left: Coastguards practising a cliff rescue at Cove Bay, just north of the school, 1970s.

Above: A Fire Service practice in 1992.

Left: Auxiliary towing vehicle leaving Nissen hut station, probably 1940s.

Opposite: A winter climbing trip in the Cairngorms in 2010.

guaranteed to a greater or lesser extent contact with the local communities they served, helping to counter the self-centred isolation that Hahn regarded as a threat to the health of country boarding schools. Jocelin Winthrop Young remarked in the mid-'80s that he had very seldom heard any criticism of the demands of the Services on the school or its pupils, and that in his opinion their success was 'in the greater part due to the enthusiasm of the students'.

Some Services have come and gone over the years, as is natural when new possibilities are explored from time to time, but the principal activities – the Coastguard Service, the Fire Service, the Mountain Rescue Service and the Community Service – have continued since their inception at various times since 1935. Traditionally Wednesday afternoon has been set aside for training in the services, and this time is jealously guarded from the encroachment of other activities by those involved.

THE COASTGUARD SERVICE

The idea for what was initially called the Watchers Service came from the Founder himself and brought together neatly the nautical emphasis of the school's early years with the Hahnian virtues of vigilance, patience and vision. It began to take serious shape when two captains of HM Coastguard came to a school meeting at which they announced that in return for the building of a Coastguard Hut, and a willingness to man it, a telephone connection and life-saving gear (pistol, rockets, breeches buoy) would be provided. In 1936, a wooden hut was opened, built by boys under the guidance of Mr (later Sir) George Trevelyan (a friend of the Richter family and Geoffrey Winthrop Young). In the December 1938 edition of *The Gordonstoun Record*, the principles of the Service were laid out in a lengthy prospectus. Initially, the Watchers was open also to boys of the surrounding district, and an early breakdown of numbers reveals twelve boys from Gordonstoun, fifteen from Hopeman village and fourteen from the communities of Duffus and Drainie. Although training centred upon nautical skills, communications and the use of life-saving apparatus, the Watchers also acted as a focal point for other joint activities with local boys, including sports, ground agility, the occasional lecture and musical events.

The prime active contribution of the Service was manning the Watchtower in bad weather. This could last continuously for many days and nights, with the watch changing every four hours. During the evacuation to Wales,

The first Watchers' Hut (top), built by boys under the guidance of George Trevelyan, and its opening in 1936 (above).

Below: The third Coastguard Watchtower or Lookout on the day of its opening by HRH The Duke of Edinburgh, 24 September 1955. Designed by Sir Martyn Beckett and made possible by a benefaction from Antonin Besse, this eight-sided tower has three floors, the first of which is a sleeping room; above it is a living room and, on top, a look-out room and open gallery.

Coastguards
abseiling at Cove
Bay, 1980s.

2 am though . . . One night I was called out some time after midnight to go on watch because the weather had got bad . . . I remember walking from the Round Square with another boy, presumably one who was to go on watch with me, along a very noisy gravel path in front of Gordonstoun House to get milk and tea and such from the kitchen for our night in the Watchers' Hut. We were passing below Mr Hahn's rooms when the window flew up and he shouted, "Who's there?" in a peremptory sort of way. When he had discovered who we were and why we were there, he shouted "Can you catch? I will throw some biscuits to you." We discouraged him from this rash scattering of largesse as it was a black night and raining, so he said, "Come to my rooms in the morning to get some" . . . We went on our way to the kitchens and collected provisions for the night . . . I remember dipping milk out of the ten-gallon churn in the store room without stirring it so that it was extra nice and creamy. Then we walked in the dark about a mile to the hut on the cliffs.' Bush then goes on to relate how in his final year he was at last allowed to be the one who fired the rocket line carrying a rope to an imagined wreck: 'There never was one, I admit, but there always might have been and we drilled earnestly.' During that year, Princess Elizabeth and Prince Philip came to inspect the Watchers' Drill: 'I don't know exactly what happened, but the rocket, instead of flying over the wreck, represented by two boys on a rock half-covered by the tide, went straight at them and they jumped, one to each side and the line hit the rock and went between them. "He missed them", remarked the Prince. I wonder what it would be like to be hit by one of those rockets? When you fired one, it burned all the hair off the back of your hand and the fluffy bits on your jersey.'

Improvements to the equipment and housing of the unit were continual in the post-war years. The use of life-saving apparatus and cliff ladder was a constant feature, and there must have been relief in 1949 when a spotlight was acquired; previous night exercises were undertaken by the light of a single lantern. Another arrival was 'Blundy', a 1929 Austin, described as 'a fashionable car of its time', and the attendant worry of how to make best use of the petrol ration, with the requirement that watch-keeping must continue during the vacations; boys who lived locally accomplished this. By now the Service had between 50 and 60 members. David Gibson, Captain of the Watchers in 1955, remembers being called out to rescue a sheep that had fallen on to a cliff ledge about twenty feet below the top: 'We dropped two rope ladders, one to each side of the animal, thus "penning" it in. I was lowered and managed to secure two ropes before the poor beast was hoisted up.'

the 30 miles between Plas Dinam and the sea prevented this, but training in sailing and rowing along with rocket drills continued (with a tree treated as an imaginary wreck). On the return to Scotland, a replacement lookout was built, constructed from the wheelhouses of two old sailing ships, and soon after a telephone was installed. Watches were undertaken in the foulest of weather; even thigh-deep snow was not enough to prevent a watch being maintained. There was a momentary break in 1947, however, when Hahn announced to an astonished school that the use of a nearby firing range by the army would preclude watching. Compromise was quickly reached: during watches the army camp would be informed, and the firing party withdrawn.

'If you were on call, you could be dragged out of bed at any time of the night to go on watch', remembers Alan Bush (1946–49). 'If one was on the night watch, one was excused all the morning classes the next day. The morning watch missed them anyway. The afternoon one was the most unprofitable from the skiving point of view, but they were all pretty good and one watched and drank endless cups of tea. It is quite hard to keep alert staring into black nothingness at

The opening of the new Watchtower (1955) was marked with a visit by the Duke of Edinburgh. The Services Centre opened in 1960, providing a base for the three Rescue Services and allowing the Watchers to abandon the old Nissen hut that had hitherto been the Service's base. The use of a lorry gave additional mobility in a group that numbered well over 40 students. The cliff ladder was replaced by various rope-based descent and ascent routines, and the lorry by a series of Land Rovers, latterly equipped with winches. In 1972 the Watchers was retitled an HM Auxiliary Coastguard Unit and now became known within the school as the Coastguard Service.

For a while after girls arrived at the school, the Coastguard Service remained boys only, not least because of worries about unsupervised overnight stays in the remote watchtower, but by 1989 the Service had become mixed. The balance of training between Cliff Rescue, Radio Training, First Aid and Search Techniques remained constant over the 1980s and 1990s. However the use of rockets and flares faded from the repertoire, partly as a result of the increased role of helicopters in sea rescue (the breeches buoy was withdrawn in 1989). The maintenance of watches in foul weather, and especially on Sundays, when there were more visitors to the coastline (both in the water and on the beach), continued to give a sense of purpose as did the introduction of pagers. The local Sector Officer based in Lossiemouth played a significant role in training. The contribution of Don McKelvie, for example, was enormous over a period of at least twenty years.

The amount of time that the local Sector Officer (later Sector Manager) could give to the Service eventually came under pressure from other unavoidable demands of the job. On one occasion in the 1990s the then Station Officer discovered that he had for many months been cheerfully using a cliff technique discarded long ago elsewhere! The school remains grateful, however, for all the support given by busy professionals.

Matthew Tawse (formerly Gibbs, Round Square, 1980–85) speaks highly of the character-forming effects of Coastguard duty: 'The harsh weather conditions and the fact that I was constantly tested physically and mentally in the Coastguards, on Expedition and on Cruise, have served me well in later years. We were given a huge amount of independence whilst on Night Watch up at the Coastguard Tower. The occasions when we were left to talk via radio with the Coastguard . . . and with passing ships, as the storms thundered past and the sea roared below us, are nights I will never forget.'

Coastguards on exercise, 2007.

In the early 2000s there were large cutbacks in funding for Volunteer Coastguard units across the country, and it was at this point that Gordonstoun lost its Cliff Rescue function. It has taken time to recover a sense of purpose and appropriate range of training. The reintroduction of preparation for a national Royal Yachting Association Radio Certificate has provided part of the answer, and currently every student in the Service undertakes both this and a first-aid qualification. Training in search techniques, with frequent drills involving local search teams, allows students to work closely with other volunteer units. National Coastguard training programmes have been adapted for school use, and recently funds have been approved for a long awaited refurbishment of the Watchtower. Thus there is every reason to be confident of the outlook for the future of this most visionary of Services.

THE SURF LIFE-SAVING SERVICE AND INSHORE RESCUE

The Surf Life-Saving Service (SLS) started in the early 1960s. In 1978, Ben Goss joined the Service, and he has vivid memories of reel and line drills and beach and sea work in all weather conditions. Per Gwalter (1979–83) remembers his bracing experiences with the Service with some enthusiasm: 'Most of my closest friends and I joined the SLS and became hardened to the freezing exercises and Surf Life-Saving exams we had to do in the Scottish winters. The Service was excellent and involved all sorts of water-based activities, including canoeing around coastlines and riding the waves on surf skis.' Soon, though, once the Sea King

202 Unit at Lossiemouth was available for call-out in emergencies, there was little real need for beach drills and a new group called the Inshore Rescue Unit (IRU) was created, incorporating elements of canoeing, motorboat work and some of the functions of the original SLS.

'I arrived in Moray in January 1981, ostensibly as a Geography teacher', writes Sue Wrenn Fenton. 'I had just crewed a ketch from the Isle of Wight to South Africa and was immediately press-ganged by Big Ben Goss into joining the Surf Life-Saving Service; was he thinking Baywatch? I had been secretly harbouring alternative preferences about Service on a Wednesday afternoon, but apparently the school motto *plus est en vous* applied to the staff as well as to the pupils. So started almost ten years of involvement with SLS, latterly as Service Commander. The Service morphed into the Inshore Rescue Unit (IRU) over this period and further spawned the breakaway groups of the Special Boat Service and Corps of Canoe Lifeguards.

'Training included RLSS pool lifeguard training in the school pool as well as the Surf Life-Saving Association (SLSA) surf rescue drills. I first tackled the intricacies of the reel-and-line in winter, on the grass outside the Sports Centre; this decided me to visit surf clubs in Cornwall, Wales and Australia in my summer holidays to see the action for real. However inspiring these visits were, there was never anyone else on Hopeman beach to rescue, even in "summer" (i.e. when the water temperature crept above the magic ten degree mark and the Royal Air Force Search & Rescue crews

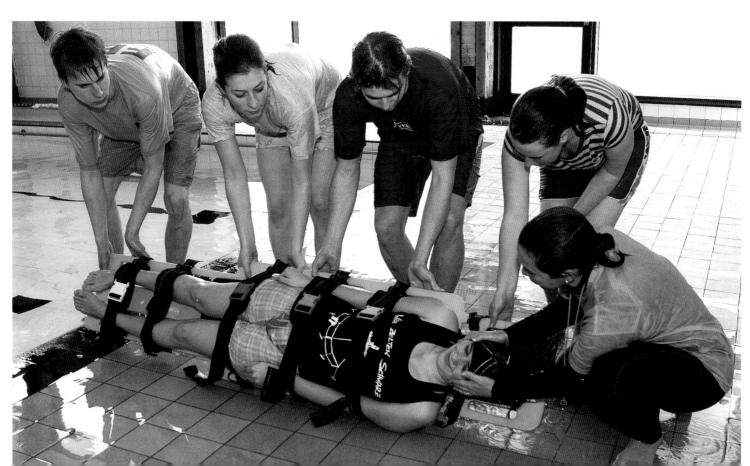

'I managed to wriggle out of the IRU when expecting a baby – wet suits didn't seem to fit any more, and it was awkward climbing down ladders on the harbour wall. However, my daughter is now a rescue diver and has been a crew member with the RNLI; she is a far better swimmer than I ever was.'

THE CORPS OF CANOE LIFEGUARDS

The Gordonstoun Corps of Canoe Lifeguards had its inception in the late 1970s as a subgroup of the Surf Life-Saving Service (which has itself now evolved into the Pool Lifeguards). Under the leadership of Ben Goss, the Surf Life-Savers introduced kayaking to broaden the breadth of the Service's activities. Soon a small group was formed to concentrate on this area, developing personal kayaking skills and looking at ways to use the kayak in a swimmer rescue or a search situation. In 1980, for example, Grampian Police called out the kayak group to help look for a missing person. They searched a local loch near Fochabers and eventually found and helped to recover a body. This traumatic event highlighted the effectiveness of kayaks in this role and the high level of proficiency of our students, prompting the idea of creating a dedicated kayak unit.

In 1981 the kayak group was taken over by Tony Gabb, who had recently joined the school, and under his leadership it grew in size and broadened its remit. In 1982 it became a separate Service; contacts were made with the BCU Canoe Lifeguards (part of the British Canoe Union), and a training programme was implemented to train students to first achieve the BCU 3 Star Award (for personal skills on moving water) and then the BCU Assistant Lifeguard Award, which focuses on rescue skills for other canoeists and for swimmers in difficulty, as well as on search techniques for rivers and coastlines. It also includes training in basic first aid and life-saving techniques.

The next major call-out was in 1985 when an elderly lady and her son were swept away while visiting Randolph's Leap on the river Findhorn, when a wall of water rushed down the gorge – the result of very heavy rain in the Monadhliath mountains where the Findhorn rises. The son had managed to climb out, but his mother had not. The Canoe Lifeguards searched the river while the Coastguards and Mountain Rescue unit searched the shore of Findhorn Bay and part of the coastline. With the river in spate, two members of staff searched the Sluie Gorge and then met up with the rest of the Service to search on down to the bay. By now, dusk was falling and this happened to coincide with low tide. Just as the search was about to be abandoned, a body was discovered tangled in a mass of branches and

were allowed to abandon their immersion suits.) However, I have fond memories of eating water melon on the beach after the stringent SLSA exams, while entertaining formidable senior examiners from the deep south.

'The unit regularly resuscitated "Annie and her baby", learnt to use oxygen therapy, and undertook extensive first-aid training. Visits were made to the yellow RAF helicopters at neighbouring Lossiemouth and to the Robert Gordon Survival Centre at Stonehaven where we were bounced around in the North Sea in liferafts. Back at Gordonstoun, demonstrations of reel-and-line were given in the lake (!) and on the lawns. One year, for Open Day, we staged a mock shark attack at Cove Bay. Students were trained for the Royal Yachting Association power boat exams in Hopeman harbour, and the unit provided safety cover for dinghy sailing and windsurfing at Findhorn. Members of the Service undertook a relay swim across the Moray Firth from Cromarty to Nairn to fundraise for the Royal National Lifeboat Institution. We made regular visits to the Buckie lifeboat and occasionally joined in with Sunday training sessions in the Firth. Call-outs were few and far between, but one winter weekend saw us scouring the Dornoch Firth for a farmer's missing wife; the armada of boats and canoes failed to find a body. The farmer's wife was later reported as having flitted to New Zealand.

'Being a Service Commander involved far more work and planning than being a Head of Department; the spectre of Wednesday afternoons hung over me for many years after leaving Gordonstoun. However, I was helped by a succession of able Heads of Service, both girls and boys, who were selected each term.

Below: Corps of
Canoe Lifeguards at
Lossiemouth in 2006.

Below right: A Canoe
Lifeguards demonstration
at the school's Open Day
in 2004.

other debris. Various members of the school assisted the police in the recovery of the body, and handed it over to the saddened but relieved family.

A key requirement for those joining this Service is that they should genuinely enjoy kayaking in all its forms. Heading onto the sea on a grey cold November afternoon is not to everyone's taste, and this provides a natural filter, meaning that the Service is made up of really dedicated and determined individuals. When the surf is rolling on

Wednesday afternoons, formal training is generally abandoned to make the most of the conditions. Learning to control a kayak in surf is a great way to develop kayak skills and is also a lot of fun. There are also plenty of opportunities to practise rescuing each other!

In the winter term the programme generally concentrates on pool training sessions together with classes on first aid, ropework for rescues and life-saving skills to try and ensure a solid all-round knowledge and skill base. However, students are equipped to head out onto the water if the need arises.

Other calls for assistance have included searching the Culbin Forest coastline for a missing yachtsman, but call-outs of this nature are few and far between and are becoming even rarer, given the increasing reluctance of the emergency services to enlist the help of youngsters in potentially dangerous situations. Other opportunities have, however, been identified, including providing safety cover for open-water swimming events, helping to coach younger students and visitors in kayaking, completing beach clear-ups and the like. Additionally, the Service aims to provide its members with a sound understanding of kayaking skills and safety that they can pass on after leaving school, when they join university canoe clubs or other groups.

THE SPECIAL BOAT SERVICE

After the school was gifted some laser dinghies and two Dory power boats in the early 1980s, dinghy sailing at Findhorn emerged as a senior activity twice a week for what David Bell describes as 'adrenaline junkie students'. Soon after, windsurfing at Findhorn was introduced and overseen by Richard Hadfield. With the extra equipment and additional activities, Ben Goss saw the possibility of starting the Special Boat Service (SBS) as one of the Wednesday afternoon Services, thus combining two of the central planks of the Hahnian educational project: seamanship and service.

The SBS has in the past been involved with HM Coastguard in searches, rescuing cruisers that have broken free of their moorings in the fierce tides of Findhorn Bay, and rescuing other dinghy sailors from the Royal Findhorn Yacht Club as well as providing safety cover on many occasions, but memorably for a sponsored swim by the Gordonstoun Inshore Rescue Unit across the Moray Firth in the late '80s and teaching other students how to sail. David Bell took over dinghy sailing (see page 133) after his arrival at the school in 1986, and soon after also took charge of the SBS, since when its function has become almost exclusively one of providing training for junior pupils at the school and standby rescue services for sea-based activities and events carried out by students at the school.

The first two vehicles pressed into service as fire tenders in Wales: an Austin 7 (top) and a Cadillac (above).

THE FIRE SERVICE

The Gordonstoun fire unit was started in 1942 by a boy at the school in Wales after it had been evacuated from Moray to Montgomeryshire during World War II. Stephen Philp, at Plas Dinam, provided his own 'fire engine', which was an Austin 7 car, painted red and equipped with a ladder. He and his group of volunteers initially trained on the Austin, until he provided another car, this time a Cadillac. Convinced of the importance of this nascent firefighting crew, Philp took it upon himself to write to the local commander of the National Fire Service requesting that the school unit be accepted as an official addition to the local force. In response, the commander sent Column Officer Rowlands to inspect the boys' unit.

'On the appointed day,' recounts Stephen Philp, 'we put on a display which involved the tender arriving in front of Plas Dinam House and entry being made by ladder into a first-floor room, from which a supposedly unconscious person was lowered by rope to the ground while the first-aid reel was brought into play. The whole school, including the Headmaster, Kurt Hahn, and the entire staff, were present to watch what I suspect many secretly hoped would turn out to be a huge joke. However, I am pleased to say that C.O. Rowlands was sufficiently impressed to recommend that we be incorporated into the National Fire Service.'

Students on a powerboat course led by David Bell at Findhorn in 2005.

Left and below: the NFS Beresford Stork Light Trailer Pump at Plas Dinam, Wales, in 1945.

Once the Fire Service had joined the official organisation, members of staff became involved. 'Although at the outset my heart had not really been in it,' recalled Norman Pares, 'a great affection for the Fire Service was born in me by the amazing keenness and enthusiasm of the few boys who started it all in Wales. We had considerable *esprit de corps*.' Since that time, many generations of teachers at Gordonstoun have been drawn into the Service by the infectious enthusiasm that it generates. Just as the original fire unit was formed at the initiative of the boys, so the

The school pump in action at the Admiralty warehouse fire, Newtown, in December 1944.

modern fire unit at Gordonstoun depends for its spirit on the vigour and commitment of today's students.

It was a condition of the National Fire Service in Wales that the Gordonstoun fire unit should be available not just in term time, but throughout the year, which obviously posed a problem during school holidays. According to the account of Henry Brereton, 'the inhabitants of Llandinam were approached and a sufficient number of men volunteered . . . The boys trained alongside the farmers, the blacksmith, the gardener, the estate agent and a number of masters.' Michael Brownson (1941–44) remembers that the enrolling of adults from Llandinam meant that the authorities also made a payment to the boys for turnouts – 'not large sums, but enough to buy the occasional cake from Ma Davies's shop by Plas Dinam gates, making it the only school service where members got paid.'

In December 1944 the new unit was called upon to help fight a large fire at a naval warehouse on the banks of the Severn at Newtown. One boy, H.D. Dawson, wrote in *The Gordonstoun Record*: 'We left for Newtown wondering what sort of fire it was, large or small, and what sort of building. We were not long in suspense, for we saw the glow about a mile before we reached Newtown. It was a three-storey warehouse; part of the roof and both upper floors had already caved in.' Norman Pares describes this same fire: 'It was bitterly cold with ice on the roads. We manhandled our large pump on the beach of the river Severn and ran our hose over a narrow footbridge to the fire.'

Although the equipment and many of the techniques of firefighting have changed since the Gordonstoun unit was started in 1942, the original underlying aims remain the same: service and education. Members of the Fire Service learn lessons and skills of huge value, principal among which are: working with others in a team, following a discipline that depends on co-operation, communicating effectively to achieve their purpose, setting aside personal priorities in favour of helping others who urgently need help, learning to trust the work of others and to be trusted for their own work, and handling machinery and equipment with confidence. For the Fire Service is neither a game nor a sport, but work in which young people know unequivocally that they are needed. For those who are both teachers and firefighters there is no more attractive way of nurturing in young people a sense of responsibility towards the community in which they live. Timothy Barker (1962–64) gives a clear account of the benefits he believes he drew from his time as a firefighter: 'Gordonstoun enabled me to develop self-confidence and esteem and I know that it was the influence of the school that led me to have a successful career working with the Probation Service . . . The Fire Service was brilliant and taught me to deal with emergencies in a calm and clear way. I was involved in house and bush fires. The discipline of working in dangerous and difficult situations was very important and again prepared me for working with some very dangerous and demanding clients.'

At about the time when the school returned to Moray from its wartime location in Wales, responsibility for the management and organisation of fire brigades across the UK was being handed back to local authorities. By 1948 the Gordonstoun firefighters were under the control of the North Eastern Fire Brigade. For the next 25 years the unit at Gordonstoun was sustained by enthusiasm and affection, and by just enough call-outs to make the boys feel that there was a job to do. This extract from *The Gordonstoun Record*, written by Matthew Wright in 1957, refers to a visit to the school by the Firemaster and illustrates the mixture of enthusiasm, exasperation and encouragement that flavoured the relationship between the school and the NEFB: 'The Firemaster was able to allay our fears, for we had felt he was not using us as much as he might have done. This in fact had been true for two reasons. Firstly, he did not like our policy of taking both his appliance and the school's own to every fire; and secondly, he objected to the number of boys and staff, besides firemen, who appeared at

fires. We have agreed to discontinue the use of the school's machine for firefighting, and to discourage spectators. He, on the other hand, will equip the Austin towing vehicle with an 80 gallon tank, hose reel, and an aluminium light pump . . . And now we have made contact again with the Firemaster, we can hope for even more work next year.'

The hope 'for even more work next year' was a key feature of the attitude of boys to the Fire Service. More than just a wish for excitement and a break with routine, it was a genuine capacity for energetic hard work under difficult conditions, and a great willingness to be of real assistance in a world run by adults, bearing out Kurt Hahn's observation that 'the call "you are needed" never fails'. It was the conviction that they had something to offer that helped boys and staff persevere with their training through the weeks, and sometimes terms, when the siren was silent.

In the late 1940s and 1950s, several of the call-outs to bigger fires were to farms; these tended to be similar in character, with the firefighters spending long hours in dirty and uncomfortable conditions, dogged by water supply difficulties, but cheerfully willing to stay on long after the flames had disappeared to carry through the arduous task of clearing up burnt straw and fallen roofs. On 21 January 1953 there was an extensive fire at Myreside Farm. P.J. Walz described it in the *School Bulletin* for that year, and his account will be familiar to any firefighter who has attended a lengthy farm fire: 'The wind was fresh and, since most of the doors had been burnt away, strong draughts swept through the building, furiously aggravating the flames and filling the barns and passageways with scalding gusts of smoke and sparks . . . Since the whole of the building lay to the leeward of the fire, it was our first duty to prevent the fire spreading further. Only then could we turn our branches upon the doorways and, by cooling the stone and the heaps of flaming straw around it, advance foot by foot towards the flaming apertures . . . What was left of the many hundreds of bales of straw we tossed and picked apart, soaking every bit. We left the farm at about 12.30 and got back to drink our well-earned cocoa.'

In the late 1950s Gordonstoun School was spread across various locations; Altyre House, near Forres, developed a relatively independent existence, and by 1960, when it was amalgamated into the main site, Altyre had been proudly running its own fire unit on a private, or 'estate', basis under Pat Whitworth, a young Physics master who had been at the school since 1957. 'During my two years at Altyre', reflected Whitworth, who had been in the Gordonstoun unit as a boy, 'we had rather more call-outs than Gordonstoun. This may have been fate, but I am more inclined to put it down to the

Gordonstoun firemen training with the Manchester Fire Brigade in 1968.

station at about four in the afternoon, set off the fire alarm and waited for the boys (firemen) to arrive. As they had all their clothes/gear there, sometimes they'd arrive from the washroom or activity with very little on, much to the amusement of the visitors and Hahn.'

In the summer of 1963, at the invitation of Chief Officer Oare of the Manchester Fire Brigade, a group of Gordonstoun firefighters spent nine days at the city's London Road Fire Station. During their stay they joined the training sessions at the training school and rode to fires on the appliances alongside the professional firefighters. These summer visits to Manchester became a regular arrangement for the next ten years. One of those who went, M.B. Howard, gave an account of his experiences in *The Gordonstoun Record*: 'The 1964 Summer visit to the Manchester Fire Brigade was as successful as the pioneer visit of the previous year. Vigorous training with the full-time trainee firemen and visits to local sites and to high fire risks were liberally supplemented by a number of interesting fires which we attended with the regular crews. Calls received during our stay included domestic fires, derelict property, a railway station, motor accidents, flooding, and many other incidents, including a "ten-pump" fire in a warehouse, involving a force of about 70 firemen.'

In 1972 the Gordonstoun unit turned out to ten incidents; in 1986 call-outs numbered 107. The steady increase in call-outs per year over this period was the result of a '24-hour call' arrangement made in 1976 (with Divisional Officer Thomson, over lunch), whereby the school unit was summoned every time the Lossiemouth station was responding to a call. Gone were the days of the occasional call-out; now they could (and did) happen with some frequency at any time of day or night. As very few of the staff involved were drivers, they were initially under some strain, but as more staff joined the Service, a more workable rota was devised, allowing the drivers to be released from the requirement to stay within a few minutes' dash of the fire station.

Former Gordonstoun firefighters who were in the Service in the late 1970s will remember the night calls in the dead of winter that started with the duty driver being telephoned by Control from Aberdeen, after which he or she would go from house to house waking the boys and girls on watch, before scrambling to the station in the darkness, hoping against hope that the appliance would start. This procedure was transformed in 1982 by the arrival of pagers (which allowed both driver and crew to be alerted direct) as well as the provision of appliances that really would start from cold without being cranked or towed.

fact that we were a freelance brigade with no official ties to anybody. If we smelt smoke in the air, off we would go and nobody indicated that we were not welcome. All our equipment was secondhand and our hose frequently sent water to places en route that were not in need of it, but we had the incentive to keep as efficient as possible and I do not think that we ever let anyone down.' Gordon Currie (Altyre, 1954–59) remembers that when Pat Whitworth was at the school he set up a system so that when the fire station siren went off, the engine of the fire truck started and the garage doors flew open automatically: 'Hahn loved to show this off to visitors and quite often took them to the fire

The Grampian Fire Brigade showed their confidence in the Gordonstoun unit not just by the provision of steadily improving equipment, but also by committing training officers to visit the station on a regular basis so that recruits and firefighters followed a thorough and sustained programme. This was reinforced by a closer link with the full-time station in Elgin, where groups of boys and girls had training sessions every Wednesday afternoon. In the late 1980s firefighters were invited to spend a working week at Aberdeen fire stations to gain city experience and to improve their training; thus began a regular arrangement whereby Gordonstoun firefighters, singly or in pairs, could work and train alongside professional firefighters away from the school, as they had done back in the 1960s at Manchester.

As more and more incidents were attended, the Gordonstoun fire crews grew to know the Lossiemouth crews well and to understand how best to work with them as a back-up unit. For numerous boys, girls and staff it became a valued experience to be able to work alongside the firefighters from Station 38 under their sub-officers, and frequently with the Elgin crews as well. What the school's crews have achieved on the firegrounds over the years has been firmly supported through the leadership, patience, and friendship of these crews in Moray.

Girls joined the school in 1972, and by 1975, memorably, the Gordonstoun Fire Service deployed the first female firefighters in the country. As it was the only fire station in the UK at which trained firewomen were riding to calls, the press took a considerable interest in this development, as did other fire brigades. Any doubts that had been expressed about the capability of women in an operational situation were soon dispelled as the girls proved themselves to be thoroughly competent as firefighters.

Anthony Montgomery, who ran the fire service from 1968 to 1990, writes about an extensive and memorable fire at which girls were present in force, though not yet as official Brigade firefighters: 'The fire on Ben Aigan above Craigellachie in 1976 was to prove significant for two reasons: first in terms of firefighting, the unit showed itself able to establish and maintain a relay of ten portable pumps (and branches) stretching from the Spey to the summit for seven days and nights; we had finally shed our amateur image and found ourselves accepted on a par with other retained units. Indeed at night most other units were withdrawn from the fireground. The second reason arose from the extent of the operation: for the first time the Divisional Commander had to make use of a light aircraft to determine his plan of action. The result of this was a call for volunteer helpers: although principally from the RAF (who supplied them with cans of water dated 1947!), it provided a unique opportunity to field a crew (by minibus) consisting entirely of girls from Gordonstoun: although fully trained and immaculately turned out, they had never, hitherto, been allowed to engage in firefighting. Their competence – and endurance – turned out to have been the deciding factor as far as the Fire Authority was concerned in taking on women in a firefighting role not only at Gordonstoun, but throughout the Brigade.' The Station 39 (the Gordonstoun unit) log book records that Bridget Koch was in the crew riding to a house fire in Coulardbank Road, Lossiemouth, on 19 October 1978, and was thus the first trained female firefighter in the UK to respond officially to a call.

Girls very soon became integrated into the fire unit on equal terms with the boys. Here is an extract from a description by seventeen-year-old Charlotte Platts of what it was like to be at the fire that gutted the Anderson & England furniture store in Elgin during the night of 10 December 1984: 'Just after we were mobile, an "informative" message came through from ADO Morrison. It told of two buildings used as furniture shops, and well alight. We heard about six different pumps being called, getting mobile, and arriving. As we neared Elgin we saw the smoke becoming thicker and the glow brighter. As we approached the fireground the flames were shooting about 50 feet into the air. ADO Morrison directed the appliance round to the back of the row of shops on the opposite side of the road (Lossie Wynd) to the fire. He told us to set into the lake (Cooper Park) with hard suction and to cover the flat roof from being set on fire by drifting sparks. We ran

Fire Service training: left, in 2007; below, Zara Phillips in 1999.

Attending the 1983 Orton rail crash.

The Duffus House fire on 15 September 1983.

out a couple of lengths and had water on, but made no impression because of the height of the building, so we pitched the ladder, but were about five feet short. 37-2 (Elgin's crew) were set into the lake about 50 yards from us, so we joined some of their crew in pitching their bigger ladder which got the height. I went up behind one of the crew from 37-2. We pulled the hose up, but it was too short so the others added a length at the foot of the ladder. I backed up the branchman while he dowsed down the roof and the sparks on it.'

Through the 1980s and 1990s the standard and range of equipment supplied to the school by Grampian Fire Brigade became ever more sophisticated: the old brass branches, canvas hose and unreliable machinery were long forgotten, instead there were turbo-diesel appliances, aluminium ladders, modern clothing and lockers full of effective equipment. There was a confident and productive relationship between school and local authority, and firefighters at Station 39, fully aware that they were appreciated beyond the school, worked proudly to maintain their side of the partnership. The strict requirement continues that after the age of sixteen a firefighter's exam has to be passed, which is no mean feat. Students have to reach a high standard in their drills to demonstrate competence in firefighting before they can 'go on the run'. The frequency of call-outs means that many firefighters become familiar with the need to exercise adult skills in situations that take them well beyond the conventional range of school experience. They also have to follow safe

procedures and work in an orderly team. Staff who join the service are obliged to meet similarly stringent requirements: training as volunteer firefighters, undertaking the demanding HGV driving course in order to become drivers of the appliances and shouldering the responsibility of being on call in addition to their other school duties. As in previous decades, the training for both staff and students is carefully monitored to meet the Brigade's standards.

Call-outs are varied and unpredictable: false alarms, chimney fires, car fires, road traffic accidents, floods, kitchen fires, farm fires, whin fires, house fires, garage fires. Some can be trivial, some substantial and memorable such as the Ben Aigan fire near Craigellachie in July 1976, the Orton train crash in February 1983, Duffus House fire in September 1983, the fire at Elgin Court House in May 1986, Newton House fire in February 1992, and the sinking dredger at Lossiemouth harbour in October 1992. One member of staff, Michael Evans, gives an evocative account of a call-out on 17 March 1990 when he was driving one of the two Gordonstoun appliances: 'Our unit was deployed most effectively (I felt) at a large forest fire (reportedly six square miles well alight!) at a young conifer plantation in the hills between Huntly and Dufftown. We attended with two appliances and full crews. Approaching the fireground, my appliance was diverted through Rhynie to the Dufftown road to assist with the damming of the river Deveron for helicopter scoops. However, we found the Elgin crews had this accomplished and fully under control so we returned to the fire. We found it by now contained though not yet fully under control and our crews were able and sufficient, with officer support, to provided the night cover essential for the by then exhausted regulars to gain the necessary sleep in readiness for the next day. Our crews spent the night on constant foot patrol with radios and portable sprays, energetically dealing with areas that were spreading and re-igniting and reporting any changes of wind direction. Finally, we went off duty eighteen hours later when in daylight the professionals returned and helicopter water bombardment resumed. The energy and enthusiasm of our fresh young crews were particularly appreciated by those tired regulars that night. And more than one senior officer expressed the feeling that their investment in our equipment and training was now being handsomely repaid.'

In the Watch Room at the Fire Station, generations of students have given support to the fire crews during and after call-outs. This necessary back-up involves receiving and transmitting radio messages from and to Control in Aberdeen, maintaining the station's log book, informing house staff about firefighters' involvement in call-outs,

The Fire Service assisting at a road traffic accident in Rothes in 2005 (above left), and a call-out to flooding in Elgin in the late 1990s (above).

Left: All Grampian Fire and Rescue Services vehicles have been white since the early 1990s, partly as a response to research suggesting that white is more visible than red, and the Gordonstoun tender is no exception.

arranging meals with the Refectory, recording by name all comings and goings of firefighters, and maintaining security in the open fire station. While all firefighters not in an active crew may do this job, it has often been a particular responsibility and enthusiasm of those students who cannot or choose not to be active firefighters.

During the 1990s and after the turn of the millennium, there was a steady decline in the number of call-outs for fire brigades across Britain as the sustained work of fire prevention and building regulations took effect, and the Gordonstoun unit became more strongly involved in fire prevention, damage control and salvage techniques. The station became a back-up unit for full-time firefighters in Elgin as well as for the retained firefighters at Lossiemouth and Forres, with the Elgin firefighters taking a more prominent role in training. Today, students visit the impressive new station in Elgin one week in every five to be trained in areas such as the use of cutting equipment, flash-over training and working at height. Health and Safety regulations and Child Protection issues were shrewdly handled by Grampian Fire Brigade (now known as Grampian Fire and Rescue Services) so that the Gordonstoun unit could still respond to most calls, though with a built-in delay for road traffic accidents. In 1999 and 2002 there were call-outs to major flooding incidents which required crews to be out for many hours over a number of days.

A major equipment change in 2003 was the replacement of the second appliance by a smaller 4 x 4 vehicle that has more versatility in off-road situations and can be driven by adults without an HGV licence. This has now been replaced by the school's first ever brand-new, purpose-built appliance – a Mercedes Vito fitted out to the Service's exact specification– which arrived in September 2010. Modern personal gear such as 'banana' suits (known as PBI Gold) and goggles with prescription lenses are supplied by the Brigade promptly, and the volunteer station at Gordonstoun is maintained in line with the other stations in the region.

After the retirement of Anthony Montgomery as Service Commander in 1990, David Spooner, who had assisted Montgomery for many years, took over. Richard Devey is currently in charge of the Service. The Gordonstoun unit remains a central part of school life, and comprises almost 40 students arranged in three watches. Although call-outs are increasingly scarce, enthusiasm for the Service remains high among both students and staff, who remain ready and willing to respond when the pagers give the alert. The future of the unit seems secure, though with perhaps a growing emphasis on fire prevention rather than firefighting.

Below: Michael Shea with the bloodhounds, 1956.

Bottom left: Wizard, Sonnet and Hamlet with their schoolboy handlers, 1956.

Bottom right: excerpts from 'The Bloodhound Diaries' kept by boys between 1936 and 1956.

BLOODHOUND SERVICE

The bloodhounds, which were kept in the kennels at Duffus House and looked after by the boys, were first acquired in 1936 and were a great favourite of Kurt Hahn. It was typical of him that a wild character called Nicholas Powell, given to such daring deeds as cycling round the top edge of the harbour wall at Hopeman, was encouraged to siphon this energy into becoming a bloodhound handler, even winning a field trial at Eaglesfield with 'Mr Hahn's Hamlet of Gordonstoun'. The hounds were used as an adjunct to the Mountain Rescue Service, available to help the police in searches for missing people. David Gordon, forester, was involved in their care and he tells how the boys would collect the black cat from Duffus House and release it in front of the bloodhounds to give them a good run. Roy McComish, Housemaster of Gordonstoun House, recounted how he was woken at 3 am by Hahn saying 'Seven Moray Sea School boys are missing on Dava Moor. Can you come at once and take a rescue party?' Two hours later McComish was on Dava Moor, having dispatched teams of boys in specific directions, when he saw the Rolls Royce taxi of Messrs McIntosh of Elgin approaching. It was, of course, Hahn himself, but what was more surprising was that he was submerged by bloodhounds in the back, licking his face

and interrupting his conversation with the boy-handler beside him. The uniformed driver was fuming. Soon a party of seven cheerful Sea School boys turned up. Everyone congratulated everyone else and the boys were loaded into the overburdened taxi for the return journey. McComish himself was on the moor for another three hours waiting for the return of his rescue parties. The dogs were generally rather unpopular with the staff and became even more so after they had eaten Lady Dunbar's chickens. They were evacuated to Wales in June 1940, and returned to Moray with the school after the war. The Service came to an end in 1959, the expense of the hounds eventually judged to outweigh their usefulness.

28th June. Disaster overtook us, when one of the bitch puppies caught a disease, and didn't eat, her temperature was up to 105.5°, and we called in the vet, who said he could do nothing. The next day the temperature was down, but it died, just before lunch. Subsequently four of the puppies died. The vet's diagnosis showed they had died from a rare and incurable disease — "Rubatths Disease." The vet had never come across it before, and I think that we will call in the II from Craigellachie, in future — who knows ... supplied some

Form No. 4

Chief Constable's Office,
Newtown, Mont.

TEL. NO.: 393

25th June, 1942.

Mr. K.M. Hahn,
Gordonstoun School,
Plas Dinam,
Llandinam,
Mont.

Dear Sir,

I understand that on Sunday, the 21st June, you very kindly offered the assistance of two of your students and a bloodhound in tracing a small girl who was missing at that time. As you will, no doubt, know by now the girl was found, very largely I think, thanks to the bloodhound.

I should like to convey to you my thanks for the help given, and will you very kindly thank the two boys on my behalf. I only hope they spent an interesting and instructive day in undertaking this practical work.

Yours faithfully,

H. Lloyd. Captain.
Chief Constable.

P.T. Would you be prepared for a bloodhound to work in adjacent counties, if required? All expenses paid, of course. H.

THE MOUNTAIN RESCUE SERVICE

In May 1951 Ian Lawson arrived at Gordonstoun for an interview with Kurt Hahn for a teaching position at the newly leased premises in Forres: Altyre House. Two months earlier he had been climbing in the Torridon Hills with the St Andrew's University Mountaineering Club when an RAF Coastal Command Lancaster, on a bearing to land at Kinloss, crashed into the hills near the village of Kinlochewe. The incident revealed the primitive nature of rescue arrangements at the time: another plane, having spotted the wreckage from the air, had to land at Kinloss, some 50 miles away, and report on its searches by telephone to the public callbox at Kinlochewe. There was no local team to send out on the search.

Deeply impressed by what Hahn told him of the existing Coastguard and Fire Services at the school and by Hahn's conviction that Rescue Services based at the school should be at the disposal of local communities, Lawson tentatively suggested a third Service: Mountain Rescue. Unlike the Gordonstoun estate, Altyre, while not far from sea, did not have easy access to a harbour, and with the mountains close by, it seemed entirely appropriate, when the plan was approved soon after, for Mountain Rescue to be run out of Altyre. Ian Lawson and Andy Clelland were given permission to set it up: 'Our only "resource" was our climbing rope. So off we went to the stables and practised abseiling on the outside staircase of the Battery Room, using the door handle as the abseiling point.'

Bobby Chew, formerly housemaster at Duffus House but also an experienced mountaineer, was now at Altyre, and the first call-out of the service (in December 1951) afforded him not a little *Schadenfreude*. While Kurt Hahn was very attached to the Bloodhound Service, Chew had always expressed his scepticism as to their usefulness in mountainous territory. One day, Hahn lost one of the hounds while out on an exercise on Dava Moor, and immediately asked Lawson to take the new Mountain Rescue Service up there to find it: 'I went up to Dava Moor on a bitterly cold night, with snow falling, to be briefed by Dr Hahn who was waiting in his familiar black taxi cab. The next morning we were lucky enough to find the hound on the railway line by Dava Station. He had been scooped up by the evening train's snow plough and flung aside. He was conscious, but in some danger, lying immobile only six inches from the track, with a train shortly due. Having been told not to move the dog because of his condition, I lay on top of him to protect him; the train was huge and very frightening at such close quarters.' All was well, however, and the dog was taken home on a stretcher, in due time making an almost full recovery.

A vertiginous descent in a stretcher exercise at Cove Bay in the 1960s. The Mountain Rescue team has always been particularly adept at this difficult type of rescue.

By 1953 Altyre had developed a trained Mountain Rescue unit and was invited to incorporate it into an ATC Squadron (2255), which had logistical advantages, not least the use of an RAF lorry fuelled and serviced at RAF Kinloss. John Fleming (ex RAF) took charge of the new Service. 'Mountain rescue expeditions', reflects Calum Anton (Altyre, 1953–57), '. . . formed a large part of our training in mountaincraft. Night exercises in particular were pretty onerous, especially for those of us who just wanted to climb hills. Imagine if you will, being dropped off on the A9 at the Slochd and told to get over Dava Moor to somewhere near Dulsie Bridge via two predetermined intermediate points – in the middle of the night! Some of these exercises were joint ventures with Kinloss Mountain Rescue, and one thing that sticks in the memory is the tins of self-heating soup. I wonder if you can still get these?'

The team's first call-out from outside the school came in 1956 when a lay-preacher from the Abbey in Fort Augustus was reported lost in the hills. Search parties, including the Gordonstoun ACF and the bloodhounds, scoured the hills for several days, but the missing man was never found. The links with the Gordonstoun Bloodhound Service led to further joint exercises and the sharing of resources. In 1958 the bloodhounds were called out twice: once to help trace a man who was ultimately 'found', having not actually been lost (a perennial problem for all Search and Rescue teams) and once to aid the police in the hot pursuit of three desperate bandits. The resulting man-hunt was spread over two days with the baying school hounds at one point chasing a fugitive up a gully and across a river. During this period the number of call-outs was small with occasional requests from the police for help and some happily provided assistance to 'lost or injured' Gordonstoun students. In 1958 the grumble was 'why does no one take responsibility for calling us out?' The suggestion of spending holiday weekends at the bottom of Ben Nevis, waiting for accidents, was vetoed to prevent accusations of 'appearing like a pack [sic] of vultures'.

In the autumn of 1960, after the merger of Altyre with Gordonstoun, the newly formed Gordonstoun Mountain Rescue Service took up its home in the recently built Services Centre. Ordnance Survey maps of the time marked this as the local MRT Post and therefore a site of both equipment and expertise. Hahn always had the view that training, although valuable, did not have the same impact as applying skills in a real situation. Unfortunately (or fortunately, to look at it another way), it has always been difficult to find sufficient opportunities for the eager young climbers to practise their hard-won skills. The onus was therefore on the team to seek out an additional function.

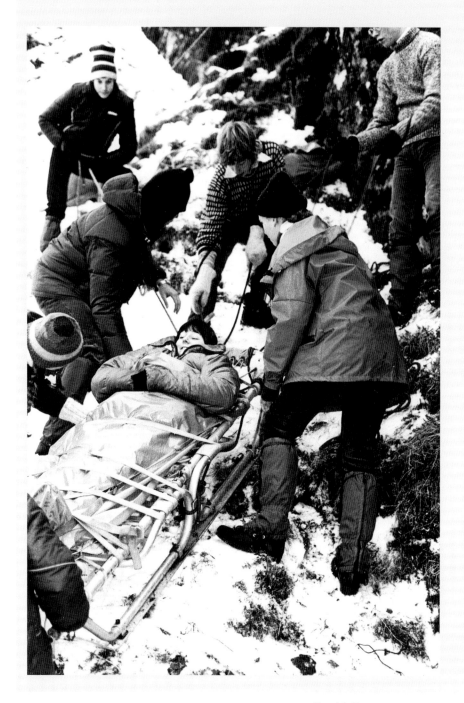

Mountain Rescue training on Beinn Fhada Kintail, 1984. It can be necessary to evacuate a casualty on a stretcher over relatively long distances and difficult terrain, making this a demanding exercise requiring a whole team of trained rescuers.

In some ways the 1960s were the golden era for the school team. In the early '60s the slopes of Cairngorm were to produce a reliable source of casualties, and throughout this period the Gordonstoun team provided regular first-aid patrols for the embryonic ski area. There were additional call-outs to help other school groups. In 1960, for example, one fourth-form party bound for Blackburn Bothy in the Ben Alder area was declared missing, and at 11.15 pm the Mountain Rescue team was

Group of students braving characteristically glum weather conditions above Glen Strathfarrar.

At the top of a climb called 'The Gutter' in Glen Nevis on a Mountain Rescue climbing trip, July 2009.

summoned from school. Happily the missing group was found safe and well camping in a wood. Externally generated call-outs also occurred, and teams had to cope with several searches in very taxing winter conditions. There was even a joint training exercise with instructors from the National Outdoor Training Centre at Glenmore Lodge. In 1968 the Service was inspected by the Warden of Ullswater Outward Bound and soon after assisted with a particularly unpleasant accident in the Lake District, during the Easter vacation. The subsequent report into the incident referred to the 'inspiration and leadership' of Jim Rawlings, then in charge of Mountain Rescue at the school, and singled out the Gordonstoun team as 'potentially one of the best in the country. All it needs is more experience of active rescues in the mountains.'

In 1971 the Cairngorm Disaster, in which several student members of an Edinburgh school group tragically lost their lives when caught in an early winter storm on the Cairngorm plateau, produced a dramatic increase in the formation of mountain rescue teams throughout Britain, so that now, every mountain area in Scotland has its own dedicated team, and there are Search and Rescue helicopters based at Lossiemouth on 24-hour standby. This tragedy and its aftermath also affected the attitude of many who might previously have called the Service out

and so further limited the opportunities for students to provide genuine assistance.

The training regime followed by the Mountain Rescue team has retained a rigour and a core of skills dating back to the Altyre days. Of paramount importance, of course, is fitness. John Hamilton (team leader during the 1970s and '80s) felt it essential that Mountain Rescue students should be able to 'cope with long arduous days in the hills' and members of the team have often been among the fittest students in the school. Training expeditions over the years have frequently incorporated long days in the mountains. In 1954, for example, Mountain Rescue groups ascended thirteen peaks over the Christmas holidays in exacting winter conditions; in more recent times groups have completed all six of the 4,000-foot peaks in Scotland in a weekend, and traversed two of the Torridonian 'giants' – Liathach and Beinn Eighe in one day. One exceptional MR student completed 'the Munros' (all the Scottish peaks over 3,000 feet high) before he left school – becoming at the time one of the youngest persons to do so.

John Pownall recalls the days when he and John Hamilton were involved in the Service: 'The Lower Sixth year was then a sort of rest year between GCSEs and A levels, giving opportunities for cruises, four-day expeditions, the Three-Peaks Race, etc. Then along came AS levels, modular

A levels etc., making life more difficult. John Hamilton and I were determined that team members should be experienced hill-walkers, so most weekends saw us on the great ridges of the Highlands, Beinn Eighe and Liathach in Torridon, the Five Sisters, the Cluanie South Ridge, Ben Nevis, the Aonachs and the Grey Corries, the Mamores, Glencoe, the Ben Starav group, the Cruachan horseshoe and many others – magic days with magnificent views . . . Another John Hamilton special involved getting up at 4 am to climb Ladhar Bheinn in Knoydart, having breakfast back at the tents, then back-packing tents, etc. over Luinne Bheinn and Meall Buidhe, the same day . . . I have clear memories of nights spent wondering if the tent would survive the howling gale, sodden retreats from Fort William or Torridon, the failed snow-holing trip to Ben Wyvis and drives back from the west in a wet, smelly minibus to be greeted by sunshine in Moray . . . The summer term would not have been complete without the four-day trip to Skye with its memories of wearing out hands and boots on the Cuillin peaks, seeing Brocken spectres as we climbed the Inn Pin (the Inaccessible Pinnacle – the only Munro that can be scaled only by rock-climbing) and always the ridge twisting in front of the seascape over to Rhum.'

Mountain Rescue has always enjoyed a high reputation in the school. Jane Hewitt (Hopeman, 1975–79) already had a great love of the outdoors before arriving at Gordonstoun, and it was not long before she had set her sights on becoming a member of the Service: 'For the whole of fourth form, my main ambition was to be selected to join the Mountain Rescue team. I was aware that the summer fourth-form expedition to Torridon was vital and was devastated to be in a group that got lost, having been sent off with an incorrect map reference by the senior boys helping with the expedition! The fog and then torrential rain came down and one member of our group became delirious with exhaustion, talking about going to catch a bus in her home town. Eventually we made our way back to the starting point and set up camp there (rather than at the agreed overnight camp site) where the staff later found us, much to their (and our) relief! Fortunately, Jim Rawlings still invited me to join the Mountain Rescue team, and he and his wife Ella became my lifelong friends until their deaths a few years ago. Jim was a true "man of the mountains" and passed on to me and many others a deep love of the Scottish hills. During my four years in the Mountain Rescue, we trained every Wednesday afternoon, usually on the cliffs

Below: Stretcher-lowering exercise in Quarrel Wood, 2008.

Below right: Two members of the Mountain Rescue team descending Sron a' Choire Ghairbh above Loch Lochy on a weekend expedition, 1988.

at Primrose and Cove Bays near Hopeman, taught new pupils how to abseil, assisted with expeditions, put on demonstrations on open days and went on some fantastic expeditions, from ice-climbing in the Cairngorms to providing assistance and radio cover for the World Championship in Orienteering in the Queen's Forest near Aviemore in September 1976.'

Beyond fitness, other crucial skills include first aid and the use of stretchers, radio work, and a range of mountain skills, allied to search techniques. First-aid skills obviously become vital once your casualty is located. In the 1950s students prepared for an internal school exam under the guidance of Nurse MacDonald. Students today are trained and entered for a nationally recognised HSE qualification. Manoeuvring stretchers on hill and mountainsides is an acquired skill – even professional teams approach a stretcher exercise with trepidation. Gordonstoun students become highly competent in this exacting practice, and it has rightly been a showpiece demonstration over the years. In these days of helicopter rescues, the technique is less frequently used, but the exercise is the perfect example of the need for accurate planning, careful teamwork and trust when operating under stressful conditions, i.e. while hanging halfway down a cliff. John Pownall recalls memories of snow- and ice-climbing 'in the almost deserted Northern Corries' and a particular exercise when the team was practising stretcher evacuations on the hills in Glen Feshie: '[there was] one awful moment when I inadvertently dropped a snow shovel, which sped down the snow, narrowly missing Ron Pickering, snugly strapped in the stretcher!'

The early students at Altyre, Forres, are to be commended for their radio work. At crucial moments, even modern-day radios can be maddeningly unreliable, but when the 'lightweight radio' weighs ten kilograms, frustrations over lack of function must have been so much greater. Radio sessions teach some useful techniques but the most succinct advice for operation – 'engage brain before opening mouth' – remains sound and widely applicable.

Specific mountain skills include climbing techniques, understanding the weather and developing the ability to navigate in all conditions. All of these involve cultivating keen judgement and high levels of self-reliance which will continue to bear fruit long after a student has left school. Winter conditions in Scotland can be as harsh as anywhere in the world. Winter skills and climbing in the Northern Corries and further afield have again become a popular activity and many Mountain Rescue students have left with an enviable breadth

of experience and knowledge of technique. This background has helped many in the transition to the less supervised world of university climbing clubs.

Over the last 25 years the main involvement of the team in rescue situations has been in large-scale, protracted searches, when Grampian Police or the Cairngorm Rescue Team have called in the extra numbers the school can provide to help in long days of combing forests and hillsides, looking for missing people. The occasions when help is requested remain few, however, and, as in the past, the staff and students involved in the Service have to work hard to maintain the team's enthusiasm and profile to ensure that external bodies do call when the need arises.

The modern Gordonstoun Mountain Rescue team is fortunate to have a group of staff who are all keen mountaineers and have the necessary qualifications to allow them to take students into the hills in all conditions. The equipment and specialist clothing now available are hugely improved in terms of lightness, 'breathability', strength and functionality. However the mountains have not dramatically changed, the weather is not radically different, and physical and mental challenges remain. The team is involved in providing safety cover for the burgeoning industry of charity events in the mountains and local forests. It has recently built strong links with the Search and Rescue Dogs Association, regularly helping with their training exercises. Perhaps in the future the school might even acquire its own rescue dogs, recalling Kurt Hahn's beloved bloodhounds!

Ice-axe training in the Northern Corries of Cairngorm, 2002.

SKI PATROL

The Gordonstoun Ski Patrol was started in 1963 as a branch of the Mountain Rescue Service under the close supervision of Jim Rawlings. The Service provided first-aid cover from the Cairngorm Sheiling at weekends and during the Easter holiday when they were based for a week at Aultnancaber. However, the rapid growth of the ski area in the late 1960s and early 1970s led to a massive rise in the numbers of skiers on the slopes and the creation of a new full-time Cairngorm Ski Patrol which assumed full responsibility for the safety cover on the mountain. This move sadly brought the school's involvement to an end.

Mike Gibson (Hopeman, 1966–70), remembers well the days 'when fledgling ski resorts were springing up at Glencoe, Glenshee and the Cairngorms. From the car park at Cairngorm you went up to the shieling in an old bus equipped with chains; there you were whisked to the top in the then state-of-the-art sideways chairlift up the White Lady, or the newly installed T-bar up Coire Cas. At the top of the White Lady a rope tow driven by an old donkey engine went even higher. Later the chairlift extended down to the car park rendering the bus obsolete. There were no machines for preparing pistes, that was left to the elements or, on race day, the endless pounding of racers and their entourages. Skis were mainly all over two metres long and although of compound construction they still had rigid lever bindings and were strapped to your ankles with cords; boots were of leather although the latest versions sported clips rather than laces. It was against this background that the ski patrol from Gordonstoun operated!

'Headquarters was the Aultnancaber bothy on the Rothiemurchus estate at Coylumbridge (now home to a clay-pigeon ground). In those days it had some manky chairs, bunk beds, primitive arrangements for ablutions and for cooking, and the whole place, although freezing, reeked of wood smoke; we loved it! It was also strategically placed near the Rank Hotel with its Woodshed bar and ice rink, one of the hottest venues in town, where it was rumoured the twin attractions of booze and pretty girls could be found. Keeping us all in order was the much-loved "Daddy" Jim Rawlings, indomitable mountain man, in real life the metalwork master who presided over the Nissen hut workshops that were beside Cumming House. We were equipped with PNX, a prototype Land Rover that was a hybrid between long and short wheelbase. Like all series 1 Land Rovers it screamed blue murder at anything over 50 miles per hour, so, fond though we were of her, a transfer of several hours in the unheated canvas-clad rear was quite an experience. Carried prominently on her roof was the latest MacInnes stretcher, a lightweight portable stretcher especially designed for hill and cliff rescue. In those days, too, we had school drivers, senior boys who had passed their driving test and a further examination under the eyes of a member of staff; you can imagine how exciting having charge of a school vehicle was for a seventeen-year-old and how terrifying a prospect this would be for any modern teacher filling out the inevitable risk assessment forms!

'On a Ski Patrol morning we rose early, ski gear on, breakfast taken, a little after-shave here, a racy scarf there – well just in case, you never knew who you might meet – then up the hill in PNX. We skied with rucksacks with the Red Cross prominent so that we could be readily recognised; there were at that time no other first aiders on the Cairngorms so we represented an important resource. We all had advanced first-aid certificates and many of us had been on courses to train with other teams, in the Lake District, for example. We had much training in winter mountaincraft and were proficient with radio, map and compass. The Royal Navy had also provided liaison training with their rescue helicopters. Our sacks contained bandages, blow-up splints, blankets and much more besides, although, to the chagrin of many who stopped us, no brandy. We also had skins for our skis so that we could go uphill to the aid of skiers or climbers stranded off the beaten track. It was highly satisfying to be of genuine assistance to skiers or climbers, as we frequently were,

Above: Winter Skills Expedition, Coire na Ciste, Cairngorm, 2008.

Ski Patrol showing off their new 'hoodies' at Sweethillocks, on the Gordonstoun estate, 2008.

dealing with sprains, cuts, pulled bits and pieces and sometimes even breaks, often caused by horrible snow and unforgiving equipment in the hands of relative beginners experiencing Scotland's weather conditions that were and still are, quite challenging. The one thing that hasn't changed since those days is the blood wagon, a tin tray with poles on either end for skiers to transport the wounded off the hill to safety. The biggest risk to safety at that time was loose skis. With no brakes to slow it, a ski travelling at speed and at head height is a formidable weapon, and they did, on occasion, inflict deep cuts needing stitching.

'Missing climbers necessitated a concerted team effort to search and with luck locate and take to safety. It was climbers who often exposed us to our first experience of tragedy, whether because they had succumbed to hypothermia or were victims of rock climbing accidents. We would then have the sad and unenviable task of recovering the body for the authorities; that was always a sober journey.

'Jim Rawlings was a great mentor and friend, with an exceptionally light touch in how he handled his team of highly motivated but sometimes boisterous charges. We were allowed to freely experience the delights of the then new Aviemore centre and Coylumbridge. When our over-exuberance and occasionally over-indulgence let us down we were gently reprimanded but then later given some vile task to complete as penance. We were extremely proud of the task we performed, and very proud that we represented Gordonstoun. We took our responsibilities very, very seriously. There was so much of a service ethos in the team that we operated in rotation throughout the Christmas and Easter holidays (nothing to do with the fact that it was really good fun, of course). What started in the Cairngorms has stayed with me to this day and has been passed on to my children. Every spring we journey to the ski slopes and have a marvellous time enjoying the snow, and it all began with Ski Patrol.'

The mid-'80s saw a succession of very cold winters and while the Alpine Ski Areas continued to flourish, several new Nordic Ski Centres at Glen Isla, Glenmulliach and Clashindarroch were established. Cross-country skiing became very popular, a development reflected in the number of ski schools and shops promoting the activity as well as the creation of a very busy twelve-race competitive calendar which ran throughout the winter. Gordonstoun students were right at the forefront of these initiatives and the school produced some outstanding Nordic skiers several of whom competed at national level. The highlight of the 'boom' was the Gordonstoun Relay Squad's victory in the

A student demonstrating the new roller skis acquired for the Ski Patrol in 2005.

Under 18 Relay at the end of the five-day army championships held in Clashindarroch.

In the light of these developments, the renaissance of the Ski Patrol, but this time with a distinct Nordic bias, was planned. Once again this initially worked as an offshoot from the Mountain Rescue with all members of the team receiving units of training in skiing skills on a rotational basis. As the popularity of the recreational and competitive outlets increased, it was felt that there would be enough opportunities to justify the creation of a new service and the Nordic Ski Patrol was born.

In the first few years the pattern of weather remained consistent and the growth of the competitive programme continued with the school taking responsibility for the Gordonstoun 50km – the longest race in Scotland – and the Scottish Schools Championships. Students received training in navigation, first aid, ski maintenance, timing and administration skills as well as becoming highly competent on Nordic skis. They prepared tracks using the skidoo, cleared fallen trees, and provided safety cover within the forest. On the Alpine front, officials and gate keepers were provided for the Scottish Schools and the Inter-House Ski Races.

Unfortunately the fickle nature of the Scottish weather, after so much promise, dealt a severe blow to the whole of the ski industry by delivering a succession of depressingly mild winters. This trend continued throughout the late '90s and into the new millennium. The numbers of active skiers plummeted and the competitive programme dissolved: all of the major championships were removed from Scotland to the Alps, and the dates were now mid-term.

Given the mild winters and the absence of the essential commodity – snow – the Ski Patrol had to re-design itself and to make a number of significant changes. The first was the purchase of a large stock of roller skis, which now enable all of the relevant skills to be taught during the autumn and summer on tarmac surfaces within and outside the campus. Secondly, in order to maintain an active Service function, the Ski Patrol diversified so that it could also provide marshals, timekeepers and officials for cross-country running races; thirdly, more emphasis was placed on the teaching of first aid. On-snow opportunities were still taken whenever possible and the winter of 2008–09 gave cause for renewed optimism. This was then followed by a good season in 2009–10, the best in Scotland for 50 years. The snow came at the start of the Christmas holidays and for nearly five weeks there was skiable snow on Sweethillocks in the school grounds. At Clashindarroch, about an hour's drive away, there were over 100 skiable days. Conditions for track skiing and ski touring were outstanding and even the hills just outside Elgin had a distinctly Norwegian feel to them. There are at present positive moves to re-establish the competitive programme, and the successes of two local youngsters from Huntly at the Vancouver Games have done much to increase interest in the idea.

Left and below: ACF camp near Crail in Fife, summer 1952.

THE CCF AND COMBINED SERVICES DAY

In September 1951, as Altyre House opened, an Army Cadet Force (ACF) unit and a Scout troop were formed. Cadet training took place with the help officers and NCOs from the local regiment together with one or two members of the teaching staff, notably Colonel John Downton. John Downton was an ex-army wartime colleague of Bobby Chew who had worked with him at Glen Feshie before taking up a teaching position initially at Altyre and subsequently at Gordonstoun itself.

In 1958 this developed into a CCF (Combined Cadet Force) unit headed up by Downton and involving a number of other teaching staff, assisted by visiting staff from the Queen's Own Highlanders (Seaforth & Camerons) and the legendary QMSI (Quarter Master Sergeant Instructor) McKenzie, who was on full-time attachment to the unit and lent colour and authenticity to Wednesday afternoon training sessions and parades. In those days, it comprised two wings – Army and Navy. Training followed the programme laid down in the national CCF training manual. The staff involved as junior officers attended courses at Frimley Park near Sandhurst to confirm their commissions. Drill, weapons training, battlecraft, map-reading, day and night exercises and weekend training expeditions all played their part.

'The manual was full of acronyms,' recalls James Thomas (CCF 1965–75), 'among them TEWTs – Tactical Exercises Without Troops – were popular, and one we particularly enjoyed: NEWDs – Night Exercises Without Dark! This allowed blindfolded cadets to simulate night attack manoeuvres and movements in the daytime.

Annual camp at the start of the summer holidays was a major event in the CCF calendar and memories of the widely differing locations are still vivid. Orkney – wild and beautiful – Stromness Battery is the only place we know where the winds are strong enough to produce waves in porridge! Northern Ireland where the CCF cadets were among the last inhabitants of McGilligan Camp before it was used for internment and where we signed for a three-ton lorry in the same way as for a compass or a water bottle! The days of risk assessment were a long way off. We had a productive, safe and exciting stay nonetheless and returned to Gordonstoun with all the troops and officers in good shape. Cultybraggan in Perthshire – the home of the Gordonstoun lookalike obstacle course and great trout fishing too! It was here that while the army instructors thought that the Gordonstoun obstacle course was inspired by the army, the Gordonstoun contingent were clear that it was the other way round. Either way, Gordonstoun won the competition convincingly. Germany at Saltau – perhaps the most challenging time with the whole contingent on manoeuvres with the regular soldiers in training – and spending some 36 hours working from armoured personnel carriers.

'A key strand of the CCF training at Gordonstoun was the series of weekend and night exercises held on Dallas Estate near Knockando by kind permission of Clodagh Houldsworth, a long-standing member of the Gordonstoun Board of Governors. We had the use of Dallas Estate around the old farmhouse at Altahourn and this provided a tremendous facility for training and an ideal remote HQ. The cadets had some great times there as the use of blank ammunition and thunderflashes under controlled conditions was permitted in those days – even bulleted blanks for the Bren guns were allowed for use by the officers to add authenticity. While compo field rations were a short-lived treat, they made the expeditions to Altahourn and Dallas all the more realistic.'

The CCF presented a good opportunity for training, confidence-building, teamwork and travel. The majority of boys at the school spent at least part of their time in the CCF, with some leaving to join other Services as they grew older. The CCF continued until 1975 when Colonel Downton

Annual inspection of
CCF in the mid-1970s.

retired, and the range of activities and the number of other Services at the school had increased substantially.

In the early days following Altyre's amalgamation with Gordonstoun (1960), the flagship day for parents (the forerunner of today's Open Day) was Combined Services Day. This grew out of what at a traditional public school would have been the spectacle of the school CCF (Army, Navy and Air Force) marching past a high-ranking officer and then demonstrating service manoeuvres. Combined Services Day continued as an annual event over the lifetime of the CCF, incorporating parents' meetings with teaching staff, a full social day and demonstrations given by all the Gordonstoun Services – the Fire Service rescuing a casualty from a burning building, the Mountain Rescue team abseiling at Covesea and demonstrating rescue techniques on the cliffs, the Coastguard Watchers firing rockets and demonstrating a breeches buoy rescue from a shipwrecked vessel, the Surf Life-Savers braving the cold summer waters of the Firth to rescue a drowning swimmer, and members of the Gordonstoun Scout troop demonstrating camping and cooking skills on the North Lawn.

This was always a well-attended and exciting day that allowed parents to be shown the extent of the Services at Gordonstoun and to see their children involved in these activities. For those Services that were less easy to demonstrate, such as Conservation and Community Service, there were static exhibitions.

FROM THE ATC TO THE RAF

'I'm going to be a pilot', said Caroline Day (now Flight Lieutenant) to her parents over the phone from Hopeman House: 'Silence on the end of the line, eventually followed by a line of questioning about why this bold career choice had been announced. The truth is, I had never even considered a career in the military, let alone in an aircraft until I was taken gliding at RAF Kinloss by the Gordonstoun Air Training Corps. The ATC (and by that I mean Mr DaBell) encouraged me to apply for a flying scholarship which allowed me to complete 25 hours of light aircraft flying. When I returned from the course, I knew that I would join the RAF. Although the medical team found my arms too short to be a pilot, I have been a Navigator or Weapons Systems Officer in the RAF since December 2002, and am so grateful that I discovered my career through the Gordonstoun ATC.'

THE AIR TRAINING CORPS (ATC)

Having started in 1951 as a unit at Altyre, Forres, under John Fleming, 2255 Squadron went into abeyance when he left, just before Altyre closed. When the Gordonstoun CCF unit was disbanded in 1975, its buildings were taken over by a new ATC Unit (given the same squadron number as the original unit at Altyre), again linked to RAF Kinloss under the Highland Wing, and run for many years by Laurie Beaton. Gerald FitzGibbon was an early recruit: 'I joined because there was no longer a CCF. It was quite boring after the CCF as there was not much drill or shooting. We spent a lot of time in the classroom learning aircraft recognition and other not very exciting activities. However, there was the fun of flying and learning to glide at Milltown airfield [east of Lossiemouth]. Also I remember Prince Andrew getting the chance to go in the Jaguar simulator at Lossiemouth and he was allowed to take a friend; unfortunately not me. I had a go with Mr Beaton in the summer of 1976. It was an amazing experience and culminated in my doing three solo flights in an open air glider. However, I then started to get bored with things military and opted for Community Service.'

Laurie Beaton was a very keen and proficient gliding instructor and for many years, while running Squadron 2255, was also the officer in charge of the gliding school at Kinloss after it moved from Milltown. Drill parades, field exercises, rifle shooting and flights in Nimrods were all part of the ATC staple diet. For a number of years in the late 1980s, small-bore shooting played a prominent role, largely to satisfy the demand by boys and girls who had come from Ardvreck Preparatory School which had a strong reputation for this sport. One of the girls, Polly Murray, after leaving school, went on to become a member of the British biathlon team (combining shooting and cross-country skiing). About this time the RAF replaced the traditional gliders at Kinloss with motorised Vigilants. These were easier to get in to the air and thus generally reduced the period of time required for a cadet to reach the standard of competence required to fly solo, the most cherished achievement of many members of the squadron.

A gliding lesson in the early 1980s at a small gliding club near Spey Bay.

Left: Working with children with special needs at Kestrel House, Elgin, 2005.

Below: Helping at the Community Service Christmas party, 2006.

COMMUNITY SERVICE

Gordonstoun's Community Service clearly does not share the potential for glamour of the Rescue Services, but the opportunities it provides are just as close to the heart of the school's ideology and decidedly part of Kurt Hahn's original vision. He was passionate in his belief, first at Salem and then at Gordonstoun, that one of the failings of modern society was that people did not care for another as they should, that those in trouble or in need of help were too often ignored. To counter this tendency, he determined that the pupils in his schools should always be encouraged to go out into their local communities to offer their assistance as volunteers.

Service in the local community, pioneered at Gordonstoun, is now a feature of many schools, in both the state and the independent sectors, and Gordonstoun has for many years been instrumental in organising national biennial conferences of what was originally called the Independent Schools Community Service, and has now been renamed the Community Action Working Party. At these conferences, which attract key public figures as speakers and are now also open to state schools, student and staff delegates have the opportunity to share and discuss experience on the ground.

Hahn was Jewish by birth, but having been a Christian by conviction for some time, eventually became a member of the Church of England in 1948. As many will testify who heard him speak, particularly at services in the Michael Kirk, his favourite parable was that of the Good Samaritan, the moral of which is, of course, that one should love one's neighbour whoever he or she may be, especially when they are in need. The boy put in charge of involvement with the local community was called the Captain of District and he headed a group of volunteers. It was not until the late 1960s, however, that this activity formally became one of the school Services under James FitzGibbon, who headed the Community Service until his retirement in 1993, when he was succeeded by Georgina Souter, who runs the Service to this day.

When the Community Service first began, volunteers were on the whole given little or no training, and the huge contrast between the lives of largely healthy students from comfortable backgrounds and those of the people they visited, often in their own homes, was sometimes stark and potentially upsetting. But testimonies about the reality of the effects on pupils of this contact bear out Hahn's belief in the benefits to the giver of helping others in this way. In the 1970s, the Service won the admiration of the Elgin Social Services department by restoring a condemned and filthy hovel. The three boys involved also won the friendship of Jock, aged 70, although he was amazed and bewildered at the appearance of clean sheets and horrified at the 'wasteful' burning of his ancient blankets. (Visits to individuals in their own homes do not now take place. These days this work is the preserve of professional social workers.) The local Social Services department subsequently requested and received help in the renovation of two private houses for mentally handicapped people, and of

Astra Cottage, a home for homeless men. A Red Cross nursing course at Dr Gray's General Hospital, which ran until the early 1990s, trained volunteers from the school in basic nursing procedures so that they were able to work as orderlies on the wards. These days, when so much more care is community-based, students' visits to institutions are largely confined to nursing homes, where they have the opportunity to build relationships and interact with old people, an experience that is much appreciated on both sides. Somewhat in the spirit of Hahn's encouraging of a *grande passion*, a recent and extremely successful project came out of the enthusiasm and drive of one student, who suggested the idea of presenting radio programmes for Wave Radio, the in-house station at Dr Gray's, and did so, with impressive results.

Back in the 1970s and '80s, activities included visiting and providing sports facilities at Gordonstoun for the residents of Andrew Thomson House, a home on the outskirts of Elgin for children taken into the care of the local authority. As it had no gymnasium or sports field, the Community Service provided referees and life-savers one evening a week at the school sports centre for the children; on another evening two pupils would visit them in Elgin. 'The children here, aged ten to fifteen, are either offenders or beyond parental control and school control', wrote one volunteer in his Community Service log book. 'We assume the role of houseparents and to me the important thing is to get to know the kids and to build up a relationship of a fair amount of trust and contact with them. I feel I have

benefited from being here as it has given me more insight into the problems and ways of so-called "delinquents", who are after all just kids like the rest of us, but who are not quite so lucky.'

Today, students in the Lower School attend Service Awareness sessions, which include developing communication skills through role play with older pupils and trips out of school to see the kind of activities undertaken by the Community Service. In Year 11, those students who become members of this Service are given induction courses. There are several initiatives involving work with children and teenagers: sixth-formers visit Hopeman Primary School as teaching assistants, notably working in Music, Drama, Art, foreign languages and PE. Others work with special needs students in Elgin High School; recently, for example, they have been building up a blog. And there are peer support sessions at Gordonstoun for young carers, where groups of children who are shouldering adult responsibilities in the care they provide themselves to family members, are given a rare chance, for a term or two, to take part in a range of activities in the sports hall. For the last ten years, the school has had particularly close links with the Princess Royal Trust for Carers. Many students work in the Oxfam shop in Elgin, and involvement with Riding for the Disabled is now long-established and thriving. Each year, Service members organise and host a Christmas party for the people with whom they have been involved throughout the year. Membership of the Service stands at 60, the largest Service in the school.

Above: The Community Service Christmas party in 2008.

Below: Helping in a playgroup for two- and three-year-olds at Lossiemouth Community Centre in 2005.

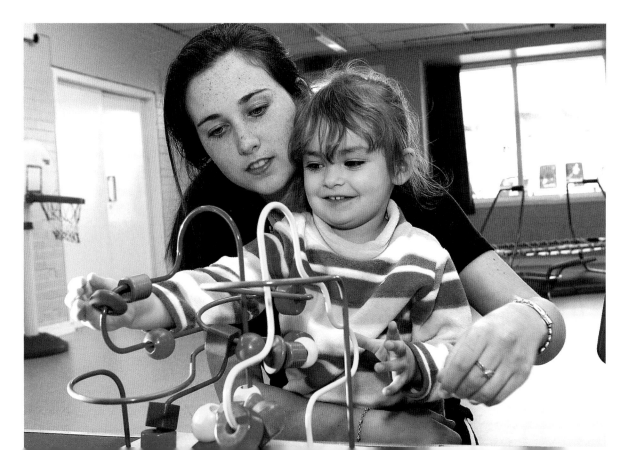

CONSERVATION SERVICE

Although the Conservation Service was not formally established until 1969, there has always been a lively interest in natural history at Gordonstoun and the rich variety of ecosystems around the school, not least as a result of the many outdoor activities in which pupils engage. Humphrey Taylor (1948–53) writes that the reasons why he chose to go to Gordonstoun 'included the fulmar petrels, terns and other wonderful birds on the cliffs and beaches, and the roe deer in the woods.'

Over many years, a figure of huge importance for anyone at the school interested in the natural world was Bex Richter. Ekke von Kuenssberg, who was a junior boy at Salem when Richter was a senior boy there, remembers him as an already impressive naturalist keen to share his knowledge: 'he it was who encouraged me to look at plants and animals with new eyes, and drawings and photographs with a box camera were all part of the enthusiastic enterprise.' As a Biology teacher, Richter accompanied Hahn in Scotland from the beginnings of the school, always enthusing those around him, as Jocelin Winthrop Young recalls: 'Bex was, of course, in his element and in a short time he had turned me into an ornithologist, which I have remained ever since . . . He generally had a sick bird or beast in the house . . . The succession [of injured birds] culminated in Duffus with a guillemot and a bat at the same time. The guillemot he saved and we set it in the sea at the old harbour. The bat tended to escape and create chaos with the ladies in the house. It was finally freed from its cage by persons unknown. Hahn? Bex used to take us out at night to listen to the stags roaring. Hahn's brother Rudo came on a visit and went out with us and roared back; he sounded very convincing to us, and also, apparently, to the stags!'

Unlike his fearless mother, Bex was a quiet and retiring character, but his passion for natural history knew no bounds. He was a first-class biologist of the old school, studying local habitats and identifying and recording plants and animals within them. After a year he had set up seven survey groups in his Natural History department and took many expeditions to study woodland, coastal warren, seashore, heathland, sand dunes, open fields and marshes. 'An Ecological Survey of Gordonstoun and the cliffs of Covesea and Sand Dunes' by one of the boys involved appears in the June 1938 edition of *The Gordonstoun Record* – long before the word 'ecology' was in common usage. All of this sparked enthusiasm for some unusual projects, such as collecting and mounting all the species of mosquito to be found around the estate. Bex himself, who was among the

Member of the Conservation Service clearing ground for the new garden in 2007.

longest-serving members of staff at the school and retired in 1972, became an expert in local *Bryophytes* and *Coleoptera* and left collections of national importance.

In the late 1960s Gordonstoun was looking for a project for European Conservation Year (1970). A series of paths called the Winding Walks, which had been laid out at Fochabers by the Duke of Richmond and Gordon in the late 19th century for the enjoyment of local people, had fallen into disrepair. These were footpaths and bridges in the gully of the Small Burn at Whiteash Hill, with rhododendrons and ornamental conifers planted alongside. With the help of the Conservation Corps, the tangle of growth was cut, footpaths repaired, new steps and bridges built and a car park made. The Winding Walks were re-opened by General Sir George Gordon Lennox in June 1972.

The Conservation Service was re-started by David Welton in 1982 and flourished for the rest of the decade. Much of the work was centred around the school grounds and Bex Richter was involved, although he had officially retired ten years before. The Scottish Conservation Project Trust provided equipment and the use of a Land Rover over the winter months. By 1986, approximately 200 nesting boxes for various species of bird were fabricated and installed around the estate and four duck rafts on the lake, all of which required regular maintenance. The nesting boxes proved to be hugely successful, not just for small birds, but also for owls, kestrels and bats.

'In the lake,' recalls David Welton, 'the growth of broad-leaved pondweed (*Potamogeton nutans*), exacerbated by the lack of through-flow, proved to be one of our most challenging projects, and this problem was tackled in the 1980s by means of a massive inter-house competition called "Save the Lake". The students spent the weekend dredging the lake, and were judged on the size of the heaps they amassed.' From then on the lake was managed largely by the introduction of weed-eating grass carp, which are periodically restocked, and a lot of elbow grease from members of the Community Service regularly removing new growth.

Other projects included bee-keeping (several hives were kept up near the Technology department) and tree-planting on the estate which involved working closely with members of the Gordonstoun grounds staff, and footpath maintenance, all of which formed part of the service's weekly work. In the early '80s, an old potato store was renovated and converted into the Conservation Service Visitor Centre, providing a focal point for activities.

A Nature Conservancy Council project to remove rhododendrons from the slopes of Beinn Eighe was attended by a party of juniors. One year later, the Service was involved in making a woodland trail at Darnaway near Forres and with work on the Sluie walk beside the river Findhorn. But perhaps the lasting memorial to the service was the re-opening in 1988 of the Hopeman to Lossiemouth coastal footpath which involved many hours of 'gorse-bashing' before the path and steps could be re-instated.

Jeremy Barclay, who succeeded David Welton in 2000, brought his own individual style to the Conservation Service. He involved the students in the Service in many joint initiatives with community bodies nearby – in Forres, Burghead, Spey Bay and Rothes and with the Forestry Commission in Culbin Forest. When the Dava Way (between Grantown and Forres) was being created, the Service cut back rhododendrons, dug out ditches, repaired fences, cleared paths and built steps. Barclay continued the 'Spring Clean Day' in March when all Gordonstoun students, not just those in the Conservation Service, were involved in clearing rubbish from the countryside surrounding the school, especially along the section of coast lying just north of the school. But his greatest achievement was persuading the school to allow the Conservation Service to establish an

organic garden. The Service was given the use of a piece of land behind the Medical Centre and Cumming House which had just been cleared of trees, and Barclay was involved in the digging out the tree stumps which remained as well as the hard slog of digging over uncultivated land; drainage was put in, tons of manure brought in to create the initial vegetable beds, a polytunnel was put in, and the area was fenced to keep out marauding rabbits. The first year's crop of potatoes was sold to members of staff, and the proceeds used to buy seeds for the following year.

Steve Potter, who took over of the Service in 2008, continued improvements to the garden. When he left Gordonstoun, Barclay had donated his own garden shed to the organic garden and it was used, along with another larger one to store gardening equipment close at hand. More vegetable beds were created and the first seeds propagated in the polytunnel. A keen plantsman, Potter had plans for a pond to promote greater biodiversity and for bee-keeping. After his untimely death in October 2010, preparations for the beehives continued and efforts to create the pond were soon underway. The current Conservation Service has about 30 members from Years 11 to 13, who have been working hard to spread the eco message in Gordonstoun.

Above: Working on the South Lawn borders in 2002.

Right: Installing new birdboxes with Jeremy Barclay, 2003.

6

SPORT AND EXPEDITIONS

'No boy should be compelled into opinions but it is criminal negligence not to impel him into experience' KURT HAHN

SPORT

Kurt Hahn greatly valued sport, regarding it as a crucial educational tool that promoted teamwork, leadership, cooperation and communication skills as well as contributing to physical fitness and health, and he saw much in the way in which games were played in Britain that he admired and wished to incorporate into his educational model. No major team sport, however, has ever been compulsory at Gordonstoun. From the earliest days, there has always been an alternative.

When Hahn was at Salem, he took on Bobby Chew, 'imported from Cambridge', as Ekke von Kuenssberg put it, 'to teach sport and *the* game [hockey]'. Von Kuenssberg relates a trip to Britain during the Easter holidays of 1932 when a combined hockey and athletics team from Salem, played fixtures at Marlborough, Eton, Inverness, Loretto and Glenalmond. There was a side to sport in British public schools, however, that Hahn found not just antipathetic, but thoroughly counterproductive, namely the glorification of sporting heroes to the disbenefit of all other participants,

Above: Morning athletic break on the North Lawn in front of Gordonstoun House, 1950s.

Left: Kurt Hahn by the tennis court on the South Lawn, 1938.

Opposite: A girls versus boys cricket match at Gordonstoun, 2007.

Kurt Hahn playing tennis, 1934.

and the humiliation of those who were never going to be brilliant sportsmen. 'Make games important,' instructed one of the Seven Laws of Salem, 'but not predominant'. Hahn hated the fact that the captain of rugby was very often the Head of School. Colours, in his school, would be awarded for proof of good character and ability to take responsibility rather than for sporting prowess. 'He didn't like schoolboy heroes,' remarks Jim Orr, '. . . he enjoyed the challenge of boys who didn't find games and studies easy.'

Norbert Kampf, who was at Gordonstoun in the late 1950s, testifies to the fact that no-one at the school was ever obliged to take up a team sport, though this did not mean that boys were let off physical exercise: 'A report I had brought with me from Salem to Gordonstoun voiced the hope that up there in Scotland, the school should try . . . to make a man of me, all those who tried having duly failed. My resistance to sport in general was great. At least I was not forced to play rugby or cricket. But I found no mercy as far as athletics were concerned. A particular horror was the obstacle course under the severe eyes of an ex-Sergeant Major who must have been delighted to see how clumsily a German behaved. The rope across the pond alone was a torture for me, I cannot remember how many times I fell in the water.' Indeed, it was because Hahn was determined that pupils should learn to draw the very best from challenging themselves physically outdoors that he made sure that a range of activities was always available. Sport was just one facet of this conviction.

Hockey, Hahn's favourite sport, being played on Sweethillocks in the 1960s; the Aberlour House rugby team, late 1940s; and a high-jumper, 1952.

Gordonstoun offers a broad variety of sport reflecting the school's belief that every student should be able to find some activity in which he or she can become proficient and find enjoyment, and therefore benefit from the enhancement of self-confidence that participation in sport can bring.

The traditional practice in many independent schools was for one sport to dominate each of the three terms. One weekday afternoon was usually the preserve of the Combined Cadet Force, and the remaining four were dedicated to the particular sport for that term. At Gordonstoun it has always been accepted that the main team sports should be allocated only two weekday afternoons for training or practice, and that, even on Saturdays, Service, expedition or cruise commitments may take precedence over representational sport.

Jane Hewitt recounts the choices she made in the 1970s: 'although I took part in the usual mainstream hockey, tennis, swimming, etc. (without much success!), I much preferred the more unusual sports such as orienteering and took part in several regional competitions. I chose Geology as an O-level subject, and later an A-level too, mainly so that I

could go on even more expeditions. Bryan Pennington was our inspirational teacher and led expeditions to Arran, Skye, Lochinver, the Lake District and further afield to the Grand Canyon and Italy.'

Hahn himself was a keen sportsman, playing tennis and enjoying high-jumping, but his favourite sport was hockey. He had had some success at the game while at Oxford, and in later life always wore his Christ Church colours when playing. So keen was he to introduce hockey to Salem that the Salem Hockey Club was started before the school opened, with an inaugural match in October 1919 (Prince Max played in goal and Fräulein Ewald was much praised as centre half). In the early days of Gordonstoun, Hahn at first still played outside right in the team; 'a boy always accompanied him just outside the touchline with a thermos flask of coffee,' recalls Jocelin Winthrop Young. 'From time to time he would stop playing and refresh himself with a gulp or two. Then he might have to speed back into the game to reach a pass coming his way.' One of his better-known exhortations to fellow players, recalls Ian Lawson, was 'Run, run, with the speed of ten antelopes!' Several old boys remember the extraordinary sight of Hahn careering down the hockey pitch: 'Whatever the weather,' wrote Jim Orr, 'he always wore his Homburg hat. He even wore it playing hockey, but it would fly off as he pounded down the right wing.' In 1936, however, when he was 50, Winthrop Young dropped him from the team – it is a testament to the fair-minded nature of Hahn that this was possible.

Joseph Pease gives an account of sporting activities at the school in 1938: 'We played rugger on Thursdays and hockey on Fridays. Hockey was played on the field now known as King George's Field. For rugger we went up the track leading to the Coastguard hut for a few hundred yards and there, in a very exposed position, was a football field. The field had no protection from the wind, which blew almost at gale force across it on most winter days. There was no need for forcible encouragement of those who were not keen. If you slacked at rugger you froze. We played rugger and hockey in all weathers . . . The only conditions that warranted cancellation were heavy snow when visibility had been reduced to zero.'

One of Hahn's inventions was the athletic or morning break. Josh Miner was highly impressed by this when he took up a teaching post at the school in 1951: 'Four mornings a week, during a 50-minute break between classes, each boy engaged in two of half a dozen events – sprinting, long-distance running, high- and long-jumping, discus and javelin throwing. He competed only against himself, trying to better his previous best performance.

Watching a physical duffer find that through daily effort he could do better than he would have expected possible, you could see him shed what Hahn called "the misery of unimportance".' That pungent phrase must strike a chord with anyone who has failed to make a mark in sport at school and is typical of Hahn's clear understanding of the unhappiness that comes from being excluded from success and his desire to avoid such discouragement and dampening of potential in his school. Humphrey Taylor (Round Square, 1948–53), whose last year at the school coincided with that of Hahn, writes: 'I have fond memories of his kindness and many eccentricities. I still have his note to me when I was captain of the undefeated hockey team urging me to pick a rather troubled boy for the school team, not because he was good enough but because it would be good for him. How many other headmasters saw that as more important than winning?' Hahn was convinced, as Josh Miner puts it, that a boy's 'new-found confidence would carry over into his peer relationships, his classroom performance, the quality of his work on his project . . . He often told the school, "Your disability is your opportunity."'

George Welsh, in his early years, continued the tradition of the athletic break on the South Lawn and produced gymnastic displays of stunning standards of discipline and agility, both for parents on Open Day and for the general public at local gardens' open days. Welsh also oversaw and nurtured hockey at the school over generations of pupils, undaunted by the often difficult conditions in Moray in January and February, and produced impressively competent sides, more than capable of competing against any school in Scotland, and for many years taking part in the Public Schools Hockey Festival in Oxford.

Physical disability was never a bar to participation in sport at Gordonstoun. Simon Graham (1952–56), who was one of the first boys to go to Altyre having had polio, writes: 'I was able to play hockey and tennis and touch-judged at rugby. Gustav Aherns, Head of House [Dunbar], used to pull me round morning run so that I did not miss all the hot water. I went on expeditions and climbed Cairngorm with a rumbling appendix. We bicycled back 40 miles and I had it out the next day. Four years of great fun and comradeship.'

Another anecdote from Josh Miner clearly reveals Hahn's position on winning: 'It was over the high jump that I had my one and only tangle with Hahn. Scottish high-jumpers were still using the old scissors method, and when I taught our boys the new rolling style, they began to break records at every competition. Crowds came to watch them, and I developed a beautiful case of coach's swollen head.

One day, Hahn called me to his study and said sternly, "Josh, I don't think we should go to the games at Dufftown. It's fine for the boys to discover they can outdo themselves. But now we are turning them into performers." When he saw that I did not understand, his gaze softened a bit. "We want to develop people through jumping," he said, "not make jumpers out of people." ' And George Welsh remembers returning from the Scottish Schools Championships in 1966 after his first year at the school, delighted with a clutch of gold medals, only to be greeted by Hahn asking how the other boys had got on.

Hahn realised that sport could act as a binding and cohesive force within a school, but he disliked cricket, as he felt it produced 'prima donnas'. In spite of this jaundiced opinion, the game has flourished at the school. One of the earliest players was Prince Philip, who, in 1938, was in the team with two future headmasters, Bobby Chew and Henry Brereton. Kempe, like Hahn, was a tennis player, but since his tenure, both Michael Mavor and Mark Pyper have worked to improve the standard of cricket. Having been captain of cricket at Loretto, played at Cambridge and coming from Tonbridge, Mavor saw this as an area he could contribute to directly and he took charge of coaching the junior team. In 2000, a cricket tour was organised to the Caribbean, a dinner held to raise funds, a South African and two Australian exchange students were recruited to bolster the team and a cricket professional from Arundel Castle in Sussex was appointed. There is also, now, a full-time hockey coach at the school.

The construction of the Sports Hall, which incorporated a swimming pool, covered training area and squash courts, hugely expanded the opportunities for sport in the school. It was funded almost entirely by Bernard Sunley after a visit he made to the school shortly before his death, and opened by the Queen in 1967 while Prince Charles was at Gordonstoun. Forty-three years later, after her three sons and two of her grandchildren had attended the school, the Queen returned to open the new George Welsh Sports Hall. George Welsh joined the school having served at the army PT school in Aldershot, and became something of an institution, retiring in 1984, but continuing to be involved in the life of the school until very recently.

Before the introduction of PE as a curriculum subject from the mid-'80s, the school relied largely on enthusiastic amateurs on the academic staff to take charge of and coach sport. From about 1979, as girls' numbers continued to grow, a number of young female teachers arrived at the school, some of them enthusiastic games players,

Below: Basketball and cricket practice in the newly refurbished sports hall, 2010.

Above: The Queen at Gordonstoun in September 2010 for the opening of the newly renovated and substantially extended sports facility, now named the George Welsh Sports Centre. Professor Bryan Williams, Chairman of the Governors, walks at the Queen's side; behind her, left to right, are the Duke of Edinburgh, the Headmaster Mark Pyper, George Welsh and, half-concealed, Mrs Jenny Pyper.

Right: HM The Queen, with HRH Prince Charles behind her (then Guardian and in his final year at Gordonstoun), opening the original Sports Hall in July 1967; to her right is the Headmaster, Bobby Chew.

continues with girls' hockey and boys' football. Cross-country running and athletics have always relied on local competition. Pupils regularly participated in the Moray Schools and the Highland Schools athletic championships and still today take part in the North of Scotland Schools cross-country running championships which are frequently hosted by Gordonstoun.

It is also a long-established tradition for Gordonstoun to participate fully in club leagues. Teams play in the Highland ladies', men's, mixed and junior tennis leagues and the Moray Firth squash leagues. Cricket is played against local adult sides. League matches are usually midweek evening affairs involving post-match socialising with opponents over light refreshments, a welcome contact with adults who have no direct connection with the school. Most golf fixtures are with local clubs and schools. The construction of the floodlit all-weather playing surface led to many more fixtures with the Moray Hockey Club, increasingly involving mixed teams of boys and girls, thus providing the stronger female players with the opportunity to really stretch their game. Girls have also excelled at individual sports, particularly athletics, swimming and cross-country running.

In the summer term, tennis has for a very long time been the top choice for both girls and boys. Throughout the 1980s and early '90s, girls were particularly enthusiastic participants in the annual coaching week, benefiting from the tuition of visiting professional Peter Darbyshire, whose sessions started before breakfast and finished well after close time.

William Boyd (1965–70) summed up his experience of the summer term at Gordonstoun thus: 'Summer term meant tennis. The school tennis team was a member of a league that operated in that area of the north east. We could play against clubs in Inverness, Forres and Fochabers. The great advantage was that these games were played mid-week, in the evening. There was something unreal about these matches. The six of us in the team would get into a minibus at about half past five on a Wednesday or Thursday evening and be driven to a small country town. There we would be dropped at the local tennis club. The matches were so regular no master accompanied us. For some reason – perhaps it was to do with the nature of the league – we often played mixed doubles, sometimes against women's teams. Here, at last, was life as most people led it. I have the most idyllic recollections of these warm summer evenings: long shadows cast across the red clay courts, the sonorous "pock, pock" of the balls in the air, the punctilious courtesy of our game ("I'm not sure if that was out – play a let!"), a few idle spectators – two girls, a dog, a ruddy man with a pipe. And then, afterwards, in the small clubhouse,

particularly of hockey. The fact that the staff were able to play with the girls and demonstrate their skills earned them respect, and, under their tutelage, the standard of girls' sport improved substantially. Hockey and netball became the girls' main team sports outside the summer term and they continue to be played to a high standard. Particularly after the construction of the all-weather playing surface in the early 1990s, mixed hockey became popular with the best female players finding no difficulty keeping up with the strongest of the boys.

In keeping with Hahn's aim that the school should be involved in the local community, there have always been numerous sports fixtures against other schools in the area, a policy which was probably also a matter of pragmatism, given the remoteness of Gordonstoun from other independent schools. In the early days rugby, cricket and hockey were all played against local schools. This practice with the glowing perspiring wives of dentists and solicitors, all of us still in dusty tennis whites, drinking half pints of ginger beer shandy, chatting, laughing, in the palpitating dusk. There was to us boys, a tender, bourgeois eroticism about these encounters, which was much analysed on the bus ride back to school. We often got back late, well after ten, with the school in bed, all curtains drawn vainly against the sunny northern evenings. We felt immensely proud of our exclusivity and were the source of great envy. Although I was a very keen sportsman at school, I find it quite easy to understand why tennis is the only game I play today.'

Sports tours are a well-established tradition. A boys' hockey tour in 1969, led by George Welsh, was immortalised in William Boyd's television screenplay *Dutch Girls* (1985). Tellingly, when a reunion of the players was organised in London in 2009, all but one of them managed to attend, from all over the world. There have subsequently been many hockey tours to mainland Europe, particularly to Salem and Heidelberg, and a couple of these in the mid-'90s involved both the girls' and boys' teams. Rugby also has a strong touring tradition both to Europe and beyond, notably, Australia, South Africa, South America and Sri Lanka. In recent years, there have been girls' netball tours to Spain (combined with tennis) and two visits to Dubai. In 2009 girls' hockey and netball teams visited Barbados. In 2010 the boys' hockey team went to Amsterdam and the boys' football team to Barcelona.

Whilst touring abroad, the participants frequently stay in local homes, thus gaining exposure to cultures different from their own. Hosts normally organise sightseeing visits to places of interest. Rugby players have done voluntary work in shanty towns around Capetown, for example, and hockey players have visited art galleries and museums in Heidelberg and learnt a great deal about the history of this medieval German town. Brief tours within the British Isles are undertaken by all the main team sports as well as squash.

In the 1990s the number of sports at the school was deliberately expanded. The aim was to give pupils the best possible chance to find a sport which they could enjoy and at which they could improve and achieve. For boys, for example, football gradually achieved equal status with rugby and is now played to a very high level. This increase in options reduced the numbers playing many sports, but standards did not suffer as a result. Participants are usually enthusiastic and often able and this has fostered a club-style camaraderie which is a notable feature of Gordonstoun sport. Probably as a result of this relatively relaxed can-do atmosphere, the numbers of pupils who go on to play club sport after leaving school are considerable.

EXPEDITIONS

One of the aspects of Moray that drew Kurt Hahn to found his school there was the accessibility of the mountains. 'Expeditions', he claimed, 'can greatly contribute towards building strength of character.' In the March 1936 issue of *The Gordonstoun School News*, Hahn records his hope 'one day, to establish a preparatory school in Glenmore Lodge, near Aviemore', a Victorian hunting lodge used by the school as a base for forays into the mountains. That never happened (it was the first home, in 1948, of the Scottish National Outdoor Training Centre, now in a purpose-built centre a few miles away, still called Glenmore Lodge). But the impulse to send pupils 'to conquer Glenmore for Gordonstoun', as Hahn put it, was certainly carried through. Here are the accounts of the first two expeditions into the Cairngorms:

'*February 2nd*. We arrived at the Lodge in snow, and, after eating our lunch, we climbed Meall a' Bhuachaille (sometimes referred to by the English as the "hill behind the house".) On the way down, we ran into a snowstorm, but owing to Mr Chew's excellent sense of direction, we soon reached the Lodge. We spent the night in extreme luxury with fires in the bedrooms and late breakfast next morning, and all sorts of other things which the Spartan life of Gordonstoun does not leave room for, even on Saturday nights.

'Next morning, we climbed Cairngorm itself . . . On the way up we saw some deer and some ptarmigan, which excited Dr Richter extremely. When he had finished, we returned by way of what our mountaineers called a "snow-couloir", and which ordinary people would call a "big ditch down the mountain full of snow." Soon after we had returned to the Lodge, Mr Hahn arrived with a party of boys who proceeded to eat most of our tea. When they had done this, we all drove home together.

'*February 16th*. We arrived in snow for the second time to find that Mr Chew had been at the Lodge for some time. After lunch, we dammed a stream as the weather was too threatening to attempt to climb a hill. Next day a terrible discovery was made at breakfast time. We found that the provisions were running short. The sausages fell far short of our requirements, and the butter was merely a pity. After our very scanty breakfast, we went up the valley to Coire Lochan. When we arrived there, we found that there was too much hail to go on, and we turned back.'

Many of the school expeditions to the surrounding countryside of Moray and the hills beyond involved the use of bicycles and some were very ambitious. In June 1936, Henry Brereton took a party of eight boys on a four-day expedition from the source of the river Findhorn to its mouth. They cycled to Forres and took a train to

Rope climbing in the early days: Gwinne's Chimney, Pavey Ark, Langdale Pikes, Cumbria (above) and Slingsby's Route, Scawfell, Cumbria (above right), both late 1930s.

Right: An extract from Bobby Chew's diary, probably relating to the same occasion.

Newtonmore. From there they walked up into the Monadhliath hills, climbed Carn Dearg, where Abhainn Cro Chlach, the chief Findhorn tributary, rises and then walked the 90 miles back to Forres along the river. In Forres they collected their bicycles and cycled to the mouth of the river. A report of the trip noted thanks to Mrs Brereton for carrying their blankets by car from one campsite to another – no sleeping bags in those days. The young Bex Richter took a party to Orton on the river Spey. They climbed Ben Aigan and then cycled down the Spey to see a colony of nesting terns before cycling back to the school, noting

wildlife all the way. Jimmy Fraser (1949–52) provides a compact reminiscence of an expedition to the Cairngorm plateau from Wester Elchies: 'Led by Bex. Being eaten alive in our tents by midges. "The smoke from smouldering lichen will keep them at bay," said Bex. So we ended up only half eaten alive, but with streaming eyes, and half suffocated!'

Taking students out on expeditions to the Scottish mountains has always been a key element of the Gordonstoun curriculum. In the early days there were always members of staff who were experienced expeditioners, having completed trips to the Alps or even the Himalaya. Among these were Bobby Chew, Freddie Spencer Chapman and John Kempe.

John Ray was the (much-admired) expeditions master at Altyre in the 1950s, teaching history for the first half of the week, and overseeing expedition training from Thursday to Sunday. 'Sunday was for Voluntary Expeditions' recalls Ray. 'A list on the notice board would quickly fill and the school bus, a converted army truck which the boys called "the biscuit tin", would head for any of a score of marvellous mountains. We might visit the corries at the head of Glen Feshie, or the hills above Affric or Strathfarrar. With an early start, Ben Nevis was within range. The plateaux of Macdui and Braeriach were closer by. The colouring of the seasons, the skies and the weather made every day a new adventure. The training element, whether map-reading or exercises on Dava Moor, was intended to stretch the party. Small groups of thirteen-year-olds, dropped off at points on a desolate or shining moorland road after due preparation, would be told to be at a map

hird pitch very hard work . I could just reach the important hold
. jockeying up the right leg , - but only succeeded after two
or three experiments . Gerry , - who was second , could not hope
to reach it but by skilfully jamming a knee in the crack managed
eventually to wriggle up so high . Michael came up by the same
method . Then an easy pitch .
Later a nasty and akward chockstone to get over . I found this hard
work . My second refused to foolow me and insisted on coming up insid
the chock stone . Result tremendous confusion of ropes and general
tangles and jams . Eventually cleared .
Final pitch under an overhang went fairly easilt although
Gerry attempted to come out the wrong side . A good first day .

Wednesday . Went to Pavey Ark . Crescent followed by Gwinns
Chimney . Great specualation between Michael and myself as to weather
Gerry would go along the crescent on all fours. Fortunately
he felt safety was important , and adopted this method much
to Michael's satisfaction , - he having used same method three days b
before .
Gwinns Chimney and the top pitch went well . Top pitch well
photographed .

Thursday . Visited Scawfell . Very tempted to go a Gully on the
Wastwater Screes , but safety first our Motto !
Toiled up to the lunching stone . Craggs deserted and we
clambere up to the bottom of Slingsbys route.. First pitch easy . Ce
second pitch the step across found none too easy till one
discovered that a press hold was the key to it . Not too

Above: An expedition to Lairig Ghru with Jack LeQuesne, 1940s or '50s.

reference, maybe ten or twelve miles across the Moor, for pick-up sometime before dusk. In the course of the day they would chase mountain hares, plough through peat hags, face a blatter of rain, get lost and find themselves. Somehow they always reached the rendezvous, usually weary and triumphant. The trick was to judge that this particular party, with this leader, in the day's weather conditions, would all arrive.

'Mr Chew soon checked up on safety. Early in November, a colleague and I were to take a class to the Cairngorms. John Gillespie's party was to stay at Aultnancaber near Coylumbridge, mine above the forest at Ryvoan. We were to climb Bynack More and the other Braeriach. Next morning the parties set off, but by 11 am the wind rose and swung to the northwest. We turned back into the bitter wind blown sleet and soon had a good fire going in the bothy. The high plateau was blotted out. Leaving a lad in charge, I walked and ran down the seven miles, relieved to find John's party also safely returned and cooking up. A few minutes later, Mr Chew arrived. Driving to a cocktail party at Nairn, 40 miles north, he had noted the sudden change of weather, deserted the party and come to check up. Driving me back up the track, a relationship of trust had begun to grow.

'It was the very start of "outdoor education". There were no qualifications for Mountain Party leaders, no "health and safety". Everything hung on judgement, experience and trust. Over their school lives, many of the boys became competent mountaineers, inured to Scottish winter conditions, exulting in the experience of a day on the high tops, or basking in the sunshine beside the tent in some remote glen.'

'It says something', remarks John Ray, master in charge of expeditions at Altyre, Forres, 'that 55 years later, I have vivid memories of the four Altyre boys in this photograph: Charles Blackwood, Alastair MacEwan, George Courtauld and Cameron Mackenzie.'

AN EXPEDITION FROM ALTYRE

John Ray was held in great esteem by his young charges. John Breckenridge gives a flavour of the expeditions he led from a boy's point of view:

' "Rise and shine! Rise and shine you idle lot!" came the voice of John Ray. Creeping out of our sleeping bags into a freezing February dawn, ten seventeen-year-old Altyre sixth-form boys stood outside the Shenavall Bothy – stretching, scratching, shivering, and drinking in the scene before them. The rising sun was lighting up an absolutely cloudless sky in opposition to a paling, fading moon across a white, snow covered moor. The snow-covered pines of the Strathnasheallag Forrest stood to the east, while the peaks along the ridge of the mighty An Teallach dominated the skyline to the north. Mostly covered in snow, icy patches on the sides of its peaks glittered in the rising sun. The air sparkled and our breath hung in clouds before us as it slowly evaporated.

'Minutes later we were cleaning our teeth and washing our faces in the ice-fringed burn; then walking back to the bothy for a breakfast of porridge, doorsteps of bread, butter and jam and mugs of strong tea thick with sugar and condensed milk. Breakfast over, it was time to strike camp and head for the hills. A final check of the bothy to ensure we'd obeyed the climber's code and left it tidy, along with matches, candles, tea and sugar for those who would come after us.

'Off we trudged northwards toward Sail Liath, the southern entry to the An Teallach ridge, using our ice-axes to probe the snow for crevices, streams, boggy holes and pools as we went. Singing songs to keep in step we walked as hard and as fast as possible, John leading the way like the marine commando he had been and our boots sinking through the thin crust on top of the snow with a repetitive crunching sound. The farther we walked, the steeper it got and the multiple peaks of the

mountain blended into one in our line of sight as our route turned north west. We stopped at the top of the gully for R&R (rest and re-hydration). Water drunk, rucksacks back on shoulders, on we walked.

'Climbing out of the gully we headed up the slopes of the first peak, Cadha Gobhlach – ice-axes coming into play to chisel hand and foot-holds. Breathing harder now, we scrambled to keep up with John – legs starting to tremble on the ledges, rucksacks pulling us treacherously backwards.

'John stopped on the top and shouted: "Ten minute break". As we caught up with him on the summit, we flopped back on the snow, puffing and panting. "Don't get too comfortable. We're going to traverse that gully next as we go up the Corrag Bhuidhe buttresses and walk on to Lord Berkeley's Seat." Gathering round the map, we looked ahead at the rocks and back at the map. The peaks on the ridge went on and on past Lord

Above: Wet clothing hung up to dry outside the Climbing Hut at 2,000 feet on Ben Nevis, Christmas holidays 1952.

Right: Easy Gully, Buachaillie Etive Mor, Glencoe, early 1950s.

'We regarded the Cairngorms as our playground just down the road,' writes Calum Anton (1953–57). 'The end of May 1956 saw David Orr Deas, Charlie Blackwood and I complete the six highest peaks of the Cairngorms, the four four thousanders plus Beinns Avon and Bhuird, a total of 38 miles with twelve and a half thousand feet of climbing, taking us eighteen and a half hours. When you are that age, anything is possible. A year and 41 summits later, a memorable weekend expedition to Slioch and Beinn Eighe. Innes Miller, Robin Dods and I did Slioch by night, or as night as it gets at that time of year, followed by a couple of hours sleep in the heather, then on to do all the tops of Beinn Eighe. Inevitably pretty knackered by then, so managed to fall asleep in the sunshine, stripped down to a string vest – remember them? – they were an essential climbing gear item then.'

Anton also recalls a one-day expedition in February or March 1956 (when two parties of four set out to tackle the central gulley of Coire Lochan), which would send shivers down the spine of any member of staff accompanying students today: 'Conditions were not good with fresh snow on old, and as time wore on more windblown snow started to pour in off the plateau into the coire. Our rope of four got into

Berkeley's Seat to the summit peak: Sgurr Fiona at all of 3,477 ft. It seemed a long way away. John's voice broke our reverie: "Come on now, don't stand around like a bunch of washer women. Get yourselves together or we'll never get to the top today."

'Slowly, we picked up our rucksacks and turned again toward the ridge. The going was much harder now; the ridge steeper and narrower, and icier. Ice-axes no longer a fashion accessory but a means of survival. Two long hours later we arrived at the top of the peak called Lord Berkeley's Seat where we stopped again for lunch.

'Getting the primuses going was difficult at the altitude but we managed and fifteen minutes later were washing down chunky cheese sandwiches with mugs of hot Knorr packet tomato soup. Revolting – but delicious as well. "Right lads" John's voice cut in "not far now to Sgurr Fiona where I have a surprise for you."

'An hour later as we stood on top of the peak, John said; "Now lads, we're going to have a bit of fun." His face was impassive – almost – he couldn't quite suppress a mischievous twitch at the corner of his mouth. "We're going down again – and quickly! We're going glissading. Do you know what that is? The Scottish equivalent of the Cresta run, but without a sledge. We'll glissade nearly 2,000 feet down to the frozen tarn there. It will take less than a minute – the ride of your life. Now watch what I do and follow me – one at a time – with at least fifteen seconds between you. At least fifteen seconds – I mean it"

'He reached into his rucksack and pulled out a black bin bag. "I hope you all remembered yours". Spreading it out just over the north side of the peak, he lay down on his side, holding the shaft of his ice-axe firmly in his right hand, the head grasped firmly in his left. Looking up at us he said; "All you do is let yourself go and use the ice-axe to steer and

brake. If you find yourself going too fast, just dig the tip of your axe into the snow – but don't on any account let go. See you at the bottom!" With that he pushed off and we watched him hurtle down the side of the mountain getting smaller and smaller until he shot across the ice of the frozen tarn at the bottom. Standing up he beckoned us to follow.

'One at a time we followed. When my turn came I lay down on my bin bag, grabbed my ice-axe, took a deep breath and pushed off. Scotland fell away below me. Icy wind rushed into my face. I was flying. Too fast – I pressed the tip of my axe into the snow – kicking up a huge plume of snow – which was trying to wrench the axe from my grasp. Holding on with a grip of desperation – the blood pounding in my ears I suddenly felt the ice of the tarn reach up to me and I skidded to a stop on the far shore wrapped in the shredded remains of my black bin bag.

'I'd done it!'

the throat of the gulley with the other four lower down and following to the side when I realised this was pretty stupid and we should get out of here. At the age of sixteen or seventeen, you know what an avalanche is, but having no experience of such a thing, or knowing anyone who has, one tends not to put two and two together . . . [Suddenly] a mass of new powder snow coming off the plateau above, and accumulating in the upper gulley, let go just as we turned round to descend. There was no noise apart from the wind howling in the cliffs above, only for a split second a sensation of massive pressure in my back before my ice-axe belay was torn out and all four of us began our very long and rapid descent to the coire floor. Being roped, it was relatively easy to extricate ourselves from the jumbled snow debris once we'd come to a halt, to find we were all OK apart from one broken collar bone and a few torn finger nails. Mr Hodges [Guy Hodges, newly graduated from Cambridge], on seeing us through the mist and snowstorm shooting past where they were standing, had apparently remarked – "there goes Anton glissading again", oblivious of our predicament. I for one wouldn't want to make a habit of that kind of 600-foot descent. The shoulder was strapped and we walked out, not to the carpark at the ski lift because it wasn't there yet, but all the way to Glenmore Lodge. News of this escapade was kept strictly between the four walls of the school. A close shave, yes, but also valuable experience for future climbing and particularly ski mountaineering expeditions.'

Allowing young people to explore the countryside did not always involve staff-led hikes or climbing in the mountains. In the 1950s, and to some extent in the 1960s, it was not unusual for pupils who had proved their competence and submitted a plan to set off in small groups on expeditions of their own. Bernard Kuenssberg (1962–66) remembers an occasion that epitomises the atmosphere in which staff enabled adventure, while still observing a duty of care: 'One weekend, myself and Tony Vlasto suggested sleeping in a snow hole on Ben Rinnes, so Ian Lawson said, "why not?" We cycled there, climbed high, made the snow hole, got into our sleeping bags and then heard Ian Lawson outside scrunching towards us just to check!'

Richard Bridges (Duffus, 1956–60) joined the scouts, 'largely so I could canoe down the Spey, a somewhat risky endeavour involving just three boys – myself, Peter Shiach and Dirk Kalis – in two canoes entirely unsupervised. One canoe was completely wrecked above Craigellachie and once we had fished ourselves out we tackled a local landlady for a bath – "that'll be two and saxpence in advance!" After we had had

Above: Practising ice-climbing at The Ice Factor, Kinlochleven, 2009.

Left: Winter expedition in Kintail, 1984.

Year 10 kayaking expedition on the river Spey in 2010.

our baths which were much needed as we were pretty cold, Peter Shiach arranged for us all to be whisked home.'

Twenty years later, the Spey had lost none of its allure. 'Nowadays,' writes Stuart Huyton, who was a sixth-former in 1975, 'the Spey welcomes all water users, not only anglers, but in the early '70s things were different. There was an ongoing battle between anglers and canoeists which would not be resolved until the famous Wills' Trustees v Cairngorm Canoeing and Sailing School court case in 1976 which finally cleared the way for anglers, canoeists and rafters all to have access to the river.' This was the background against which three boys from Altyre House and one from Cumming House decided to construct a raft and see how far down the river Spey it would get over a weekend. The raft was designed by Robert Barbour and consisted of six oil drums, staves, planks and ropes all topped with a Vango Force Ten flysheet to provide shelter. It was constructed on the South Lawn with a modular design to allow it to be disassembled and shipped, in the school lorry, to the shores of Loch Insh where it could then be reassembled. Huyton continues, 'The intention was, in true nautical fashion, to cruise for 24 hours

a day with the crew taking shifts. This plan was abandoned on the first night when the raft encountered a low-hanging branch which very nearly brought the expedition to an untimely end. The branch knocked down the flysheet and a good number of items were lost into the river. On seeing a vital cooking pot beginning to sink, one of the crewmembers who had managed to catch his own spectacles, which had been knocked off, most valiantly dropped them and rescued the cooking pot instead to the communal good. After this it was decided to make camp during the hours of darkness.

'The river is not always calm and deep so there were times when the crew had to leap overboard to negotiate shallow stretches or where all hands were needed on deck to navigate through rapids. Nevertheless . . . [by] the end of the weekend the raft had managed to sail all the way from Loch Insh to Nethybridge, which is a distance of approximately eighteen miles. No mean feat.'

In the 1970s and early '80s there were far fewer people climbing the Munros. The great Munro-bagging surge didn't really get under way until after Hamish Brown's account of

doing the Munros in one long walk. At that time the third- and fourth-formers had four-day camps in such places as Glen Affric, Glen Strathfarrar, the Coulin Forest and Strathossian – magnificent areas that they were then fortunate enough to have virtually to themselves. John Pownall recalls those halcyon days: 'Memories spring to mind of impromptu games of cricket at Strathossian and of one student catching so many fish in the river Affric that we almost got tired of fresh grilled trout for breakfast. I have memories also of an anxious night in Torridon watching the river rise towards our tents while the Headmaster, John Kempe, slept soundly, totally unperturbed.'

House expeditions were very popular. Pownall recalls the friendly rivalry that grew up between houses prompted by Angus Scott's (by several accounts somewhat embroidered) tales of Munros conquered by Bruce House. Pownall remembers exciting trips with Bruce to An Teallach and the Five Sisters, for example. Anthony Jones and Round Square took up the challenge with the Cluanie South Ridge (Anthony's first Munros) and the hills around Loch Arkaig. Angus Miller (Jones's successor) carried on the tradition with long days walking from Derry Lodge in the southern Cairngorms. Altyre House's trips to Ben Nevis became an annual event, weather permitting. Not to be outdone, the girls of Hopeman and Windmill also tackled Ben Nevis, some of them along the Carn Mor Dearg arête.

At this time, the training of students in preparation for expeditions and the assessment of a member of staff's suitability to lead expeditions to the hills were, by present standards, pretty rudimentary. In the wider world, and in response to incidents such as the Cairngorm Disaster in 1971 (see page 154), ways were being sought to develop outdoor activities as a method for building character, while ensuring that the physical risks to young people were minimised.

All this led in the 1980s to a more structured outdoor programme, under Tony Gabb's guidance. This allowed students to progress through training and a range of expeditions with the ultimate aim of equipping every student with sufficient skills and experience to be able to plan and undertake a trip to the hills unaccompanied by staff at the end of Year 12 (lower sixth). A greater emphasis was also placed on staff training with staff being encouraged to participate in the Mountain Leader Training Scheme and achieve awards for leading groups in summer and in winter, as well as for teaching rock climbing and other outdoor activities.

Heather Thomas-Smith recalls with great fondness the expeditions she went on, first from Aberlour House in the late 1970s, and then from Hopeman and Gordonstoun House

in the first half of the '80s: 'Aberlour offered that all important introduction to form expeds and many happy memories remain of "Tattie" Hanson's survival expeds round Cape Wrath, exploring Erraid and the Ross of Mull, eating winkle sandwiches, madcap adventures in medieval costume or summiting Ben Rinnes for the Queen's Silver Jubilee despite unseasonable hail and snow. If enjoyed and cherished, such grounding perhaps meant an inevitable draw to Gordonstoun's hillier pursuits. At Gordonstoun, third- and fourth-form expeds involved going to Torridon and later my first winter Munro in deep snow, invariably sporting the large bright orange cagoule that seemed *de rigueur* at the time and sweated damply with you whether you were stomping up a hill or rowing the cutters as fast as possible out of Hopeman harbour.'

Summer Climbing Tours. Above: On Curved Ridge, Buachaillie Etive Mor, Glencoe, 2009. Opposite: Savage Slit, Northern Corries, Cairngorm, 2010.

Further progress was made in the 1990s with the appointment of John Trythall as Gordonstoun's first full-time Sail Training and Outdoor Education Co-ordinator. The two roles were separated in 2007. Ibrahim Park is now Outdoor Education Co-ordinator and has worked hard to ensure that Gordonstoun's outdoor education programme is an example of best practice, with all staff being fully qualified and the safety of students being viewed as paramount. The school has made great efforts to avoid withdrawing from adventurous activities in a climate in which health and safety regulations have led many to decide they are just not worth all the effort. Risks are carefully managed but as far as possible the excitement of outdoor activities is preserved, and the considerable benefits to young people of being involved in challenging activities are highlighted and explained to parents and other interested parties whenever possible.

Roped climbing has often been the saving grace for students who do not necessarily appreciate the delights of traditional team games, providing both a physical outlet and the opportunity to learn lessons regarding teamwork and trust. Staff involvement has always been high and particularly in the early days of the school the dangers to be encountered were not to be underestimated. In the 1950s, Peter Dean, a staff expedition leader, recalled, in *The Gordonstoun Record*, a memorable description of the hazards of climbing given to him by another climber:

'What happens if you do slip? [when second on the rope]'

'You fall – and provided your rope technique is sound you come to little harm.'

Above: Year 9 expedition on Cairngorm, 2003.

Below and opposite: Year 9 backpacking expedition, Glen Affric, June 2006.

Duke of Edinburgh's Award expedition from Linn of Dee to Loch Morlich, 2010.

'But what happens when the first man falls off? He cannot have a rope above him.'

'No he hasn't but if he peels off when he is 30 feet above his second, then he can only [sic] fall 60 feet which, although it is quite a way, is preferable to falling perhaps 200 feet . . .'

'So the number two can always hold the leader?'

'Yes. He will probably suffer from rope burns on his hands but unless the rope breaks the leader will, in all likelihood, get away with only bruises.'

This phlegmatic approach was matched by the rudimentary nature of available equipment. Modern students, in their helmets and 'sticky' boots, complaining of the discomfort of their sit-harnesses, would probably be traumatised by a shoulder belay or a 'classic abseil'. Numerous early acolytes will have clear memories of the friction burns generated by the rope in these standard procedures.

Many of the early climbing trips took place among the mountain crags of Scotland – Cairngorm, Glencoe and Torridon or sometimes, during school holidays, in Wales or the Lake District. There are surprisingly few early records of the local sea cliffs being used for practice. However by the 1960s the focus of British climbing generally had started to shift from finding interesting ways up mountain cliffs towards devising technical routes up smaller cliffs. The coast near Gordonstoun thus became more relevant, and in the late 1960s the cliffs between Cove Bay and Covesea were thoroughly explored. The double-legged stack of Gow's Castle, below the Coastguard Watchtower, rated 'severe' and 'pleasant' in the Scottish Mountain Climbing guide, has probably not been climbed since Gordonstoun boys tackled it, because of natural erosion of the soft sandstone. There was also a reference in the SMC guide to Cove Bay where 'a smooth wall of soft sandstone has seen the unsuccessful attentions of a phantom bolter'. The 1968 *Gordonstoun Record* perhaps sheds more light – 'More time has been spent on rock climbing (this term). Artificial routes have been completed at Cove Bay and there have been many ambitious attempts at new routes'.

In the 1970s, many developments occurred at the Cummingston cliffs, further west. Surprisingly only one climb is recorded by the official guidebook as being first led by a Gordonstoun student – Fracture Face Very Severe 4b – unfortunately not an attractive or popular climb. These local climbs and the opening of the climbing wall in May 1988 (following a generous donation from the family of Gordon Henderson, an old boy tragically killed in a mountain accident after he had left school) made climbing far more accessible to students. In the last twenty years abseiling and climbing have become established activities in the expedition training programmes and all students have the opportunity to discover how they cope with heights. Climbing is widely recognised as a way of building confidence as well as developing the ability to manage

Left: Tony Gabb demonstrating rope climbing technique at Covesea to a student, 2006.

Below: A climbing trip on the Isle of Eigg including Julian Lines (in red), c. 1984.

Below left: Julian Lines on the Cummingston cliffs, west of Gordonstoun, 2005.

JULIAN LINES, one of the finest rock climbers in the UK, was already an exceptional mountaineer when he was at Gordonstoun. Before he left he had climbed all the Munros [the Scottish peaks over 3000 feet high], becoming at the time one of the youngest people to do so.

'When I was eleven, in the spring of 1980, I went on a walk organised by my prep. school along the West Highland Way. I was in awe of the snowy mountains such as Ben Lui and Ben More. On the last day we tackled the mighty Ben Nevis. On the way up the track, I got talking with Simon Roberts, an old boy who had gone on to Gordonstoun. He had a big purple Alpiniste rucksack with an ice axe attached to it, and he told me he was in the Mountain Rescue team. From that day on, I knew where I wanted to go to school next.

'Once at Gordonstoun, I was initially a little disheartened, as I couldn't join the Mountain Rescue team until the fifth form. There were form expeditions and house expeditions during the autumn and summer terms, but these were never enough to satisfy my desire to be in the mountains. However some of the younger teachers, such as Tony Gabb, organised voluntary expeditions and winter skills courses during the winter time. And in later years Tony Gabb and John Hall used to take me ice climbing – acts of great generosity, as the responsibility and the risks were high and they went out in their own free time. During the summer term we were allowed to go off in small groups (a minimum of three) for backpacking weekends. With a couple of like-minded pupils, we took the train from Elgin and alighted at Dalwhinnie on a Friday night. We returned on the Sunday by which time we had walked over 50 miles and climbed nine Munros.

Right: Hopeman House expedition to Badaguish, Glen More, 2004.

stressful situations. The sheltered climbing wall (albeit in an unheated area) provides a controlled introduction to this activity – from the introductory prep. school challenge climbing competitions to senior students taking their first steps at lead-climbing. All students now learn the basics of rope management, abseiling and climbing techniques on 'the Wall' before moving to the actual cliffs.

Those students with a passion for the sport and who wish to take the activity even further use their activity time and any extra sessions to train and improve their technique. Recent students have gone on to flourish in various mountaineering contexts: at 26, Polly Murray (Windmill, 1987–91) was, in 2000, the first Scottish woman to climb Everest; at the cutting edge of British rock-climbing, Julian Lines (Bruce, 1979–84) achieved, in 2003, a spectacular first ascent of the 'Icon of Lust' route on the Shelterstone Crag above Loch Avon, described in *Scottish Rock Climbs* as 'probably the hardest slab climb in Britain'. Tristan Bamford (Cumming, 2003–07), writes, 'What I am really grateful for is that the school introduced me to my biggest passion – climbing. My first lesson was on the school climbing wall. In 2005, I was ranked second in Scotland . . . and I have become absolutely hooked on mountaineering.' Perhaps most importantly, there will have

'Gordonstoun is fortunate in having the small sandstone sea cliffs at Cummingston close at hand, and it was here that I first learnt to climb and went out with the Mountain Rescue Service before I had joined up. I remember my first climb when I was helped into my harness, knot-checked and belayed by a girl in the team. There were no teachers double-checking knots or belays, and it made me think how professional the pupils in the Mountain Rescue team were, when my life was literally in the hands of a seventeen-year-old girl.

'Once I was a member of the team, I went on many expeditions into the hills, of which the most memorable was when we were camping on a high plateau in the Cairngorms and the wind picked up in the night and started to blow the flysheet away. I went out into the dark to find some boulders, but then got lost on my return trip, eventually finding the tent but no boulders; two of us proceeded to hold the flysheet down with our cutlery whilst the third guy slept through it all.

'However it wasn't all expeditions. The team was always on call and we did many stretcher-lowering exercises in the hills with 500-foot ropes and also on the cliffs close to school. On one occasion, I was barrow-boy (the person who hangs from the bottom of the stretcher), but as the stretcher was being lowered over the edge, the rungs got caught in the soft sandstone rock and dislodged a piece that fell on my thigh; it was painful and I said to the pupil in the stretcher that I ought to be in there! I could barely walk when I reached the bottom. And here I am still enjoying the outdoors 30 years on.'

Ocean Spirit in the Svalbard archipelago, the northernmost territories of Norway, 2007.

been countless unsung incidents in which training received at Gordonstoun has led to the correct mountaineering decision being made in testing conditions.

The number of events organised by the school during holidays has grown enormously, and for a while the exchange programme, Service projects, sporting tours, and so on, led to the temporary demise of the climbing tour. Fortunately, in recent years, it has been possible to resurrect these opportunities to visit more distant parts and for students to gain wider climbing experience. Once again students have been able to enjoy quite prolonged visits to the bigger crags of Scotland and the Lake District – both in summer and winter. In autumn 2007 a combined mountaineering and sailing team took *Ocean Spirit* to within 600 miles of the North Pole to explore Spitsbergen and the Svalbard archipelago. This joint venture allowed far more than the honing of previously learned skills; 'an experience like this,' wrote Lukas Albeitz in *The Gordonstoun Record* in 2007, 'gave us the opportunity to look outside the

boundaries of our own lives and gain an insight into the wider world'.

SKIING

One sport which is not readily on offer at most schools is skiing, but pupils at Gordonstoun have a unique opportunity to learn this exhilarating form of exercise. Sweethillocks, within the school grounds, is in cold winters sometimes skiable, and the Cairngorm and Lecht ski centres are located within driving distance.

In the late 1930s, the school had the use of a small house called Lyngarrie on the river Nethy, from which cross-country skiing trips were embarked on. David Byatt remembers skiing in the Cairngorms as a schoolboy in the late '40s. Although skiing in the Cairngorms was not routinely organised at Gordonstoun until the 1970s, Angus Miller remembers helping with ski instruction there in the mid-'60s, and joining up with the boys in Grantown where hired skis were picked up. And many of the denizens of

Altyre, Forres, enjoyed skiing, encouraged, no doubt, by Bobby Chew, himself a practised mountaineer and skier.

Alpine skiing was a particularly popular sport at the school from the mid-'70s, with skiing occasionally taking place in all three terms. Such was the demand, that the school purchased a large number of sets of skis, and a small team of enthusiastic pupils was recruited to help maintain the equipment which was then hired out each week for a small charge; the money thus collected allowed replacement equipment to be purchased. The scheme saved precious time previously spent hiring skis on the day at Grantown, reduced costs to parents, and allowed many more pupils to develop a new skill and to enjoy the confidence the sport gave them.

The standard of skiing varied and ski lessons with local ski instructors were arranged for all levels. The school ski team often performed well in various competitions, including the Scottish Schools Ski Championship, which the school won in 1979 and 1980. The ski team has continued to do well over the years. The inter-house ski race, held on a weekday at Cairngorm, was always an enjoyable outing for staff and pupils alike, even in adverse blizzard conditions. The general public often commented on the high standard of the skiing shown by Gordonstoun pupils taking part.

When Alasdair Gordon-Rogers arrived at the school in 1976, nobody was doing cross-country skiing, and in Scotland as a whole the sport was not well known. He introduced it and, in 1977, a few staff and a small number of pupils took a tentative interest in it. By 1987, however, cross-country skiing had become a part of school life, and it continues to be a popular option among both staff and students.

In the 1980s the Scottish intake substantially expanded. Many of these pupils belonged to families who skied regularly in Scotland, and not a few of these had received race training with either the Scottish or Cairngorm Ski Clubs. The demand for such training to continue while they were at Gordonstoun grew until, at the end of the '80s, it was eventually agreed that serious racers could receive training on a weekday afternoon. Thus, on Wednesday afternoons in the spring term, a minibus full of boys and girls carrying picnic lunches set off for the Lecht to do two hours of concentrated coaching in race technique through gates. The benefits of this training were swiftly evident in a series of impressive results in both the Scottish and British Schools championships including a year in the early '90s when the boys won both, and the girls were placed third in the Scottish competition.

For many pupils, a lifelong love of skiing began on Sundays at Gordonstoun. Depending on the weather

forecast, the decision to go on the Sunday had to be made by lunchtime the previous day, as in the late 1970s and early 1980s it was not unusual to have three coachloads of pupils (some 150 youngsters) skiing on Cairngorm. Allocating and fitting the hired skis earlier in the week, organising packed lunches, coaches, informing the boarding house and academic staff, booking ski instructors, and briefing staff bus supervisors all had to be undone if Sunday skiing were cancelled. 'If the cancellation was based on a horrendous forecast for Cairngorm and this subsequently coincided with good weather at school on the Sunday,' recalls Gordon-Rogers, 'I had to hide from collective chastisement at the start of lessons on the Monday. A typical Sunday involved an early rise and a 7 am breakfast . . . a lot of list checking and ticking, and a holding of breath as Cairngorm came into view from the bus in case it was stormbound. If it was, a morning of skating in Aviemore placated some of the frustrated skiers. At the ski slopes after a warning about safety, organising ski school and race training, the pupils hit the slopes for a day of unsupervised skiing. The worst moment was at the end of the day making sure everyone was back at the buses before returning to school with an exhausted but happy crowd.'

Sunday skiing continued through the 1990s and beyond in the same vein as in the Gordon-Rogers era. However, recently the substantial increase in the number of activities available at school on Sundays and health and safety concerns about unsupervised skiing have reduced the availability and demand for this leisure pursuit.

A party of novice skiers on Cairngorm, accompanied by David Snell, 1949.

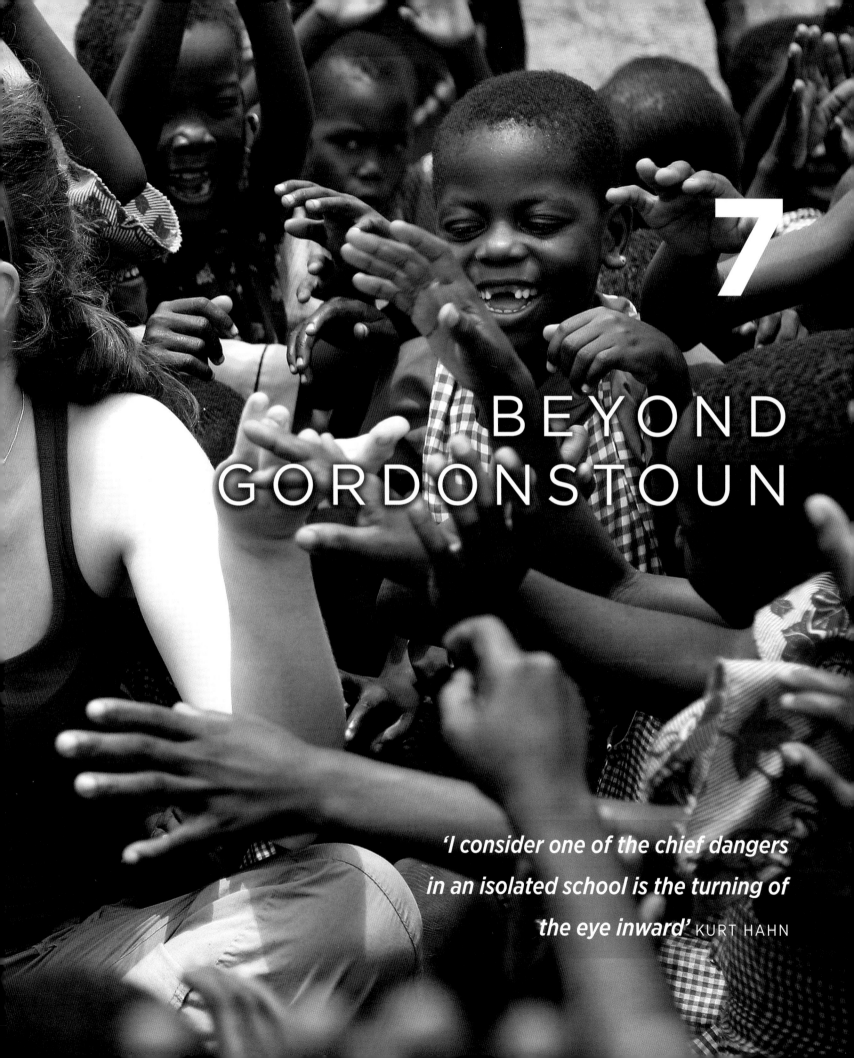

7

BEYOND
GORDONSTOUN

'I consider one of the chief dangers
in an isolated school is the turning of
the eye inward' KURT HAHN

SALEM WAS, OF COURSE, the first school in Germany founded by Hahn (with Prince Max von Baden), but he was also instrumental in the establishment of Birklehof Schule in the Black Forest region in 1932. Then, after the war, in 1949, Hahn advised Duke Friedrich of Schleswig-Holstein on the establishment of the Louisenlund Foundation in northern Germany. In Britain, Hahn's influence on schools has been disseminated almost entirely through former pupils and teaching colleagues. Box Hill School in Surrey was founded in 1959 by Roy McComish, a former Housemaster and Art teacher at Gordonstoun. In Devon, Battisborough School's ethos, under the guidance of Headmaster David Byatt from 1960–1970, was again Hahn-inspired (Byatt was a former Guardian at Gordonstoun and later returned to become Second Master and subsequently Warden). Rannoch School, in Perthshire (1959–2002), was founded by three former Altyre staff, Dougal Greig, Pat Whitworth and John Fleming. In 1962, Hahn played a major part in the founding of Atlantic College in South Wales, the first of the thirteen United World Colleges. The foundation of Dunrobin, across

Above: The first Round Square Conference, with a now rather frail and elderly Hahn in attendance, Gordonstoun, 1967.

Left: Constructing water tanks in a Karen hill village in Thailand as part of a much-needed sustainable water supply, 2010. Surface water is diverted into the tanks and then travels through gravity-fed pipes to two more tanks in the village.

Opposite: A break in the hard manual work involved in reinstating a well and constructing a water storage scheme in the Sinai Desert which will allow traditional ways of existence, such as herding goats, to continue.

the Moray Firth in Sutherland (1965–72), was directly encouraged by Hahn and involved masters who had previously taught at Gordonstoun – Nevill Mangin, Simon Hall and Ian Lawson.

Abroad, Aiglon College in Switzerland was founded in 1949 by John Corlette, another former pupil and member of staff at Gordonstoun. Corlette's educational ethos was very similar to that of Hahn: just as Hahn valued the place of silence in the school day, for example, so Corlette instituted a 'Meditation' at the start of each day, a practice still followed today. On the other side of the Atlantic, the Athenian School in Danville, California, was created in 1965 by Dyke Brown who had been educated at Salem in the early 1930s. Brown's educational philosophy was partly driven by his experience of working for the Ford Foundation on youth development, but perhaps even more strongly influenced by Hahn's ideas.

Kurt Hahn had always intended that there should be a growing network of 'British Salem Schools', each spreading its influence beyond the school boundaries in its own area. It was not long before there were ambitions on the part of others to widen the influence of Hahnian ideals still further and to promote international understanding not just by welcoming pupils from abroad to Gordonstoun, and the handful of other Hahn-inspired schools, but by actively promoting travel to different parts of the world either to provide some kind of assistance or to experience education in another culture.

After World War II, Jocelin Winthrop Young became the founder Headmaster of Anavryta School in Greece. In 1954, he was involved in an aid project organised by Salem School to offer assistance in the aftermath of the 1953 Ionian Earthquake, and it was this experience that prompted him to consider the formation of an association of schools that could offer assistance where help was needed. In 1962 he visited some ten schools started variously by Hahn, his colleagues or his pupils to make a proposal: that there should be an annual conference to discuss and coordinate future aid projects.

On 4 and 5 June 1966, Winthrop Young (by now Headmaster of the main school at Salem) and Prince Max von Baden invited friends and acquaintances from all over the world to meet at Salem to celebrate Dr Hahn's eightieth birthday. There were speeches, concerts, parties and bonfires. The main item on the agenda was a proposal to found the 'Hahn Schools Conference'. Other Headmasters present were Captain E. Tsoukalas (Anavryta), Dyke Brown (Athenian School, California), Roy McComish (Box Hill, Surrey), David Byatt (Battisborough, Devon), the Headmaster of Louisenlund (Schleswig Holstein, Germany)

and Henry Brereton, by now Warden at Gordonstoun. The first meeting was held a year later at Gordonstoun and it was here that the name was changed to 'Round Square Conference'. Hahn had been against the name 'Hahn Schools Conference', saying 'I have made many enemies and you'd do better without my name'. In those early days, it was the Headmasters rather than the schools who belonged to the conference. Jocelin Winthrop Young, Founder Director, was the principal organiser until 1992, when Terry Guest, formerly Headmaster of Lakefield College School in Canada, was appointed Director.

For some years the conference continued to be attended by Headmasters and governors alone. Then in 1974, when it was held at Cobham Hall in Kent, pupils were invited to attend for the first time, and the young people increasingly played a part in deciding the theme for a conference and organising the discussions. The name soon became simply 'Round Square' and in 1980 the Round Square International Service (RSIS) was created to promote and organise overseas voluntary service projects.

Today the Round Square Conference usually takes place over a period of two weeks with either pre- or post-conference tours organised by the schools in the host region, and the meetings themselves taking up five days. Each year the pupil-led conference explores a different theme, with keynote speeches followed by smaller group discussions. There are now many more conferences within the Round Square regions: in Europe for example, there is an annual senior Round Square Conference but also many junior ones. In the USA there is The Conference of the Americas, which now includes schools in Latin America. So extensive has the global membership become (now in excess of 70 schools), that with a delegation of nine from each school, there are few schools around the world that can host and accommodate such a large group. The idea of virtual conferences is one possibility that has been aired. One thing on which all schools agree, however, is that the conference should leave a lasting impression not just on those who are delegates, but on the community and region in which the conference takes place and that this should be true to the ideals that underpin Round Square (which grew out of Hahn's Gordonstoun Four Pillars of Internationalism, Challenge, Responsibility and Service).

International student exchanges are a long-established feature at Gordonstoun, both with schools both inside and outwith the Round Square. Some are associated with the acquisition of fluency in a foreign language, but many have been primarily to do with immersion in a foreign culture. In the 1970s and 1980s, for example, students of German

Two pupils from a South African school on a cricket exchange visit at Gordonstoun in 2009.

Students who attended the Round Square Conference at Regent's School, Thailand, in 2010 helping to plant rice on a farm on the outskirts of Bangkok. Here children from an orphanage funded by the Human Development Foundation in Bangkok learn about growing food in the afternoons, having spent their mornings in school.

often went to Salem, Birklehof, Louisenlund or the Englisches Institut Heidelberg. Le Caousou, a Jesuit school in Toulouse, was the usual destination for those studying French. For some time a whole French set would go together for a brief exchange. Those who were not language students would often go to English-speaking schools such as the Southport School in Australia, Wanganui Collegiate School in New Zealand, Lakefield College School in Canada or the Athenian in America. Aberlour House had a regular group exchange with Hohenfels, the junior school at Salem.

There has been a substantial increase in the number of exchanges over the last two decades. This is partly the result of the massive expansion in Round Square membership, as well as an increased focus on internationalism within the school. Most exchanges are now with Round Square schools and since the introduction of AS levels participating pupils have been exclusively fourth-formers (Year 10) whereas previously most were from the lower sixth (Year 12). The exchanges take place in the spring term. Most are for the entire term, but those involving the learning of a foreign language to schools such as Salem, Birklehof, Louisenlund and L'Ermitage (in Paris) are for four weeks. In any one spring term there are generally between

18 and 26 exchanges in operation. Most recently (2011) schools in France, Germany, Denmark, Canada, USA, Peru, India, South Africa and Australia have been involved. All of these are members of Round Square. It is also common to have exchanges with schools in New Zealand, where there are no Round Square schools. In addition there are usually up to three exchanges in the summer term involving cricketers. One beneficiary of the exchange system in 1997 was Guy Jolly, who writes enthusiastically of this window on to life at the school:

'Gordonstoun is held in the highest regard in New Zealand so being selected by our Headmaster to do an exchange from Wanganui Collegiate School was a huge honour. Without a doubt the fondest memories I have stem from the camaraderie built among fellow students; and also between the teachers and students, something I had never had the privilege of experiencing before.

'These memories were developed from experiences that no other school could offer: sailing on board *Sea Spirit* from Oban to Ireland and back to Troon; enjoying a wee dram with Mr Pyper at the Headmaster's Dance and subsequently finding out that trying to spell the name "ceilidh" was actually far more difficult than doing "strip the willow"; losing 50 balls over 9 holes at the Moray Golf Club in

Lossiemouth – the world's most difficult course; expeditions in the Cairngorms amidst treacherous weather; and playing some great cricket under the supervision of Mr Barton and Mr Brown on a magnificent oval in the school grounds. I must say in the Staff v School cricket fixture I also enjoyed putting a few of Mr Brown's left arm spinners over the long on boundary! Although he did manage to clean out my middle stump in the end and rightly pointed out that he had done the same to each of my NZ predecessors over the previous three years.

'I couldn't write this without acknowledging the great time I had in Duffus House – a quality boarding establishment with some superbly talented lads in there.

'One term was certainly not enough, in fact I very nearly stayed. However, being a Kiwi working in London some thirteen years on I still have a number of mates and staff members from 'Stoun with whom I enjoy a regular (cold) pint . . . To me that's a true reflection of the calibre of Gordonstoun School, it is comprised of exceptional people of all ages year in year out.'

Service, in whatever form, has always been at the core of a Gordonstoun education, and many pupils see international voluntary work as the pinnacle of their Service contribution at the school. International voluntary work can mean many different things but for Gordonstoun pupils, and for the last 25 years, it has meant groups of students (themselves from a variety of countries) working overseas in less developed parts of the world. There are broadly two structures within which international voluntary work occurs: those arranged by Gordonstoun itself for its students, and those that are joined by Gordonstoun students under the auspices of the Round Square International Service (RSIS). On all of these trips, students benefit both from the invaluable experience of working for a common good with groups of people who are often economically and socially marginalised and from the opportunity to learn from other cultures. The sense of purpose, eagerness and willingness to do something constructive and worthwhile is palpable among those students who participate, and their experiences often have an impact way beyond the individual's time at school. Former students who left Gordonstoun many years ago often comment that their project experience was the single most important thing that they have done and regard it as having shaped their thinking about degree courses, careers and lifestyles.

In Thailand, students digging the channel to carry the pipeline from the high-level water tanks to the supply tanks in the village, in 2009 (above), and the 2010 Year 12 students photographed at the end of their three-week trip to the project (below). Each year, applicants at Gordonstoun are interviewed by senior students and a project leader who have worked on the project in the previous year to determine who will be selected to make up the next contingent.

Gordonstoun student helping at a summer school for needy children from the town of Sibiu in Romania, 2009.

An early international initiative began during John Kempe's headmastership when, with Shomie Das, he explored the possibility of setting up a project in India. Das had been Head of Physics at Gordonstoun (1966–68). Returning to India he became Headmaster successively of Mayo College, Ajmer (1969–74), the Lawrence School, Sanawar (1974–88) and his alma mater, the Doon School, Dehradun (1988–95). The last two both joined Round Square in 1981. As a result of the deliberations between Kempe and Das, a reconnaissance expedition to Sanawar took place in the early 1980s. Gordonstoun was represented by John Pownall (staff 1972–2001) and Andrew Mason (Round Square, 1977–82) and among the other schools involved were the Lawrence (the host), the Doon, Cobham Hall and Box Hill, as well as students from schools in Canada and Australia. The original intention was to assist in rescue and relief work in an area affected by flooding. In practice this was considered too dangerous, and the students were instead involved in mountain rescue training and in a village building project, which became for some years a regular Round Square International Service project – the beginnings of the RSIS. In recent years Gordonstoun students have been well represented on RSIS projects. Each year about sixteen pupils participate in eight projects working in places such as Ladakh (India), Kenya, South Africa, Thailand, Honduras and Peru.

There are now three main Gordonstoun projects: the Thailand Water Project, the Romania Orphanage Project and the Sinai Project. The Thailand Project, the longest running initiative, began in the mid-'80s. The father of a student, Jonathan Reid, was at the time working at the British Embassy in Bangkok. He was acquainted with a British expatriate, Jim Souter, who had established a business in Thailand. Souter was already involved in relief work with the Karen hill tribe in the northwest of the country and through the Reid family approached the school for assistance. This well-established project now runs to a tried and tested formula involving the construction of two sets of water storage tanks and pipeline feeders in each community where it works. The experience is physically extremely demanding for pupils, especially as they visit during the monsoon, working alongside villagers to provide a source of clean water without which infant mortality is very high. Souter still works with the Karen, and remains much involved with the Gordonstoun project.

The Romania Project has been running for the best part of twenty years. It was started in the early 1990s by the then school chaplain Peter Dewey. Situated outside the town of Sibiu, south of Bucharest, Little John's House Orphanage cares for the needs of a range of young people up to the age of eighteen, some of whom are disabled; others, in the past, have been suffering with HIV Aids. Gordonstoun pupils spend two weeks in the summer at the orphanage organising a range of sporting and hands-on cultural and creative activities. Local children also come to a summer school there and join in with the orphans. While this is less physically demanding than the Thailand Project, pupils have to be innovative, interactive and prepared for some emotional challenges. Before each trip to Romania, considerable fund-raising is undertaken to support the orphanage; like many similar institutions in Romania, its survival often hangs by a thread.

The third main overseas initiative is the Sinai Project. This started in 1999 when an A-level Geography field trip to the desert, led by Chris Ince, was mounted, and the opportunities for aid projects in the area quickly became apparent. Students either work in the Sinai Mountains with the Jebeliya Bedu, mainly carrying out the restoration of Byzantine gardens that have been damaged by landslides or neglected because of out migration. There is 40 per cent child malnutrition among the mountain peoples, and helping to create sustainable local food sources by bringing alive these fifth- and sixth-century gardens is well received locally. The other project is in the eastern sandstone desert working with the Musseina Bedu. Here the focus has been primarily on water resources, constructing dams in narrow sandstone canyons or restoring wells and making surface water tanks.

The most recent initiative has involved constructing a desert shelter in a wadi devoid of shade for use by both the Bedu and other travellers.

In all three projects, pupils are interacting with marginalised communities, whether it is the Karen people, many of whom have been refugees coming from neighbouring Myanmar, the Bedouin who have mainly failed to benefit from recent social, educational and health advances in Egypt, or the orphans in Romania whose tragic history of neglect under former Communist rule and continuing problems are well known. It is hoped that exposing Gordonstoun pupils to these issues can only strengthen their sense of concern and responsibility as international citizens and encourage them to be pro-active in response to the challenges of the modern world.

A small number of initiatives are organised as individual trips, as was the 2007 trip to Rwanda. The Rwanda connection came about through Sir Tom Hunter, Scottish businessman, entrepreneur, philanthropist and Gordonstoun parent. He was already deeply involved in supporting Rwanda through the Clinton Hunter Development Initiative. With the support of his organisation, a school in the south-east of the country was identified that was in dire need of help – it consisted of two dark classrooms in which the

Above: Digging a channel for a water supply line in a Karen village in Thailand, 2011.

Left: Clearing the ground before building a volleyball court outside Kaduha Primary School in Kirehe, Rwanda, 2007.

In the Sinai Desert in 2008, a Bedouin and a Gordonstoun student undertaking the laborious work of removing rubble and sand from a canyon using a bucket (made from recycled car tyres) so that it can be filled with water. On the next visit, the canyon will be lined with cement to improve its efficiency.

Sinai Desert, 2008: making bread from durum wheat grown in the Nile delta. The flatbreads are placed on the cut-out top of an oil drum heating over a fire and take twelve to fifteen seconds to cook, Sinai Desert, 2008.

Right: A group of students drawn from several Round Square schools who went to Peru in 2010 to help in a project which involves constructing high-altitude greenhouses in the village of Chancha Chancha in the high Andes. These enable local Andean Indians to grow a wider variety of vegetables than would otherwise be possible. Here the group is enjoying some sightseeing before returning home.

children sat on stones for their lessons. By the time the Gordonstoun contingent arrived, two large classroom blocks had already been built, and the Gordonstoun project was to transform the uneven, dust-covered and barren land around Kaduha Primary School in Kirehe into a volleyball court. This would enhance the childhood of 800 pupils at Kaduha before they went home each day to work in the fields or care for the younger members of their families.

Harriet Cross, one of the eleven students on the trip, testifies to the life-changing impact that a trip like this can have. First there was the hard physical labour and witnessing the extraordinary making-do skills of the Rwandans with whom they were working: 'Our wheel-less wheelbarrow had a stone fixed in place with cement to cover the gaping hole in the bottom of it, and when we needed a means to carry boulders that were going to be broken into shape to make the wall surrounding the court a perfect two-man carrying device was quickly made from an old wooden ladder.' Then there was the diligence of the eight- and nine-year-olds at the school: 'No-one spoke unless asked to, when work was set there was not a single word of complaint and when the class as a whole was asked a question every single one of the children was able to volunteer and answer . . . so different to the atmosphere in our classrooms when . . . people are often thinking more about how many minutes are left or decorating their prep diaries.' Included in the trip was the chance to explore the country: 'On our first day we trekked into the mountains of the Volcanoes National Park on the Congolese and Ugandan borders with Rwanda to see the Mountain Gorillas . . . to be within a couple of metres of

these giant animals in their natural environment was extraordinary.' And they also visited memorial sites to those killed in the genocide of 1994, a reign of terror that lasted 100 days and left over 800,000 people dead. One of the last locations the group visited was in the Bisesero Hills, where a group of Tutsis had tried in vain to fight back against the Interahamwe with sticks, clubs and other farm tools: 'Now all that remains of their resistance is fourteen rooms containing the skeletons of those who were murdered preserved in lime. A sight that will haunt me always is how most of these skeletons were curled up, hands over their faces; the terror of their final moments preserved forever.' Cross refers to the lesson in forgiveness writ large in Rwanda: 'In an attempt to move on and more importantly try and prevent another national catastrophe the Rwandan people were urged to accept members of rebel armies back into their communities. This is usually achieved by the ex-rebel knocking on the door of their victim's family, confessing to the murder of the father, mother, sons or indeed an entire family and asking for forgiveness and so to be accepted back into the community . . . I cannot even comprehend coming face to face with the person who murdered my family and not wanting revenge, let alone welcoming them back into the community but as one man described to me, "I am not forgiving them for what they did, I see it as forgiving my children and future generations, they are and they will always be Rwandans, they deserve a nation, a home they can feel safe in and that is why I accept the apologies." . . . My way of thinking has certainly changed; I no longer tend to hold grudges against people. Instead I realise that in the grand scheme of things a minor argument is so insignificant compared to what other people have lived through and learned to move forward from.'

GOVERNANCE

SHROUDED IN MYSTERY, as it is even in the most efficiently run and well-established schools, the concept of governance in the early days of Gordonstoun was, of necessity, reactive and pragmatic. There is a tendency in the world of education to wonder what, if anything, school governors actually do, and it would be easy to assume in the case of Gordonstoun, that, with Hahn as the founding philosopher king at the helm, their role must have been insignificant, if not superfluous.

Such an assessment is far from the truth. In the school's first fifteen years, groups and committees do indeed appear to have sprung up almost at random. There were, separately: Governors, a Board of Directors, an Advisory Council, an Executive Committee, a Finance Committee, a Management Committee and the Gordonstoun Society. What these bodies in fact represent is a highly creative tension between Kurt Hahn and those who, largely at his invitation in the initial stages, gathered around him as he embarked upon and developed what he hoped would be the first of the British Salem Schools.

So, while Hahn attracted many well-connected individuals to support his enterprise, first as Governors and later in the wider Advisory Council, a number of the Governors took it upon themselves to form a Board of Directors and a little later delegated much of their work to the Executive Committee. The tasks of this group in 1946 were illuminating and stated clearly as 'propaganda on behalf of the school, the raising of funds, the expenditure of the funds and, lastly, the general administration of the school and the framing of policy'. Hahn was frequently called to account over, for example, the unauthorised employment of additional staff or acquisition of new buildings. However, the Headmaster invariably had his way, as either the deed was already done and the objections were therefore too late, or he simply raised the necessary funds independently.

Although their names may not trip off the tongue as easily as those of former Headmasters, there were some in the role of Governors in the early years who brought a level of expertise and offered a style of service without which Gordonstoun would not have survived as a school and flourished as an educational entity.

Geoffrey Winthrop Young, celebrated mountaineer, was responsible in 1933 for persuading Kurt Hahn, who was profoundly depressed on leaving Germany, that he had to found another school. Winthrop Young removed his son Jocelin from Salem to be one of the first two students, and the same year became the first Chair of Governors. He was still very much in the frame twenty years later to ease the difficult process of Hahn's retirement and the establishment of a successor. It was Winthrop Young who first said, 'We are more than a school, we are a movement', even if Hahn, with his customary tendency to plagiarise, borrowed the phrase and used it as his own.

Peter Rowntree brought essential funds from the Rowntree Trust which saved the school during the war years and also ensured that reserves were not squandered. David Kemp Colledge, who owned a firm of dyers and finishers in Galashiels, visited Plas Dinam in 1941 and immediately became a central figure in the governance of the school. He negotiated leases on buildings both in Wales and at Wester Elchies; he brought order to the perhaps conveniently haphazard way in which staff salaries were paid; he established a system of superannuation for the first time. Throughout the financial difficulties of the 1940s, both in Montgomery and in Moray, David Kemp Colledge repeatedly felt constrained to take the reins himself to avoid financial disaster. Restraining the 'Greater Gordonstoun' aspirations of Hahn on one hand, and ensuring that the importance of looking after the interests of the staff was appreciated by both Board and Head on the other, Colledge fought and

won some major battles – a legacy for which succeeding generations should be grateful.

Kurt Hahn battled too with the officials of the Board, particularly those brave enough as bursars to try to balance the books and bring a little order to an administrative nightmare. Walter Laffan, an entrepreneur, negotiated the original Gordonstoun House lease and planned the early development of the estate. Michael Varvill, his successor, continued the challenging work and initiated major building development – Cumming House in particular – before the move to Wales, where Dorothy Whislay had to cope with the demands of teenage boys not showing the required respect for valuable historic property, while soldiers encamped at Gordonstoun behaved in exactly the same way. One of these hard-working modest heroes commented that progress had 'not been planned but simply happened'. Some surely felt a lack of direction, while others relished the unpredictable excitement which seemed to drive the whole enterprise forward. And all of this was at a time when, as Henry Brereton wrote, 'not a term passed without thoughts of the necessity of closing the school'.

With resettlement after the World War II came increasing stability. Perhaps Hahn, still ferociously protective of the educational development of the school but now into his sixties, was a little more willing to allow the Board to do its work. Under the Chairmanship of Sir William Hamilton Fyfe, the future of the school was secured by a substantial donation from Antonin Besse. Hahn retired in 1953 but was elected as Secretary of the newly formed Gordonstoun Foundation, established primarily to support the school through providing funds for those unable to pay the fees. At last the British Salem School became Gordonstoun and assumed the status of an official charity.

There was continuing consolidation throughout the 1950s, at first under the chairmanship of Brigadier Sir Henry Houldsworth, who began a period of 50 years of his family's benevolent interest in the school. His daughter-in-law Clodagh Farquharson gave unstinting service for long periods on the Boards of Gordonstoun, Aberlour House and the Gordonstoun Foundation. Sir Iain Tennant, Chairman from 1957 to 1971, oversaw a period of rapid growth and development which included the closing of Altyre, the construction of both St Christopher's and the Sports Centre and the acquisition of *Sea Spirit*, a new sail-training vessel. Lord Leven's period of chairmanship (1971-89) covered almost precisely the headships of John Kempe and Michael Mavor and thus oversaw the introduction of co-education and the improvement of academic performance, as well as the construction of many new buildings and the increasing financial stability of the school, which has been strongly underpinned by the remarkable success of the Summer School.

Over the last 50 years the development of the estate and the facilities on it has been quite remarkable. This has been due partly to generous gifts from individuals and charitable organisations, usually impressed by the school's commitment to its distinctive ethos. Fundraising became much better organised and focused following the appointment in 1983 of long-serving staff member, James Thomas, as director of a department which incorporated fundraising and external affairs. Since then a number of successful appeals have been launched, and fundraising has become an ongoing affair.

The greater part of the construction and improvement of buildings at the school has been achieved through astute financial management. Substantial projects, including classrooms and boarding houses have been paid for with surpluses generated from fee income; likewise at various times extensive refurbishments. The generation of funds in this way is a tribute to successive Finance Committees of the Board, particularly their Chairmen, and also to several highly able and committed bursars: John Ruscoe, George Barr (both of whom were titled 'Controller') and the current Financial Director, Hugh Brown.

The personalities in Gordonstoun have always reflected a wider constituency, and this is characterised by the three Chairmen who have governed the school through the twenty years up to 2010. Angus MacDonald, old boy of the school and a leading figure in agricultural circles in the north of Scotland, was a perceptive enthusiast of all that went on and continued the strengthening of the infrastructure. Vice Admiral Sir James Weatherall, also an old boy and a man whose broad perspective was enhanced by his substantial authority, reorganised the operation of the Board by establishing a cohesive committee system with specific responsibilities for all Governors, deftly steered the Boards of Gordonstoun and Aberlour House into amalgamation, and also ensured the future of large-vessel seamanship with the purchase of *Ocean Spirit*. In Professor Bryan Williams, Gordonstoun appointed a Chairman of Governors with broad knowledge of both the private and

the public sectors and considerable experience of further education. Under his stewardship the pace of development has not slackened. Building development – the Ogstoun Theatre, the Tennant Room, the new Sports Hall – has been accompanied by strategic issues of educational provision being placed ever more clearly under the microscope, while the sale of Aberlour House and the moving of the Junior School on to the Gordonstoun campus has been the single most decisive development of recent years.

Mark Pyper, Headmaster and then Principal 1990–2011, is clear about the debt owed by the school to its Board of Governors: 'If the significant but quiet work of the Chairman of the Board of Governors does not always acquire the prominent place in popular memory that it deserves, how much less do the honest toil and the unsung contribution of so many experts and generous Board Members receive the recognition which they so richly merit. Such champions are legion in the history of the school, and Gordonstoun has flourished not least because of the invaluable commitment of those who have served it as Governors, many of whom exemplify the school's motto: *plus est en vous.*'

Mark Pyper completed his tenure in March 2011. Pyper embraced the core elements of the Gordonstoun or Hahnian philosophy, while welcoming and enabling change and development in many areas of school life. Sir James Weatherall worked with him both as Chairman of the Governors (finding when he returned to Gordonstoun 'a modern, progressive and exciting school') and, from 2003 to 2011, as Warden. He remarks that among Pyper's most impressive traits were the sensitivity and skill evident in his interaction with the students in the school and the kindness and deftness with which he dealt with any personal difficulties that arose.

Simon Reid, the new Principal, arrived in April 2011. A personal interest and conviction in the educational aims of Gordonstoun since its beginning coupled with a teaching background at Stowe School, Christ's Hospital and Worksop College and his own education at Hilton College in South Africa have amply equipped him to lead a school that excels in promoting the ideal of service to others and personal development as well as strongly supporting academic endeavour.

SUBSCRIBERS

This book has been made possible through the generosity of the following subscribers:

Jeremy Adam (1978–83)
A.R. Adams-Cairns (1967–71)
Antonio del Aguila Sanchez (1980–3)
Qatrelnada Khalil Al-Khonji (2007–9)
Hamish McGregor Alexander (1955–60)
James Alexander (2008–)
Laura Allan (2006–10)
Nichola Allan (2006–8)
Zoe Andreae (2008–9)
Henry Angus (1980–4)
Jestyn Angus (1944–8)
Kaamil Ansar (1970–4)
Talal Al Ansari (1997–8)
Colonel B.C.F. Arkle MBE TD (1938–43)
Allison M Armitage (1988–92)
Anne Armitage
Mr Neil Ashcroft (1991–3)
Rupert Atkins
Ana Atkinson (1991–3)
Charlie Atkinson (1989–91)
Lucy Atkinson (2005–7)
Jonathan Attey (1987–92)
D.W. Austin (1966–71)
I.W. Austin (1964–9)
Emily Ayre (1993–8)
Dr Simon Backett (1958–63)
Mr Neil A. Baird (1954–9)
Paul R. Ballard (1965–7)
Peter Bally (1953–6)
Anthony Barker (1945–51)
Iain Barrett (1965–9)
Oliver Nicholas Barton (2006–8)
Peter Behncke (Hogrefe) (1979–80)
Liz Bell (née Martell) (1983–7)
Wendy Bellars (née McLean), Staff (1985–8)

Esther Bello (1977–82)
Mr Kenneth Bews, Staff (1978–2010)
Vidur Bharatram (2007–11)
Vivek and Sukanya Bharatram
Patrick Bierbaum (1990–1)
Andrew Bishop (1973–8)
Julia Blakeney (1989–94)
John Bloomfield (1971–3)
P.J. Boland
Elena Bonatti Rocca
Robin Bond-Winspear (1997–9)
Pablo Born (1981–3)
Jeremy Bowen (1964–9)
Richard William Boyle (1972–5)
Major Martin Bray (1958–63)
Christian Brehm (2000)
Richard Bridges (1956–60)
Kai Britzke
Graham and Carleen Broad
H. Brockmann
Fergus Bevans Brown
Hugh S. Brown
Mr M. Brownson
J. Alistair Buchan (1953–6)
J. Andrew Buchan (1986–91)
Kirsty Buchan (née Tawse) (1999–2001)
Michael Bullen (1953–6)
David Burdett (1943–6)
David Byatt MBE
Emily Byerley
John and Jane Caithness
Jamie W.G. Cameron (1965–70)
Dr Lorien Cameron-Ross (1988–93)
Max and Josh Cannell (2006–8)
Gair F.M. Carson (1962–6)
James Cawood (1996–2000)
Sir Jeremy Chance Bt (1938–43)
Amy Louise Chapman (2006–8)

Hamish Chenevix-Trench (1990–5)
Tony Chew
Bethany Cheyne
Rebecca Cheyne
George Chinn (1997–2002)
Susie and Antony Chinn
Mrs Vanessa Christie
Drs Stephen and Ute Clackson
Rosemary Clark (née Greenlees) (1980–3)
Stuart Clarke (1981–3)
Paul Cleaver (1970–6)
Lt Col Richard Clements OBE (1974–8)
John Clugston (1952–8)
Dr and Mrs D.B. Clutton, Staff (1981–98)
Heather Cochrane, Staff (1951–87)
T. Bruce Cochrane (1955–9)
Lady Coghill
David Conran-Smith (1953–7)
Richard Thompson Coon (1960–5)
Diana Cooper (2008–10)
Lydia Cooper (2004–6)
Peter W.L. Cousens (1974)
Rodney W.W. Craig (1964–8)
Euan V. Crawshaw (1964–9)
Colin Crole (1938–47)
Canon Philip Crosfield OBE, Staff (1960–7)
Harriet Cross (2006–9)
Jess Cross (2008–11)
Tom Cross (2005–7)
Henry Crowe (2009–)
Charles A. Cruickshank (1974–8)
William Cruickshank (1969–74)
Natasha Dangerfield, Staff
Daisy Darwall-Smith (2000–4)
Richard, Harry and Kitty Davies
Richard St Aubrey Davies (1951–6)
John S. Dawson (1960–3)
Caroline Dearden, Staff (1989–99)

Michael Derenberg (1958–63)
Richard Devey, Staff
Simran Piers Dhaliwal (2007–9)
Carlo Barel Di Sant' Albano (1981–3)
Dennis Dick (1948–52)
Ben-Jacob Diewitz (1999–2001)
Mrs Constance Diggle
Dr Roger Dior (1976–8)
F.S. Ditmas (1963–7)
Robert Murray Watson Dods (1952–6)
Robin Dods (1953–8)
James T. Donald (1950–3)
John Donaldson (1964–6)
Simon Dorman, Staff (1996–9)
Alasdair Douglas-Hamilton (1953–8)
Elly Douglas-Hamilton (1986–9)
Jess Dunbar (née Baker) (1997–9)
Andrew Ehrgood
Miss Rosalind Eleazar (2001–6)
Brian Ellis (1950–5)
Peter Ellis (1946–54)
Phoebe-Jane (Peach) Emmett (1996–8)
D.G. Esson (1961–5)
W. Donald Fairgrieve (1952–6)
Kamran Farman Farmaian (1977–81)
Ian Farmer (1941–8)
B.T. Fenner
Andrew John Findlay (1957–61)
Anthony Finlay (1949–52)
Guy Finlayson (2006–10)
Marcel Alexander Fischer (2004–5)
Edwina FitzPatrick (2000–3)
Michael Flesch (1954–8)
Brian Stuart Forsgate (1961–5)
Mr J.G.A.G. Fraser (1996–2001)
Jack Frazier (2003–8)
Oliver Freiland (1994–6)
Hal French (2007–)
Lord Gainford (Joseph E Pease) (1938–40)
Stephen Gale-Batten (1969–71)
Jessie Garden
Kerith Maria George-Briant (1991–3)
Michael Gibson (1965–70)
R.G. Gilchrist (1946–50)
John Gillespie, Staff (1952–63)
Robert T.D. Glaister (1957–61)
Julius Freiherr von Gleichenstein (1993–6)
Joanne E. Glossop (née Solomon) (1997–9)
A.D. Goddard (1944–5)
James A Goodlad (1951–5)
A. Gordon-Rogers, Staff (1976–2001)
James Gordon (1958–63)
Matthew Gordon (2008–)

Fraser Govan (1984–8)
Jim Graham, Staff (1966–82)
Mr R.S. Gray (1949–53)
Charles Green (2005–)
Innes Green (2008–)
Jamie Green (2005–10)
Magnus Green (2009–)
Major (Ret'd) Aubrey Grey (1943–7)
Charlotte Griffiths (1991–3)
Amelie Grille (2003–5)
Madeleine Grille (2008–10)
Peter Harold Grove (1990–5)
James Gunn (1958–63)
Sverre Gylseth (1965–8)
Detmar Hackman (1948–53)
Sax Hallam (1954–8)
Neil Hamilton (1948–51)
David Hanson, Staff (1965–2001)
Katie Hardie (2009–)
Laura Catherine Phoebe Harkess (2010–)
Nicholas Munro Harkess (2006–)
Julian N. Harrison (1982–7)
Simon R. Harrison (1989–91)
Tom Edward Harrison (2002–7)
Nicholas Hartley (1960–4)
Erinna Iona Harvey-Jamieson (2010–)
Alec Hay (Betts) (1979–84)
John Hay (1949–54)
Professor W.K. Hayman (1939–43)
Alexander Hegard (1969–72)
Ian E. Henderson (1965–9)
Jeremy N. Heron (1946–50)
George Hesse (1955–6)
Jane C. Hewitt (née Green) (1975–9)
William Heynes (2006–11)
Robin Hildrew, Staff (1964–9)
Mrs Caroline Hill
Edward Hill (2001–6)
George Hill (2003–8)
Jakob Hoeflich (2007)
Andrew Hoellering (1945–51)
Erin Hoover (1974–6)
Michael Houstoun (2008–10)
Robert Houstoun (2010–)
Michael Howes (1961–5)
Ornella Hulbert (1989–91)
Peter Hulett (1981–3)
Samantha Durston Humphrey
    (née Trussell) (1979–84)
P.D. Hunter, Staff (1979–85)
Ian Huntington (1960–4)
Stuart Lindsay Huyton (1974–6)
Pippa Irwin (2002–4)

Jonathan Janson (1944–50)
Frederick M. Janzen (2009–11)
Douglas Jardine (2008–)
John Jardine (2005–9)
Gordon K. Johns (1964–6)
Fiona Johnson (née Dickinson) (1990–2)
Grenville S. Johnston, Governor (1985–99)
Heather R. Johnston (1987–92)
Maryanne Johnston (1990–5)
Marylyn J. Johnston, Staff (1971–2)
Quentin Johnston (1962–6)
Stuart L. Johnston (1982–7)
David Johnstone (1945–6)
Mr Michael Jones (1951–6)
Alfred Jordan (1985–6)
Joshua Joseph
George Joyce (2008–)
Paul Marc Andre Judlin (1971–6)
Lee Edward Kahl-Adams (2006–8)
D.H. Kalis (1956–61)
Norbert Kampf (1956–7)
Anna Michelle Kellas (1987–92)
Tim Kendall (1976–9)
Linda Kennedy (1982–3)
Annabel Kerby (1978–80)
Dennis A. Kew (1956–60)
Francis Kinloch (1958–61)
Frau Jutta Kleine-Doepke
James Knapp (1980–5)
William Knox (1955–9)
Dr Michael Koehler
Maximilian Kredel (1995–8)
Herr and Frau Dr Wolfgang and Renate Krie
Wiebke Krutein (1995–7)
Bernard von Kuenssberg (1962–6)
Finn Rieber Kuhnle (1951–2)
Jolly Kwan (2000–4)
Emma and Robi Lambie
Alastair (Ally) Lamont (1954–9)
Ian Lavender, Staff (1998–2009)
Ian Lawson CVO, Staff (1951–68)
Brian Leach (1961–5)
Francesca Leaver (1990–5)
The Lees (1991–2000)
Nick Lee (1990–2)
Tony Lennard, Staff (1998–2001)
Hugh Leslie (1995–2000)
Tim Leslie (1997–2002)
Alistair Letby (1990–4)
Johanna Letby (1990–6)
Elliot Andrew Fyfe Lewis (1986–91)
Helen Lewis (1988–93)
Edward John Lightowler (1958–63)

Lawrence Lincoln (2007)
Howard and Rosemary Llewellyn
Stephen Lockhart (1970–4)
Dr Norbert Lodde
Ann A. Logan (1979–81)
Suzanna Loh (2004–6)
Hugh Lonsdale
Mr Leslie T. Lucas
Kloe Lynas
Calum Alastair Franks Macfie (2010–)
James Macintyre (1955–60)
Rory Mackay (2002–7)
Timothy Mackern (1968–72)
Jock Macknight (1968–73)
Donald A.D. Macleod (1955–9)
James Main (1938–43)
Iain Majcher (2000–5)
David Maloney (1982–4)
Miss C.S. Marsh (1980–2)
John Marsham (1945–50)
Charlie Martell (1984–7)
Kaye Martin (1948–53)
Tony Mason, Staff (1968–89)
Kirsten Matheson (2007–9)
Mrs J. Elizabeth Mavor, Wife of Headmaster (1978–90)
Albert Christian Russel Maw (1973–5)
Mrs Delphine L. Maw
Cullum McAlpine (1960–5)
Rachel McArdle (née Beards) (1982–4)
Francis McArthur (1948–50)
Andrew McCallum (1964–9)
Captain James McClean (1993–8)
Mr Brian McComb (1951–3)
Captain Ian Andrew McGhie RN
    and Mrs Doreen McGhie
Caroline McHardy (1976–8)
Keith McIntosh (1946–51)
Hugh Jonathan Fleming McIntyre (1943–7)
Emerald McNamara (2008–)
McNie Family (1988–2001)
James McVean (1979–84)
Charles Metcalfe (2004–9)
James Metcalfe
William Metcalfe (2005–11)
Chris Miller (1962–6)
Andrew Stirling Mitchell (1971–5)
Gustav Mohn (1948–9)
Bill Mohr (1954–8)
Christopher Monahan (1996–2001)
Hugh Monckton (1962–6)
Dr Ricarda Mondry (1983–4)
Michael Monsell-Davis (1954–7)
The Reverend Anthony Montgomery, Staff (1968–93)

Iain (John) Morris (1950–60)
Luke Morrow (2002–7)
Tim, Antoinette and Joseph Morton
R.J.R. Mott (1972–7)
Peter J. Muckle (1951–4)
Peter Muller (1951–4)
Olav Munch (1969–70)
Keith K.I. Murdoch (1958–62)
Chris J.K. Murray (1971–6)
Mr Rupert Murray (1968–72)
Mark and Carey Nash
Graham Neil (1952–5)
Sean E.A. Neish (1988–92)
James H. Newsom (1987–8)
Michael Newton (1947–52)
John Nicholson (1958–63)
Dr Dorothea Niedrée-Sorg (1982–3)
James O'Toole (1970–5)
Dr Jendrik Odewald (1993)
Philip A.R. Oetker (1990–2)
Dr David and Mrs Bryn Oh (1989–91)
Hugh Osborne (1970–2)
Ben W.R. Paddick (1999–2004)
Robert Palmström (1962–8)
Kenneth Hugh Parsons (1953–7)
Gabriella Paterson (2009–11)
Jamie Paxton (2008–11)
Kim Paxton (2007–11)
Martine Peltzer (née Sturgess) (1986–8)
Nick Pisani (1976–81)
J.D.L. Playfair (1960–3)
Karl-Wilhelm Freiherr von Plettenberg (1953–4)
James Pogson (1969–71)
Janine Poley (2007–8)
Rupert and Elke Pollard (1972–5)
Anne Pollock, Governor
Miss Sarah Anne Potts (2007–9)
Laura S. Powell (1985–6)
Hugo N. Radford (2002–7)
Nicholas P. Radford (1970–5)
Andrew Randall (1955–9)
Susan Reeves, Widow of Staff Member (1965–9)
Michaela Rehorkova, Staff (2001–2)
Anne Sophie Renaud (1976–7)
Richard Renold (1953–8)
Miss Nicola Jayne Reynolds (2008–)
David M. Richmond (1976–9)
Nigel J.D. Rimmer (1957–60)
Robin L. Rimmer (1958–9)
Tim Ringrose (1982–8)
Andrew Ritchie (1957–61)
Colin M. Ritchie (1955–60)
Max and Abigail Rivers (2008–)

Roger Roessink (1977–81)
R. Roos
Isobel Rose (1979–84)
Tamara Rosenberg
John Roxburgh (1951–4)
Jean Royan, Catering Services Manager (1979–2004)
Belinda Rymer (1978–81)
Faraj Saghri
John M.S. Salloway (1942–3)
Douglas Sanderson (2006–11)
Sacha Sapera (2002–7)
Tim Saville (1959–64)
Florian Schindler (2011–)
Nigel Sclater (1956–61)
Alexander Scott (1950–2)
Jane Scriven (née Kelly) (1979–84)
Richard Seal (1985–90)
Paul Buckingham Segrott (1964–9)
James David Selka (1979–82)
John Shackles (1954–8)
Susie and Matt Sharp (2005–9)
Gordon Shiach (1948–54)
Ms Anna Shine (1974–6)
Ian Falconer Sime (1937–41)
Ian Simpson (1969)
Robert Patten Simpson (1969–71)
David Sinclair (1960–5)
Jane A. Sinclair (1996–8)
Richard I. Sinclair (1969–74)
Gregor Skinner (1949–51)
Graeme J.B. Smith (1947–51)
Ian Donald Smith (1951–5)
Oliver Smith
Cassie Soper (2006–)
Lella Soper (2008–)
Luke Souflas (2003–5)
Zisimos Souflas (2002–4)
Alain Speeckaert
David and Bebe Spooner, Staff (1970–99)
Mrs K. Springbett (1980–3)
Katherine St Clair Tisdall (2005–7)
Philip St Clair Tisdall (1966–71)
Anna Stanford (1979–82)
Maria Start
M. Stary (1944–8)
Dr Vincent Stephanopoli D'Armagnac
Cdr Andrew Stewart OBE RN (1969–74)
Anna Stewart (2008–10)
Rory Stewart (2007–9)
Pim Stones (2008–10)
Wilson and Gerardine Strachan
Emily Strudwick (2008–10)
Paul Strudwick (1967–9)

Paul Sturrock (1971–3)
Hiroaki Suda (2000–1)
Peter Sutton, Chaplain (2002–8)
Mr and Mrs L. Tattersall, Staff (1987–)
B.M. Taylor
George B. Taylor (1955–8)
Humphrey J.F. Taylor (1948–53)
John S.W. Taylor (1952–7)
The Terry Brothers (1985–2011, 1988–2011)
Constantine Theodossiou (1986–90)
Michael Thierhoff
Heather Thomas-Smith (1980–5)
B. Claire Thomas (1986–8)
James D. Thomas (Mr T), Staff (1963–2011)
Ruaraidh A.D. Thomas (1982–7)
John M. Thomson (1955–7)
Charles Christopher Thornton (1998–2003)
Henrietta Tillard (2003–8)
Oliver Tillard (2000–5)
Sandy Tod (1939–42)
Professor Christopher Todd (1953–7)
Miss Elizabeth Anne Townsend (2007–)
Rob Truefitt (1961–6)
M.H. Tunstall-Behrens (1937–42)

Leo Turley
Lydia Elspa Ulvedal (1990–2)
Jan Urbye (1954–6)
Joachim Urbye (1969–72)
Thomas Urbye (1971–2)
Roderik van Grieken (1988–90)
Ramon Varela Apraiz (1991–5)
Gabriele Varley
A.G. Ventress (1951–4)
Kieran Verster (2010)
Marc Villalongue (2006–10)
Christian Vracas (2006–11)
Bob Waddell, Staff (1959–89)
R.G. Wade (2003–5)
Harry Wallace
Hugh Wallace (1985–90)
Michael Wallace
Robyn Wallace
Andrew and Gail Wallbank
David Walser (1950–4)
Thomas M. Walser (1985)
Guy Walters (1974–8)
Roger Walters (1944–50)
Geraint Watkins, Staff (2009–)

Francis Roy Waylen, Staff (1935–9)
Vice Admiral Sir James Weatherall KCVO KBE DL
    (1949–53)
Alexander T.A. Webb (2008–10)
Derrick Webster (1959–61)
Mrs M.J. Webster
Tom Weekenborg (2007–)
Helen L.N. Weir (2009–11)
Norman Weiss (1951–6)
Mr Tony White, Staff (1953–63)
James J. Whiteford (1965–70)
Alexander Whiteside (2008–10)
Patrick Whitworth (1944–8)
P.M. Wilcox
Mr Ian G.H. Williams (1961–5)
Alan J. Wills, Staff (2003–5)
Denise Wills (née Hribal) (1982–4)
Konstantin Hubertus Kajetan Wolf (2006–9)
Mr W.A. Wood (1960–3)
Jacqueline Woodcock (1981–3)
Nancy Woodcock
Euan Wright (1990–5)
Tanya Wright
Catherine Younger (1983–8)

INDEX OF NAMES